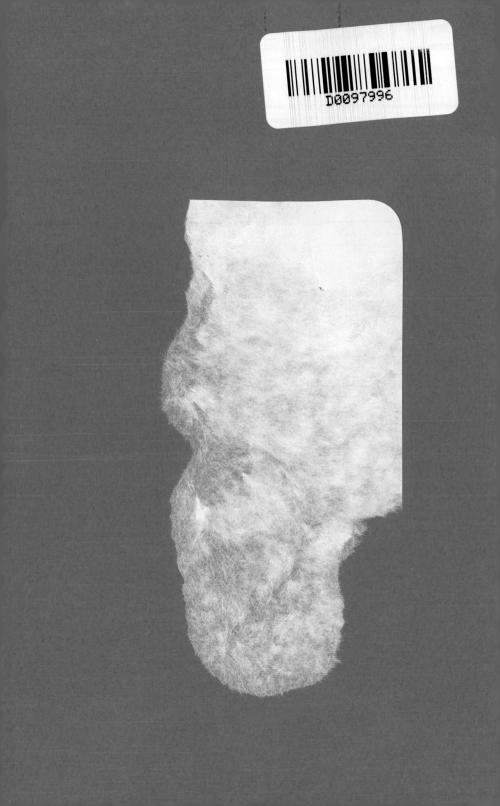

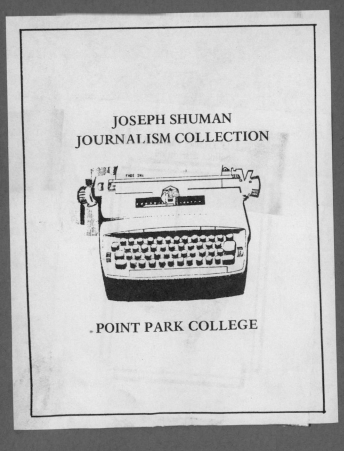

JOSEPH SHUMAN
JOURNALISM COLLECTION

POINT PARK COLLEGE

WEEKLY

ON THE WABASH

by Wheeler McMillen

FOREWORD BY

Howard Rusk Long

Carbondale and Edwardsville

SOUTHERN ILLINOIS UNIVERSITY PRESS

FEFFER & SIMONS, INC.

London and Amsterdam

COPYRIGHT © 1969 *by* Southern Illinois University Press
All rights reserved
Standard Book Number 8093–0676–x
Printed in the United States of America
Designed by Andor Braun
Library of Congress Catalog Card Number 69–15328

Foreword

The weekly newspaper is as American as apple pie and the Fourth of July.

Colonial printers were among the first to defy the authority of the King's men sent to administer royal affairs in the Western Atlantic. They balked at Parliament's Stamp Act, and they skirmished on various issues with the local establishments from Boston to Williamsburg. The weekly newspapers were the medium employed to carry to the network of societies organized by the Sons of Liberty the circular letters prepared by Samuel Adams and his radical followers, known collectively as the committees on correspondence.

The weekly press served so ably the cause of an imperfectly organized revolt that General Washington concerned himself with the collection of discarded linen cloth required to make paper for editors eager to publish the news and the propaganda messages of the Patriot Cause. Even as the first of America's great popular dailies were ushered upon the scene by Benjamin H. Day and James Gordon Bennett, a weekly newspaper, the *Washington Globe,* still carried the word of President Andrew Jackson's policies, as spelled out so vigorously by the "kitchen cabinet," Francis P. Blair, Amos Kendell, and John C. Rives, to faithful party leaders and editors throughout the land. In fact it was the weekly edition of the New York *Tribune* that raised Horace Greeley to the stature of a household god. The similar editions of other great metropolitan dailies enabled lesser editors to function as the oracles of rural America until well into the twentieth century.

Weekly editor-printers marched westward behind the explorer, the trapper, the fur trader, and the land scout, arm in arm with the lawyer, the politician, the preacher, and the merchant, in close support of the first wave of permanent settlers. By 1786 the *Gazette* of John Scull and Joseph Hall was helping to bring law and order to the village of Pittsburgh. The next year another *Gazette* was established at Lexington while Kentucky still was a part of Virginia. Cincinnati had a weekly by 1793; Chicago waited until 1833 for its *Weekly Democrat*. Meanwhile the *Indiana Gazette,* known later as the *Western Sun,* appeared at Vincennes in 1804; Joseph Charless launched the *Missouri Gazette* at St. Louis in 1808, and Mathew Duncan founded the *Illinois Herald* at Kaskaskia in 1814.

So it went until the land was filled. Each aggregation seeking to establish local institutions soon found a printing press in its midst, accompanied by an editor prepared to participate in the process of creating a new center of government and building a new community.

The same drives that brought the first primitive press into each burgeoning metropolis changed the local weekly into a daily newspaper as quickly as the community generated sufficient economic support to sustain the ambitions of the proprietor and the vanity of local boosters. For years, in fact until the beginning of the present century, there was little to distinguish the small daily from the country weekly except frequency of publication. Then as the forces of urbanization swept across America the little daily prospered with the merchants at the place of publication, acquired the technology employed by wealthy city publishers, and became watered down versions of the metropolitan press. The country weekly, relatively unchanged, reached its numerical peak at about the time William Jennings Bryan made his last national campaign to become President of the United States. The long drift into decline was concurrent with the failure of the small towns and villages which had provided the weekly's natural habitat. By 1920 the process was almost complete and a new type of weekly newspaper was emerging.

Just as the product of the country press in the years before World War I differed so much from the local newspaper immediately after the return of our troops from Europe, so had rural America passed from the age of the horse and buggy into the era of the tin lizzy.

And herein lies so much of the value of the book to be published under the title, *Weekly on the Wabash.* Wheeler McMillen was at the journeyman stage of his career when he contrived to become proprietor of the weekly *Republican* at Covington, Indiana. It was the very twilight of what so many people of his age group are determined to call the "good old days of American life." Four of Mr. McMillen's best years were claimed by the weekly cycle of activities connected with bringing to life each new edition of a newspaper. The personality of an ordinary person in this time span would have been marked forever by the impact of the trivialities of his work, in the manner that the tympan of a cylinder press becomes smudged by ink from the type forms. In fact quite a number of ordinary people, so marked, have written ordinary books about the weekly newspaper filled with anecdotes of the minor sorrows, joys, and hilarity of the backshop and the tribulations heaped upon the editor's head by a public lacking in understanding.

No ordinary man, Mr. McMillen arrived in Covington filled with ideas, many of which worked out, and with an idealism which did not elude him. In retrospect his editorship was an experiment in community leadership and newspaper economics; a study of practical politics; an exercise in applied sociology. To perform the task set out for himself it was necessary for him to know the people, to understand their problems, and somehow to relate these affairs to events in the larger world. Thus acquired were the observations preserved in this case study of small town American life, extracted as a cross section from one of our most significant periods of change. Preserved, also as if still alive (and of course some of them are), are the personalities of Covington's people moving about the town square in association with each other during the years of the McMillen editorship.

Weekly on the Wabash supports the contention that every editor is a living social document. For four years *The Covington Republican* was Wheeler McMillen interacting with his readers.

Howard Rusk Long

Southern Illinois University
October 1, 1968

Preface

Though both may appear in these pages, amusement rather than social history has been the purpose of *Weekly on the Wabash*. The events recounted took place during the years 1914–18. Midwestern small town life in those irrecoverable days before radio, supermarkets, TV dinners, or Scotch tape was far different than now.

A draft of this book was written while the episodes were still fresh in mind and while notes and files were at hand. The manuscript was laid aside as more urgent matters filled the intervening years.

Now, when the half of a century has elapsed, it has been fun to recall the people and perplexities amidst which four exciting and instructive years of youth were spent. The text of the early draft has been shortened and polished a little but otherwise left unchanged. All incidents are true, and all names except two or three are actual.

Wheeler McMillen

July, 1968

Contents

WEEKLY ON THE WABASH

1

A Town on the Wabash

A SHARP WIND sent white eddies of hard snow skittering along the sidewalk. On that last day of February, 1914, five weeks past my twenty-first birthday, I hurried along the west side of the courthouse square in Covington, Indiana.

Turning to include as much of the frigid scene as possible in one glance, I reflected that this place on the Wabash, this town of Covington in Indiana, was to be home, possibly for a lifetime. A queer old courthouse of pre-Civil War construction loomed in the center of the square. Three brick business buildings, each with a corner to itself, thrust themselves three stories high in the snow of the gray morning. Most of the other structures were one-story frame buildings whose false fronts did not disguise their squat proportions. The only man I met saluted with a mittened hand, and spoke a friendly good morning.

Half a block north of the square, I turned into the battered two-story brick building that was the last business structure on the west side of the street. Over the sidewalk a crude wooden marquee flaunted in flaking paint its legend,

THE COVINGTON REPUBLICAN.

An elderly, handsome man with silver hair and mustache greeted me ingratiatingly. He was Thomas A. Clifton, who now had my two-thousand-dollar down payment.

"Well, sir, I bid you welcome and good luck. You are on the job early, I see."

"I shall probably need to be," I said, without realizing just how prophetic this reply was.

Tom Clifton bowed and indicated a high-backed revolving chair. "Take the editorial chair itself," he invited with playful sententiousness. "The chair, the sanctum, and all that goes with it, are now yours, sir."

I sat down. Clifton opened one of a pair of glass-paned doors at the rear of the room and called up an open stairway.

"Bill! Cooper! Come down a minute!

"I want to introduce the staff. This is my son, Cooper, who works here."

The well set-up young fellow, wearing pince-nez glasses with a tiny gold chain hooked over one ear, was greeted.

"And this is Bill Harden, the foreman. Bill's the best printer in Fountain county."

Bill, a tiny man past sixty, suggested a cartoonist's model for "the common people." He rubbed his mouth and drooping mustache with the back of his hand and glowed at my handshake.

"So you're the new boss," he said.

"Hardly a boss," I replied, "I rather think we'll all just work together." I thought that was a correctly modest way to start.

"Understand you're a practical printer," the foreman ventured, questioningly.

"I know a little about the back office," I admitted, trying to imply that it was an understatement. It wasn't.

"That's good." Bill tried to button up his open vest. "Anything special you want done this morning?"

I opened a copy of the *Republican* and with a pair of long shears speared a hole in the editorial page, clipped off the single-column masthead and pasted it on a sheet of copy paper. Across a corner I wrote and underscored "DC." Drawing a pencil through one line, I wrote a substitute across the side of the sheet: "Wheeler McMillen, Editor and Proprietor," and handed it to Bill. "We might as well start with this."

The foreman adjusted his spectacles and looked at the "DC." "Double Column?" he inquired.

"If you please. The editorials will be double-column hereafter."

"Well, a little change don't hurt, sometimes," he remarked. "The Staff" returned to the composing room upstairs.

"Your first act," commented Clifton, who had owned the *Covington Republican* for twenty years. "This afternoon, if you like, I will come down and introduce you to our businessmen and others around town. I'm going back to the house this morning and see how it feels to be retired. Anything I can do, just let me know." He went out.

The new owner surveyed the "sanctum." The rough oak boards of the floor, worn from sixty years of footsteps, bore evidence of a hasty early morning sweeping; dust plainly of long accumulation darkened the chinks around the edges where baseboard and floor failed to meet. A high, unpolished Round Oak stove in the corner at the left of the entrance was glowing red at the bottom with a coal fire that promised to be alternately too hot and too cold. At the right stood an old-fashioned steel safe. A tall bookkeeper's desk leaned against the south wall by a cobwebby window that looked into the alley. Opposite the safe a pine bookcase reached to the ceiling, filled mostly with volumes of *Proceedings of the Indiana Legislature* and the *Department of Agriculture Yearbook.* A large lithograph of former Vice-President Charles W. Fairbanks, in a wide black frame, hung near the alley window. A calendar completed the mural decorations. Wainscoting, painted a dead gray, reached halfway up the walls, with dingy wallpaper continuing to the unpapered ceiling. Two low pine tables in the room were piled with accumulated newspapers, many still unopened. Four light, cane-bottomed chairs completed the furnishings, except for two battered coal buckets and a flat box half-filled with ashes. Double doors at the rear led into a corridor and to the open staircase. Upstairs were the composing rooms where type was set; in the back rooms stood the presses.

As new owner of the *Covington Republican* I drew a long breath and leaned backward in the high revolving chair. It tipped suddenly, my feet left the floor, and I grabbed at the table to avoid being spilled backwards on my head. The customary spring was absent from the mechanism underneath the chair. The unexpected blow to my poise compelled a laugh.

"I wonder if Covington will have many more of these surprises for me," I thought.

Letting the chair back more carefully, I found that it was entirely safe, and so I lifted my feet to the table for an interval of meditation. . . . "In full control of a newspaper, at last. Make it the best country weekly in Indiana. Best one in the United States, maybe. Make it good enough and everybody in the Covington territory will subscribe. Make it snappy and interesting — different from other papers. Get the news. The power of the press! Editorials that will change people's minds. Editorials that will get things done. Make Covington the best town in Indiana to live and do business in. Bring more people here to trade. Pile up the advertising. Make some money. Be a real leader in a community. Maybe in the state. Forceful. Stand for the right. Above all, get out a good paper."

Except as to plans for making a good weekly paper, the ideas were far from specific. That a good paper would pay its way and make a living I had no doubt. The *Covington Republican* was to be a good newspaper, so money would doubtless be forthcoming. And since the editor of a good newspaper was always a man of influence and consequence, realization of any subsequent ambitions would naturally follow. In some undefinable way I would come to be recognized among people as a man of ability and distinction. With an ably written editorial column, eagerly read by a long list of subscribers, I would be able to do much good in the community. Just what good, or why any good should be done, was a cloud of mist. But I wanted, anyway, to do some good, to be recognized as an outstanding person, and to produce a better weekly newspaper than Indiana had ever seen.

Reaching into my pocket, I laid my money on the table. I found two five-dollar bills and four ones; three half-dollars, including one of Newfoundland that by coincidence I had received on the day the Titanic was sunk off the shores of that island; three quarters; some dimes, nickels, and six pennies. A total of sixteen dollars and fifty-six cents. I had no other money anywhere. That was the working capital. That subscriptions, advertising, and job printing would soon amply augment the supply I had no doubt.

The price of the new property was five thousand dollars; two thousand dollars down, the remainder to be paid in semi-annual installments of five hundred dollars each, with interest at seven per cent. The impression was conveyed that the enterprise had been making around three thousand a year. The figure seemed reasonable — a thousand subscribers, paying a dollar and fifty cents each per year, along with the advertising, legal notices, and job printing. Being single, and accustomed to frugal living, there could be no difficulty in paying off the mortgage at the rate of a thousand dollars annually for three years. No detailed figures were presented, nor asked for.

Neither had any inspection been made of the town. No examination was made of its trading area, nor consideration given to the fact that nearby larger places already were beginning their drain on small business centers. Were there any local industries? The question did not come up. A young fellow had two thousand dollars to pay down for a newspaper, and here was an old man willing to take it.

Clifton, who had owned the paper, also owned the old building that housed the office, owned a home, and possessed an automobile. Not a great deal of property, obviously, to show for a quarter-century of effort; but, then, the files revealed that the *Republican* had not been a very good newspaper. That the rewards to the publisher of an ably edited, meritorious paper would be proportionately larger seemed simple and clear.

As the debutant editor and proprietor I may have known something about newspaper editing. For three years I had been reporter or desk man on daily papers. About the business end of a newspaper office and about a small town like Covington, I had much to learn. Nevertheless I was confident that I stood on the threshold of a glowing future.

That the *Covington Republican* might prove to become as much incubus as opportunity was beyond imagination.

Midnight electricity burned regularly in the *Republican* editorial sanctum for many nights. As yet, the town had presented no counter-attractions to unremitting work at the fascinating job of launching a career. Nor did the small upstairs room in their home which the Cliftons had rented to the new proprietor for $1.50 a week.

Multitudinous details entered into preparing the first edition. Many were the changes to be pondered over. I disliked, for instance, the appearance of paid "reader" advertisements interspersed amongst the personal items. A classified department was determined upon. No cash customers having demanded this unannounced feature, it was launched without them. Three advertisements were written for the classified column. One sought agents to sell subscriptions to the *Republican*. Another offered old newspapers for sale at five cents a bundle. The third read: "WANTED —— To rent modern house by May 1. Inquire at the *Republican* office."

"Going to get married soon?" new acquaintances asked, after seeing this.

The big news story of the initial issue was the announcement of new proprietorship. Two columns wide, it was set up to command attention. A statement of policy occupied most of the space.

"The first effort of the new management of the *Covington Republican* will be to make it a good newspaper," asserted the opening sentence.

The second paragraph might have been taken as either a promise or a threat. "The *Republican* will stand for things. It will be on the fence on no important public questions. We shall express our opinions freely. If readers agree with us, good. If not, an opportunity for discussion will be afforded."

That last sentence, at least, proved to be well founded. The years ahead brought frequent opportunities for discussion.

The business policies were announced with flamboyant definiteness:

A newspaper is neither a charitable institution nor an object of charity. The *Republican* will be conducted as a business enterprise. Our advertising space and subscriptions will be sold on the basis of their worth alone. We expect to make no donations as inducements for business, nor do we wish to receive any. . . . We will at no time offer premiums to induce people to subscribe. Any paper that is not worth its price is at liberty to "give away" automobiles, whales, pottery, fish bait, cheap books, porcupines, dishes or whatever it can get for 13 cents from some overloaded factory. As for the *Republican*, it will be worth the price without any additional inducements.

Framing the political paragraph of the statement of policy raised a question that had to be answered at once. The *Republican*, during all its history, had been an undeviating advocate of the policies and candidates of the party from which its name was drawn. Most of its readers were party adherents in the county. Expressions of interest in the paper's future political policy had already come from so many persons that the importance of this paragraph was plainly considerable.

Having been enthusiastic for the election of Theodore Roosevelt two years before and for the success of the Progressive Party, my sympathy stood with the ideals proclaimed by that organization. Dimly, perhaps, I recognized that the Bull Moosers of 1912 were edging back into the G.O.P. Plainly enough, in Fountain County the Progressive numbers were a small minority. A declaration of Progressive faith might be futile. It might even generate the establishment of a new party paper for the Republicans. A Progressive newspaper already existed in Attica, a larger town in the north end of the county. The question of who should have the profits from public printing and advertising was of some consequence — of just how much I as yet had only a vague notion.

I concluded to commit the paper to the Republican party. I argued to myself that the Progressive movement would eventually effect its aims under the old party banner, that the third party scheme had served its purpose as a protest, but was futile as a future political course. But, nevertheless, I would assert independence. So the statement read: "The paper will not undergo any change in its political profession. It will be ready at all times to support all that is best in the Republican party, and to do its part when there is work to be done. We do not believe that mud and clubs are good weapons in any kind of fight, political or otherwise, and will endeavor to fight cleanly and squarely. We want it fairly understood that the opinions we voice will be our own, and those of no one else."

Perhaps I had compromised a little, but I hoped that in local matters the Republican forces would prove worthy of support; or else that I might, with the strategic advantage of owning the paper, be able to dominate sufficiently to justify the statement.

"How about getting some advertising for your first issue?" Cooper Clifton asked Tuesday morning. I hadn't thought much about it, but urged the young man to see what he could do. Cooper brought in enough orders for new space that some forty or fifty dollars' worth of business, including old advertisements and legals, was measured up.

That evening the expenses were roughly calculated. Twelve dollars a week for Bill Harden, nine for Cooper, six for Malcolm Adamson, a high school lad who had been engaged temporarily to help pick up local news and do errands. That was twenty-seven dollars. The building had been rented from Clifton for fifteen dollars a month. What paper and ink cost per issue I had no idea. There had been an order or so for job printing. Subscriptions would be coming in soon. Of course, the proprietor himself had not yet gone out after advertising. Evidently there would be a profit, once things really got going.

Press day approached. The boys upstairs had been setting type furiously, until the cases threatened to grow empty. Every page was planned to be filled with home-set type. No boiler plate nor patent insides (pages bought already printed) were to contaminate the paper.

The flat-bed press, so old that no one in the office knew

its history, could print four pages at a time. The paper stock came in the proper size so that the first four pages (actually pages two, three, six, and seven) were printed in one run; then the sheets were turned and the other four printed.

One young editorial ideal had to be bent that very first week. Neither time nor type remained to set up the entire eight pages. So three columns of boiler plate were selected and the first run made. The type supply had run so short that there had to be a pause to distribute some of the first run before the composition could be completed. Some time Friday, nearly a day late from the scheduled Thursday evening, the second run began. As the first copy emerged from the folder the editor took it up pridefully, to be put away in his archives as a memento.

Readers were confronted with a first page that was a phenomenon of bad typography. The announcement and statement of policy occupied the first two columns. In the lower right hand corner a square double-column cut presented in profile the features of the new editor. I believed in personal, rather than anonymous journalism. The self-advertisement of the picture might be in bad taste, I supposed, but suspected that success in a strange territory could be promoted by getting acquainted quickly with the people. The announcement had said: "I hope to make the personal acquaintance of every citizen of Covington and the surrounding communities. Not being gifted with a memory for faces and names, it may go slowly; but in time we will come to know each other."

An oval picture of the retiring proprietor, with a valedictory of flowery sentiments from his pencil, occupied the upper half of the two center columns. Local news items completed the page.

Once the issue was all printed and mailed, I cautiously tilted the high-backed revolving chair to its limit, rested weary feet on a corner of the exchange table, and looked at our handiwork. The routine news of the community seemed to be fairly covered. Time to attain the intimate local knowledge that would permit neat, original touches on the news had to be awaited. Compared with previous issues, I thought it was pretty good. Compared with the newspaper I hoped to publish, I had to admit that this issue was pretty weak.

Carefully I reread the editorials — double-column down the left side of the second page. Whoever proclaims such events had designated the approaching Sabbath as "Go-to-Church Sunday." The leading editorial endorsed the idea. This was an opportunity to indicate the paper's sympathy with "better things."

"The better people of every community are usually found connected in some way with the churches," the editorial said. "Attendance at church, however, is but the first step to a desirable end. We must carry our Christian principles into private, civic, social and public life, if we make Covington an ideal community."

"Covington an ideal community!" A large order for one young editor.

Another editorial paid the new owner's compliments to his predecessor. A handful of colloquial single-sentence paragraphs closed the column. "The guy who knocks his home town ought to move to some place that suits him," was neither the best nor the worst of them.

A gentleman stopped his automobile in front of the office and walked in.

"I want to subscribe to your paper!" he announced.

The flow of new business from "getting out a good newspaper" seemed to be getting under way.

"How much is it?"

"A dollar and fifty cents a year — and it's going to be worth the money."

"Oh! The papers here have always been a dollar. But all right." The gentleman laid down a dollar bill and a fifty-cent piece, and accepted a subscription receipt. "You might give me a copy of this week's paper," he said. "I just this morning heard that Clifton had sold out. I swore I'd never take the paper as long as he owned it. Never did like that fellow. Mighty glad you got him out. Good day!"

I held the dollar and a half in my hand for a moment,

then shouted up the stairway for the foreman to come down.

"Bill, what's the subscription price of this great news-paper?" I demanded.

Bill wiped his mouth with a side of his hand. "It's been a dollar a year as long as I can remember," he said.

"But it says here on the masthead a dollar and fifty cents!"

"People ain't used to payin' more 'n a dollar. Dollar 'n a half has been the printed price for a good while. That's just for the foreign advertisers to see. A dollar is all that was ever collected."

Five hundred of the dollars that had been counted on as revenue from the thousand subscribers — the full amount of one semi-annual payment of the mortgage — immediately faded out of the budget. The brief call by the first new subscriber left other food for reflection. The *Republican's* circulation had gone up a total of one, not because the editorial quality of the paper had improved, but because a former subscriber for reasons unknown had hated the former editor. Evidently even in this apparently placid and peace-ful town personalities clashed, feuds developed, and en-mities were cherished. Possibly even a new editor, free from previous entanglements, without intending to do so would find himself enmeshed in old controversies; or would lose friends and business by the simple process of running an honest newspaper. Nevertheless, I reflected that a few well-selected enemies could be more useful than the lukewarm friends that a colorless course might hope to create.

2

Where Money Came From

A s SPRING came shining and blooming up the Wabash, the external charm of the quiet streets and soft surrounding landscapes began to enchant the susceptible newcomer. Too, he sensed that the village wore an inner dignity assumed from the heritage of a semi-important past.

From elder citizens I picked up fragments of history that slowly pieced themselves together into a background that shimmered with tints of occasional glory. Home from the Mexican War, a slender, handsome young lieutenant with jet-black hair and beard had come to Covington in 1850 from Indianapolis. "Lew Wallace, Attorney-at-Law," read the black and white sign he nailed to the door of a meagerly furnished office. His beauteous, spirited young mother was buried in the old cemetery up Liberty street. The future author of *Ben Hur* had lived in Covington until his ninth year; he had gone to school there, and had played hookey to swim and fish in the Wabash. David Wallace, his father, had in the meantime been governor of Indiana. The place of his childhood had become the site of his future hopes.

When law business was slack, as often it was, Wallace toiled over a manuscript that he had started years earlier, before he had gone to Mexico. Two decades more were to elapse before he was finally to put it aside as finished and to choose its name, *The Fair God*. And late at night, when most of the town was in bed, the strains of a violin might be heard floating over the square from his office. Like as not a friendly rival lawyer, Daniel W. Voorhees, also a newcomer to the Fountain County bar, preparing for his later fame in the national House and Senate as the eloquent "Tall Sycamore of the Wabash," had dropped in to beg Wallace that he play his favorite tunes, "The Arkansas Traveller," "Cracovienne," and then, for both were in love and engaged, melodious "Annie Laurie."

A man of temporarily far more brilliant fame had lived in Covington in those faraway times. Not long before Wallace hung out his shingle, the whole nation had resounded with the slogan tongued by Edward A. Hannegan — "Fifty-four Forty or Fight!" In the Senate of the United States, Hannegan, only a few years after having been a Fountain County farm hand, had matched eloquence with such giants of the eighteen forties as Webster, Benton, Calhoun. When he feared that the President, James K. Polk, was leaning toward a compromise on the Oregon question, in violation of previous stands, Hannegan had uttered a sentence that history still quotes as memorable congressional philippic: "So long as one human eye remains to linger on the page of history, the story of his abasement will be read, sending him and his name together to an infamy so profound, a damnation so deep, that the hand of resurrection will never be able to drag him forth."

Out of the Senate, Hannegan had been sent to Berlin by the unresentful Polk to be minister at the Prussian court of Frederick William IV. Soon home again to Covington — alcohol and diplomacy had not mixed successfully — the noted man was pleased to extend to young Wallace the privileges of his library. He consented that his distinguished name be advanced for nomination to humble office in the state legislature. On a rainy election night he sat with the boys in Democratic headquarters while the returns came in. He was defeated. Wrapping his flowing cape around his impressive figure, he had announced as in a melodrama his interpretation of the vote: "This is the winding sheet of my political career!" and stalked off into the night. A few days later he went to St. Louis and died before his fifty-seventh birthday.

As we passed the Methodist church one day, a companion called attention to a substantial frame house across the street, set in a wide yard enclosed by a low picket fence.

"That's Hannegan's house. Dave Ferguson owns it now. Hannegan had his office in a little building in the corner of the yard when he lived there. See that room up there — on the second floor — the corner room? That's the room where Hannegan killed Captain Duncan."

A drunken fight between brothers-in-law, Hannegan and Duncan, was the story; a brawl over nothing in particular. Hannegan had stabbed Duncan with a dirk. Duncan lived long enough to declare that he remembered having attacked Hannegan, and to exonerate the statesman as having acted in self-defense.

I was thrilled to hear of these incidents from my new town's historic past and sought to find out more about her illustrious citizens. They, too, had once been young in Covington. I wondered whether it was in me to flash a phrase that would arouse the nation as had "Fifty-four Forty or Fight!" Or write a book that would endure as well as *Ben Hur*.

A tumble-down old building, used as an ice house, was pointed out. "The old Hiigel House — great old hotel in its day. Abraham Lincoln stayed there once." I was never able to verify the legend that Lincoln had visited Covington, though the event was probable. Danville, Illinois, only fifteen miles westward, was a regular point on Lincoln's law circuit. I read an account by Lew Wallace of a horse and buggy trip with Voorhees to Danville where, in the tavern, they had heard the future emancipator swap stories with Hannegan and others. Lucas Nebeker, the dean of the local bar, told me how he had gone to State Line in 1861, where he had listened when Lincoln, on his way to Washington, had spoken a few words.

No Covington citizen of the current period was known afar, although two years before there had died the latest of the town's national figures, Enos H. Nebeker, a Republican politician who had been appointed Treasurer of the United States when his friend, little Benjamin Harrison, was President.

The office of the *Covington Republican* had itself played a small part in history. The brick building, which bore numerous marks of decrepit age, had originally been constructed for a hotel, and for many years had served as a hostelry. In the stirring times of the Civil War, the editorial room had been a recruiting office, where young fellows from the countryside were outfitted in the federal blue and sent to fight for the Union. As earnestly as they with their bayonets, I mused sometimes, I would fight with the typewriter for what was right.

Covington had been established about 1826. Pleasantly situated upon high, level land, the western edge of the town sloped steeply down to a flat alluvial bottom, a third of a mile wide, beyond which flowed the Wabash river. This stream had been the community's first outlet to the commercial world. With flatboats, and later with steamboats, the produce of the section had been floated down to the Ohio and beyond. I wondered about those early steamboats; the river seemed hardly deep enough for them. Boys said that at low water they could walk across a stretch above the covered bridge. Forest clearing and erosion had changed the river. Someone said the last steamboat to visit Covington had gone downstream in 1873.

The heyday of old Covington had been in those early fifties. That was when the canal was dug, the canal that came up the Maumee from Lake Erie, through Toledo, cut past Ft. Wayne and followed the Wabash to Vincennes and the Ohio. On Sunday walks I could easily follow the route of the canal along the bottoms at the base of the bluffs. Water still lay in the old bed in many places, nourishing mosquitoes and catfish. Northward a spur of the Wabash railroad ran some twenty miles to Attica using the old towpath for its right of way. Southward the towpath provided a grassy, unobstructed walkway through a jungle of woods and underbrush that became a favorite route for expeditions afoot.

The canal's heyday had been brief. Railroad building, which followed soon after the waterway's completion, destroyed its usefulness. Had the leading men not been so devoted to the canal, it was said, Covington might have become a larger and more prosperous town. Being skeptical of the railroad, and tight with their money, they lost to

Attica the Wabash main line, a much more important road than the Peoria and Eastern Indiana that later became Covington's chief rail outlet.

While the canal business flourished, another engineering feat, not small for those days, threw a sturdy covered toll bridge across the Wabash river. This brought new trade to Covington from farms across the river in Warren and Vermillion counties. The covered bridge, with its original timbers, was still in use, a picturesque and romantic feature in the Covington landscape. It was soon to figure in an entertaining episode.

The population of the town had reached 1,366 by the census of 1860, I discovered, and had in twenty years grown to 1,920. By 1890 it fell to 1,891, and then rose by the end of the century to its maximum of 2,213. The 1910 census had counted only 2,096. The number was still declining. On days when business was slow I was moved to suspect that I had chosen a dead-end town and would have done better to have located in a faster-growing community. That suspicion was to grow. Still, Covington was an agreeable place of abode. Every street was lined with beautiful native trees, mostly maples. Many varieties, including some fine elms, crowded the courthouse square. Among them sat the dignified old courthouse, a stone and brick structure of curious but not unlovely design that, like the canal and the covered bridge and the first railroad, had been built in that lively decade of Covington's history, the eighteen fifties.

The trees in the square one week furnished proof that the weekly press could have its moment of power. Reed Marlatt, a high school youth, had asked to be permitted to work in the *Republican* editorial office, at little or no pay, for the sake of experience. One day he counted the trees in the square, and wrote a piece about the number. The morning after the paper came out a dozen citizens were noted to be taking their own individual arboreal censuses of the courthouse yard. No one believed that there were as many as sixty-six of the trees; they hoped to have the pleasure of proving the paper wrong. They were disappointed. Skeptical of the cub's accuracy, before printing the article I had myself carefully checked the count.

Neither the colorful background of the town's history nor the charm of its physical setting proved to be more delightfully interesting than the people themselves. At least half of them came from families who had settled there in the very early days, and nearly all the others were of characteristic Hoosier stock — friendly, shrewd, and highly individualistic. The years ahead were to be an intensive course in the most fascinating of laboratories, an intimate community of human souls. A sympathetic listener and a poor gossiper, I was given to look at skeletons in many closets, often by the owners themselves, to hear of inner hopes and disappointments, and to see beneath the surface the forces that pulled and tugged through the community.

How did the people live? Regardless of Covington's history and its charm, it was most necessary to make the *Republican* pay a profit. Success, it was not hard to see, depended completely upon earning a fair share of the collective local turnover. Weeks when the bills were bigger than the income made that uncomfortably clear.

With a few exceptions, everyone in business in Covington, so far as I could see, encountered intervals when bills were hard to pay. That puzzled me. I was naïve enough to assume that in a good society any competent and industrious individual could make a fair living without too much worry and trouble. Covington was located in a favorable section of the earth's surface. The soil of the farm country around about was truly fertile. Wood and coal were plentiful, transportation sufficient. The people seemed not to be inferior to human beings elsewhere. Why should not every reasonably energetic and prudent person get along comfortably? Where did Covington get its money? And how was The Republican to get a share of this money, a share big enough to make its publisher a "prosperous citizen"? I needed to know!

Agriculture, by any measurement, was the foremost local resource. The farms that stretched up and down both sides of the Wabash, and back across each of the three counties that cornered near Covington, were steadily producing new wealth. Day and night, rain or shine, winter and summer, products of value to mankind were maturing on those farms.

Having been raised on the land, I was familiar with these processes, and could talk with the farmers in their own technical language. At the office desk I liked sometimes to lean back and envision the miracles that nature, guided by trained farmers, would at the very moment be working on the hundreds of farms around Covington. Soil and raindrops, the sun's light and warmth, and man's skilled care all summer through were converting tiny grains of corn and wheat and oats and barley into harvests, a hundredfold and a thousandfold greater than the seed. Grass was flourishing in the meadows and pastures. Little pigs and lambs were growing from tiny brute babies into maturity, to provide luscious, nutritious hams and chops for hungry workers in distant cities. Hens were laying eggs, chicks were growing into fryers and hens. Through the winters, corn and hay and fodder were being fed to lazy beef creatures that one day would yield toothsome beefsteaks and nourishing roasts.

Yes, the fertile cornbelt soil was the foremost source of Covington's livelihood. Wagonloads of wheat, corn, and oats were brought in season to the grain elevator, where Walter Moore wrote thousands of dollars' worth of checks to farmers in payment for grain he shipped to Indianapolis or Chicago, eager markets that seemed to be insatiable. Nearly every week in the year fat hogs, beeves, calves, and sheep were brought to the railroad to be freighted out; the money for them was always paid on the spot by the local livestock buyers. For chickens and eggs that the poultry buyers gathered up, and for cream delivered to the little station an Illinois dairy concern had established, cash was paid.

Other lesser sources of new money could be counted. Across the river in the gaping brown gravel pits, glacial deposits of pebbles and sand were washed, graded, and shipped in carloads to ballast railroad tracks, improve highways, and furnish building materials. Down south of town eight or ten miles there were shallow veins of coal. Some forty years earlier a railroad had been run from Chicago to this district, and the mines had been active. Now only one deep shaft was worked, but the "slope mines," tunnels into the hillsides, were numerous. Coal of fair quality was hauled to Covington and to neighboring towns in horse-drawn wagons. The motor truck had not yet come to do such work. The coal averted the necessity for Covington to export much money in order to import fuel.

The Wabash River brought new money to town, also. A few thousand dollars' worth of mussel shells were shipped out each year to button factories at Muscatine, Iowa. The mussel fishermen counted on finding pearls amounting to half the value of the shells. The river and the tributary creeks accounted for another minor source of new wealth, the skins of furbearers. Each winter the streams and woods yielded their small portion of mink, muskrat, raccoon, and skunk, for whose pelts buyers offered cash. Now and then some timber was sold from farm woodlots for posts, mine props, or lumber; though not much commercial value was left in the woodlots. The fine trees from the great virgin forest had been cut decades before.

These were the natural resources of the country around Covington. Transient people now and then spent a little money in the restaurants or hotel, and in the stores; however, the usual errand of the transient visitor was to take money away. The town had one small seasonal industry, a cannery, where value was added to peas, sweet corn, pumpkins, and tomatoes by placing them in tin cans. A very few persons were well enough off to receive revenue from investments and inheritances that added a little to the total sum of new income for Covington. Pensions for services in the Civil and Spanish Wars supported a dwindling group of veterans and their widows.

That was all. I could find no other veins that yielded wealth to increase the volume of money. Practically all of the two thousand residents obtained their livings by circulating from pocket to pocket the proceeds of the surrounding farms, gravel pits, coal banks, waters, and the lesser sources of wealth. The actual process, of course, was by no means so confined. A daily stream of money trickled out of town to wholesalers for groceries, clothing, and supplies, mostly manufactured materials, in addition to that expended by citizens in Danville or sent to mail order houses. But all the money that came in had to be derived from the sources that have been named. Thus there were "exports" and "imports";

and a "balance of trade" that I suspected was not too favorable.

How, then, did the money these resources produced pass from hand to hand? How did each household actually obtain its living?

The leading "industry" was clearly the public schools. In the town itself two buildings required thirteen teachers and two janitors, a total of fifteen. The "little red school houses" that dotted the rural territory tributary to Covington — most of them actually little white school houses — employed at least thirty more teachers for more than half a year each. All the school employees were paid from local taxes.

The second largest enterprise was the courthouse. Here fifteen or twenty officials and aids were paid from the county tax funds. Ten lawyers had offices around the square, not counting several "members of the bar" who depended for their livings primarily on enterprises outside the legal vocation. Under the Indiana constitution at that time one could become a member of the bar and be admitted to practice in the local courts with no more formality than to present a certificate of good character, so that the bar membership list was somewhat longer than the number of actual lawyers. The requirements for becoming a saloon-keeper were more rigid than for admittance to the bar. The ten legal gentlemen drew wills and contracts, tried cases in litigation, collected delinquent accounts, acted as attorneys for estates in probate, and by other such services seemed, most of them, to make fairly good livings. Half of them were regarded, by Covington standards, as prosperous. They owned good homes, drove the larger automobiles, and habitually paid their bills upon presentation. The latter was a fairly reliable local test of prosperity or, at least, of solvency; although some reputed "skinflints" were suspected of putting off creditors in order longer to enjoy possession of their money.

Six doctors attended to the ailments of the community. Two were old men whose followings had dwindled away. One of these died in poverty after a lifetime of service. None of the doctors was ever known to refuse a call, though they well knew that some families would never pay, and others paid only when shamed into it by the need for further medical aid. The two dentists kept busy. Also there were two veterinarians. Five preachers completed the "professional" class.

Two department stores occupied the three-story buildings on opposite corners of the square. Dry goods, clothing, and shoes were the "departments." Another small store, Bill and Maggie Coleman's, sold dry goods and shoes; M. Schesley dealt in men's clothing, shoes, and haberdashery; and John Peters' store was devoted exclusively to shoes and their repair.

Seven grocery stores and two butcher shops supplied the community with the foodstuffs not produced in the gardens that nearly everyone grew. Every house in town was built on a lot large enough for a vegetable garden. Two of the grocery stores attested to the hazards of that business by changing hands frequently. Two had been run by the same owners for thirty or forty years. One was owned by Billy Dennis, a genial Irishman with a notable fund of stories. Ost and Davis owned the other — Peter Ost, a German who was equally famous for his merry stories, and Albert Davis, a quiet bachelor.

Ost and Davis ran a bakery in the back of their store. Their bread was wholesome but not in heavy demand after the more modern Danville bakeries began to deliver a superior product to Covington customers. Its quality inspired a witticism in Charley Bergdahl's tailor shop. Bergdahl, a friend to everybody, was a delightful Swede whose goose and bench had been local institutions since his boyhood. Charley liked company as he worked and made all loafers welcome, even when they crowded his narrow shop until little space was left for him. He talked and listened and laughed as he cut, sewed, and pressed; when cloth had to be spread he made his guests move over.

A shockingly brutal crime had stimulated a lively discussion one night. News had just been spread about an intoxicated young miner at Coal Creek who had beaten his own mother with a club, damaging the old lady severely. The men were arguing over what would be the most suitable punishment for such a fiend. Tortures had been proposed and ruled out as illegal. Finally, someone said that "if it has to be legal, the very least I would do to the dirty cuss would be to put him in the county jail for a whole year in solitary confinement and give him nothing but bread and water."

"Yes," added Ambrose Banta, the gangling, six-foot-five deputy sheriff and jailer. "Yes, and I'd make it Ost and Davis bread, too."

One of the butcher shops was notable in a way. Its owner was the only married man in Covington who lived openly with another woman. The townspeople were traditionally conventional, but they continued to trade at his shop. Whether this was because he was so defiantly frank about the matter, or because of the dependably superior quality of his meat, never became entirely clear.

Another man maintained a mistress and was reputed to make other illicit calls, but he lived respectably at home with his own wife. Once a nosy woman who had just heard about this man's adventuring telephoned his wife and excitedly asked, "Did you know your husband was going to see So and So?"

"Yes," snapped the injured wife, before she slammed the receiver. "Yes, I know it. Just have patience and he'll soon get around to you."

Among the business enterprises were three drug stores, two hardware stores, two plumbers, two soda and confectionery shops, four barber shops, two banks, a building and loan association, always two and at times four restaurants, a pool room, three jewelry and watch repair stores, two dealers in junk and second hand goods, one hotel, three boarding houses, a notion store, two livery barns, two blacksmith shops, one lumber yard, two coal dealers, four garages and part of the time six, a large farm implement house owned by Mayor McGeorge, a harness shop, a moving picture theater, two furniture and undertaking establishments, one tombstone dealer, a music store, a shoe repair shop, a milliner, a cream buying station, the two newspapers, the *Republican* and the *Friend*, and John Duncan's one man job printing shop.

The telephone company employed six or seven people as switchboard operators and linemen. The municipally owned waterworks and power plant gave jobs to about the

same number. The town had a day policeman and a night
officer. The postmaster employed two assistants, while five
rural mail carriers earned good salaries. The Peoria and
Eastern Illinois railroad employed four or five men regularly
at the depot, and gave intermittent jobs to laborers on track
maintenance; the "Towpath" branch of the Wabash kept a
station agent.

The grain elevator, canning factory, and livestock shippers
have been mentioned. A firm of title abstractors might have
been listed amongst the lawyers because their special work
partook of the legal character. Part of the time six saloons
were in operation. One or two men were employed by oil
companies, distributing gasoline and kerosene. Three traveling salesmen made their homes in Covington.

Several of the business houses hired clerks whose services
supplemented those of the owners and owners' families.
Ten to fifteen dollars a week was considered fair pay, ample
for the maintenance of a household.

A sprinkling of carpenters, painters, paperhangers, and
masons were numbered amongst the good citizens, the best
of them being respected as much as the minor storekeepers.
These specially skilled men fell into two classes, "bosses"
who took contracts, and the others who preferred to be hired
by the day. Allied loosely to this group were the handymen,
jacks of all trades, who could do passable work at several
jobs. Common labor supported many men and their families. Few in this category expected to be employed every day,
but they were called upon to help out farmers in busy times,
to dig ditches, aid in moving, beat rugs, polish stoves, assist
other more skilled workmen, or to perform almost any not
too difficult task. One or two teamsters survived, soon to
debate the advisability of selling their horses and buying
trucks.

Every woman in Covington did her own housework, except possibly half a dozen who kept steady hired girls. For
special occasions, such as spring-cleaning and large parties,
competent women who worked out by the hour could be
obtained on short notice. Other women wage earners took
in washing, did sewing and dressmaking, were amateur mil-
liners, minded children, or nursed the sick. The majority of

teachers and many of the clerks and book keepers were women. The busiest of the better paid female specialists was the faithful, gentle, tireless old Mrs. Paisley who acted as midwife, doctor's assistant, and nurse to the mothers and babies. Though the total population of Covington had changed little in fifty years, the custom of having babies was assiduously maintained. Two women were alleged to be prostitutes, but the oldest profession was not recognized as a commercial activity.

The town was home for a dozen or so of retired farmers. All of these were elderly men, who by industry and economy had saved up enough money to leave off continuous work. Their farms had advanced steadily in value since the eighties and nineties and, they supposed, if properly maintained would always continue to be worth a little more each year. Usually they had moved from the farms to make room for sons and sons-in-law; others, actuated solely by the wish to spend their declining days at ease, rented their lands to the best tenants they could find. In this general group were a few "town farmers," inheritors of large farms who resided in town by choice and lived easily on the proceeds from their lands.

Widows, who subsisted from the estates large and small that had been left by their husbands, were numerous. Now and then a widow remarried. One was regarded as especially successful because she had outlived two well-to-do husbands. She came near to marrying a third, the richest man in town, just before he died from old age.

Of the professional men, merchants, artisans, and others, those who enjoyed net incomes above three thousand dollars a year were few. Four or five of the number may have had in excess of four, or possibly even five thousands in exceptionally prosperous years, counting one man who owned a great deal of farm land. The majority earned less than twelve hundred or less even than one thousand dollars yearly. Some must have done with less than five hundred.

Indeed, I never was able to understand how a few of the moderately prominent citizens really managed to live, although they owned homes, bought Fords, sent children to college, and their wives took active parts in the social affairs.

Some of these were "members of the bar," but apparently without law business. Their offices carried signs such as "Real Estate and Insurance," yet they were rarely known to sell any real estate, and were too seldom seen away from the courthouse square to earn many insurance commissions. Either money from law, real estate, and insurance came more easily than I knew, or these men were master economists. They had time to enter every discussion, visit leisurely in any store or office, and were never too busy to keep thoroughly informed on all the gossip of the town.

More remarkable was the fact that no family in all Covington, except for a very small number of willful and incompetent wastrels, ever seemed to lack the essentials of frugal comfort. To their small incomes were added the abundance of well tilled gardens, and adept choice of the frequent surpluses from nature's abundance. Everyone offered his neighbors whatever fruits and vegetables he could not use. Wood enough for all winter could be had for little more than cutting and hauling, and coal was cheap. Rent and taxes were moderate, so that any family without a desire for display could live on two dollars a day or even less, and many did.

Such were the sources of what wealth there was in Covington, and thus were the channels through which it circulated. After putting together this picture of the community's economic structure, I wondered what I could do that would strengthen it, to make wealth flow more freely and abundantly for the good of the people and for the prosperity of the *Republican*. In the course of time I found at least one idea; and I was not willing to concede that Covington was a dead-end.

3

Ousting the Courthouse Gang

THE SECOND Sunday afternoon in Covington was spent in the office. I had no other place to go. A bitter wind was whooping through the empty streets and rattling the office doors and windows. A bucket of coal made the old black stove glow red. The room was warm and comfortable. With the long-bladed editorial scissors at hand, I started idling through the accumulated "exchanges," the newspapers from nearby Indiana and Illinois towns that came weekly and daily in return for the *Republican*. From time to time I glanced with frank self-satisfaction at a page from the Sunday Indianapolis *Star* folded to display a single-column engraving under the headline: "Youth is Believed Youngest Indiana Newspaper Owner."

"McMillen, despite his youth, may be called a veteran newspaperman," said the two-paragraph article which mentioned the various previous connections. "He does not expect to change the political policy of the paper," the piece concluded, "but plans the introduction of some radical innovations in weekly newspaper publishing."

The appearance of the Sunday *Star*'s article was due to no enterprise on the part of that important state newspaper. I had furnished the enterprise, having provided the *Star*'s Covington correspondent with the information, a photograph, and the suggestion that probably the "youngest newspaper owner" idea would sell the story. In my private mind I had to admit that a fair measure of vanity had prompted the desire to be pictured in the *Star*. However, I believed that publicity in an Indianapolis newspaper was sound business which should add to the *Covington Republican*'s prestige and to its earning power. Actors, politicians, and business concerns hired press agents for dollar reasons; so why should not a country town editor be his own press agent?

The locked door rattled louder than before. I looked up to see a well-dressed man waiting to enter. I asked him in. He took off his overcoat and then introduced himself.

"My name is Wilkey," he said. "Elmer Wilkey. I'm in the real estate business here in Covington." We shook hands. He accepted a chair and made himself comfortable near the stove. He appeared to have called with a definite purpose and to expect to remain awhile. I guessed that he might have a house for sale, although at that period in Indiana Sunday seemed to be an unsuitable day to broach a matter of business. The surmise was wrong.

"Well, McMillen, I'm mighty glad to meet you," he said, after offering a cigar and lighting one for himself. "I would have been around sooner but I was away on business all week."

Waiting for no reply, he drove on to his point. "I understand you are going to run this as a regular Republican paper."

"That's the policy," I said.

"Well, that's fine. We certainly have needed a good, vigorous, *loyal* Republican paper in this county. The *Ledger* up at Attica went Bull Moose. I wouldn't want to say a word against Clifton, but he couldn't always be depended on to stay on the reservation. And we haven't any other Republican paper.

"You see," he went on, "I happen to be the Republican county chairman. We want to elect a Republican ticket this fall. I believe you and I can put it across."

I tried to appear mature and noncommittal as I listened to his clipped, decisive speech. Better dressed, more suave, evidently faster thinking than most Covingtonians, he challenged interest. A county chairman was influential. This aggressive, self-confident visitor could be important to the future. I determined to speak warily until the man measured himself.

If Wilkey turned out to be a square-shooter, in sympathy

with decent ideals of public service, there would be no problem. As he went on talking, I saw that he had mental dex-
terity and was likely to be quick on his political feet. Nothing wrong with that, for quick maneuvering was sometimes
the essence of successful political action. The impression
grew that here was a fellow who could see beyond his nose,
at least for a little distance, and who would play the game
the wisest way to win. Perhaps if he did not see public
affairs through idealistic eyes, he could at least be swayed.
Again, if he viewed politics solely as plunder, the only alternative would be to put up a fight.

To start a fight in a Hoosier political ring, I fully com-
prehended could be a lively undertaking for a green hand.
Nevertheless, I already had command of power. As Wilkey
had just said, the *Republican* was the only newspaper in the
county that bore the party label.

"What is the political situation in the county now, Mr.
Wilkey?" I asked.

"Well," he explained, "this is normally a Republican
county. It's close, but it belongs to the Republicans. Fac-
tional divisions beat us eight years ago. Ever since then
the Democrats have controlled the court house and the
county business. They still have the whole thing — judge,
commissioners, and everything down to the poorhouse. We
might have done something two years ago, but the Bull
Moose put out a third ticket and we lost. This year, I think
we can win. The Bull Moosers are drifting back; we may be
able to avoid a third ticket. The fact that the Democrats
have been in for eight years is an advantage to us, as well
as to them. They have naturally made some enemies. I
think the people are ready for a change."

I remarked that the people might vote for a change if
they thought it would be for the better, and asked what
would be his policy as county chairman.

"To win this election," Wilkey answered, with a flicker of
tentative humor in his cool eyes.

"And what is your program for carrying out that policy?"

"Well, we're working on that now," he replied. "I suppose we can count on your help?"

"I'm rather new here to be of much immediate help," I

evaded. "I'll want to get the lay of the land before I do much. And I don't know much about politics."

He reminded me that the matter had a practical aspect for me. "A Republican administration here will mean quite a lot to you. The county printing and advertising business is a considerable item. I would like to see you get it."

I could not deny my interest in that. I explained that although I had supported Theodore Roosevelt, I believed in party responsibility and that the time had returned to restore the Republican party. "The best support I can give the party now is to insist that it stand for honest and efficient local government here in Fountain County. Any time the Republican party fails to do that I expect to decide for myself what this newspaper will then do."

Having made that declaration I added, "If I judge you correctly, Mr. Wilkey, you believe that the best politics is to put up the best men. With that program you can count on me."

The county chairman threw his cigar stub into the coal bucket and reached for his overcoat. "I'm mighty glad to get acquainted with you," he said. "I see that you and I are going to understand each other perfectly. Well, success to you!"

I wasn't sure what he meant by saying that we would understand each other perfectly. Two or three nights later Mr. Wilkey walked in abruptly and immediately began to talk.

"We're going to win this election," he began. "We're going to win it hands down. But we'll know we've had a fight.

"I'll tell you what we've got to do. We've got to pick out the best Republican in Fountain County for each office on the ticket. Get the best man we can find to run for auditor, the best man for sheriff, and right on down the line."

I wondered whether my own idea was being brought back to me. He was enthusiastic as he went on: "The Democrats are sure they can't be licked. That's their weakness. Anybody can be licked. A lot of Republicans think we can't win, either. All right, that's going to be to our advantage. There are some mighty fine Republicans in this

county, able men who stand high with everybody, who
wouldn't take an office if you handed it to them on a silver
platter. We'll get them on the ticket. If they thought there
was a chance of winning they would turn us down, but
we'll tell 'em that it's their duty to the grand old party to
let their names go on the ticket. Help build up the party
again — you know, that kind of stuff. Then, when they
have been nominated, they won't want to be beaten. They'll
want to win. They'll go to work. We'll fool 'em. We'll
elect 'em."

The county chairman became a frequent caller. He
brought in every new idea for the campaign and talked it
out in detail. He did this more to clear his own mind than
to get my opinions, but I appreciated his apparent confidence. From time to time he brought in party workers and
prospective candidates to be introduced. We made two or
three trips together into other parts of the county. By June
we were ready for the county convention. This was the last
year for county conventions in Indiana; not long afterward
a primary election law was adopted.

The convention nominated, without contest or opposition, the slate that we had prepared. The nominee for
every office was a man of character and ability. Every section of the county was represented. It had taken some per-
suasion to get two or three of the strongest men to agree to
be nominated, but the flattering appeal that the party
needed the prestige of their names had been effective despite
their disinclination for public office. After the Democrats
had held their convention and our candidates measured
themselves against their opponents, Wilkey's prediction began to work out. Each determined not to let himself be
defeated by such an inferior scamp as the opposition had
put up. Wilkey inspired the precinct workers with a convic-
tion that with such a ticket victory was possible, despite
the recent defeats. The candidates themselves began to
believe that they could be elected. Shortly the campaign
was on in earnest.

Meanwhile the *Republican* had experienced no sharp up-
turn in its volume of business. New subscriptions came in,

but slowly, advertising was scanty, and job printing not very profitable at the local price scale. I looked covetously at the legal advertisements. One class of these came by favor of the lawyer or of his clients. These were notices required to settle estates or to quiet titles. The law required such notices to run three or four times and it set the fee at ten cents a line for the first insertion and five cents a line for each subsequent insertion. This was profitable business.

Another and more abundant type of legal publication was the public notice or report which the law required from various officers of the county and its eleven townships. The state law specified that most of these should be published in two papers of different political faiths within the county. Some had to be printed in one paper only. Under the Democratic county administration the *Republican* got none of this business. Notices for publication in only one paper naturally went to the Covington *Friend,* my local competitor, which was the Democratic county organ. If the law demanded two papers, the Attica *Ledger* was second choice. Because it supported the Bull Moose faction the Democrats regarded the *Ledger* as an ally. A Republican county administration was bound to bring the fat end of this business to my paper. Moreover, the newspaper of the dominant party always had the contract for the stationery, legal blanks, and office supplies required by county officials. The righteousness of the Republican cause became more evident as I calculated these possible additions to my income.

I looked back into the files to see how previous campaigns had been conducted. They gave me an idea. From all I could learn, political campaigns in Fountain County for longer than men could remember had been notable for personal abuse and mudslinging. The *Republican,* it appeared, had been quite adept in this method. I recalled also that it had lost the four previous campaigns.

The vote records indicated that the county was nearly equally divided between the two principal parties. Loyal Democrats always voted Democratic and about the same number of loyal Republicans always voted Republican. The victory went to the party that attracted the largest number of votes from the third element, the small number who were not governed by simple party loyalty. Those were the votes we had to win.

At the first party conference of candidates and precinct workers someone asked what plans I had for the paper's participation in the campaign.

"I can tell you one thing I am *not* planning to do," I answered. "I am not going to sling mud at anyone. I shall not mention unpleasantly a single one of the Democratic county candidates. Everyone of them has friends and well-wishers. These people will resent personal attacks. Their ill-feeling will spread to others whose votes you men might otherwise get."

"How you going to make a fightin' campaign if you won't hit at anybody?" a committeeman of the old bloody shirt school wanted to know. "Aren't you going to lambast these danged Democrats?"

"Oh, we'll murder them," I promised. "We'll attack them plenty — but in a different way. Our opponents have been in office for eight years. From what I can see, and from what you fellows tell me, the boys over in the courthouse have learned to work together pretty closely. All right, that's a gang!

"The paper will attack the courthouse gang week in and week out. But it won't take a crack at any individual member. Then there will be no personal hard feelings. Nap Cardiff's friends can think I mean Oscar Phebus and Claude Philpot, when I denounce the gang. Claude and Oscar can think I mean Nap Cardiff and Van Martin and Roy Sanders.

"We will win this election by making friends, not by making enemies!"

No one broke the thick silence for several seconds. Two or three aimed thoughtfully at the cuspidor. Then Finis Drake, a farmer from Fulton township who had been persuaded to run for county recorder, gave his thigh a resounding slap and shouted, "By golly, young fellow, you're right! We've got to get the people that change their votes to vote for us this time."

The *Republican* began its campaign quietly. A series of

short biographies praised sky-high the sterling character of each candidate on our ticket. These sketches bore heavily upon the business abilities of the Republican nominees. "An honest, business-like administration" was our pledge and slogan.

A minor decision by the incumbent Democrats became, much to their amazement, a virulent issue early in the campaign. The ancient courthouse, built in Covington's famous fifties, had become cluttered by accumulated court documents, the impedimenta of many decades, which could not legally be destroyed. The retiring county clerk, Leroy Sanders, who was also chairman of the Democratic county committee, recommended to the commissioners that these documents should be put in jackets and indexed. Then future generations could find the few that might be wanted without having to search through dusty shelves and boxes. The cost, he thought, would be only a few hundred dollars, while the officials would be thanked in years to come by all who had occasion to search old records. The commissioners authorized $500 for the work and gave Sanders a contract to proceed.

To the people of the county in general it made no difference when the courthouse clerks had to hunt for half a day to locate some old document that a lawyer happened to need. The *Republican* first reported in prominent space but without comment that Sanders had been given the contract. The next week carried no denunciation, either; merely another news story:

> Opinions of attorneys appear to be somewhat at variance as to the legality of the recent act of the county commissioners in letting to County Clerk Leroy Sanders, the Democratic county chairman, a contract for filing and indexing the records of his office. The contract provides that Mr. Sanders shall receive two cents for each document filed and four cents in case a legal jacket must be provided for it. He has employed to work by the day two assistants for the job.
>
> The belief is advanced by a number of men of law that the appropriation is questionable on the ground

that the filing and indexing of the records comes within the regular duties of the clerk for which the state law provides that he shall receive the annual sum of $2,200, plus fees amounting to about $900. If this is the case, the commissioners have merely added a bonus of $500 or more to the clerk's salary. $500 was the amount appropriated to start the work.

Others question the propriety of having let the contract to the county clerk without it having been advertised in the usual manner. . . . The matter has created widespread discussion, and many people are interested in knowing just what would have been the legal and proper manner in which to have proceeded.

Word was passed to all Republican precinct workers and candidates to start talking about the filing and indexing contract. Within a few days the county began to stir with indignation at the arrogance of the "courthouse gang" for giving such a lucrative contract to one of their number, one who also was their party's county chairman. The next issue of the *Republican* reported the public reaction and added more fuel by intimating that, because of the large number of documents and records the actual cost was likely far to exceed the $500 first appropriated and might, indeed, turn out to be more than treble the amount.

Keeping suspicion's accusing finger steadily pointed at the courthouse gang, the *Republican* hammered away. Turn out the whole corps of Democratic politicians who have been dominating the county! Elect a virtuous group of high-minded patriots whose remarkable business ability will serve the public with greater efficiency at less cost! Week after week the idea was reiterated that only professional politicians were running on the Democratic ticket, while the Republican aspirants were all business men or farmers of sterling character willing temporarily to sacrifice themselves for the public good.

Then, early in September, the Democrats dropped a bombshell. They lowered the tax rate. Due to the excellent business management by their administration, the announcement said, and to the faithful devotion of all their officials to economy and the interests of the taxpayers, the county rate for next year would be lower. Their party organs jubilantly paraded and repeated the news. The lower rate, they said, effectually squelched the false claims of their Republican opponents, and the decent people of the county would show their appreciation for such excellent Democratic servants by triumphant reelection in November.

We had to face the truth; we had been set back. The Republican workers were frankly worried. From the start their confidence had depended largely upon the enthusiasm whipped up by Elmer Wilkey and upon the rather faint hope that the people were ready to vote for a change.

While making the round of county offices for routine news one day early in October, I had occasion to ask Captain Gray, the county auditor, for a particular figure. Engaged with a visitor, he said genially, "You can find it in the commissioners' record, back there in the vault, bottom shelf on this side."

After finding the figure I noticed that the big leather book contained the official minutes of the meeting at which the lower tax levy had been adopted. I read them over without comfort. Turning idly backwards through the book some sheets of scrap paper caught my attention. A figure met my eye that had not been made public. There, in the auditor's own handwriting, was the official estimate of the receipts of the county for the following year. I hastily copied all the figures on the sheets, put the book back in place, and gave the auditor especially hearty thanks for being permitted to examine the book. It was, of course, a public record.

Back at the office, I checked and rechecked the figures. They revealed exactly what I had faintly hoped. The total valuation of taxable property, multiplied by the newly lowered tax rate, failed to equal the appropriations already made for the following year. The discrepancy was not much, but it was plenty for the purpose I had in mind.

"The lowered tax levy is a political trick," the *Republican* thundered in its next issue. "The courthouse gang is trying once more to fool the people of Fountain County into keeping them in office."

Double column down the front page the article hammered at the iniquitous duplicity of the gang in lowering the tax levy when the appropriations had already exceeded the prospective revenue. Determined that this issue could win the election I decided to blanket the county. "Print three thousand copies this week," I told Bill Harden, the foreman.

"Who's going to pay for the extra copies?" Bill wanted to know.

"I don't know who will — the Democrats, I hope. Our commitee hasn't got much money."

"Better make 'em put it down on the barrel," Bill advised. "A dollar now is better than a hundred you're hopin' for and don't get."

Sure that if enough people could see the article the voters would blast the gang out of the courthouse, I paid no heed to Bill's advice. The extra distribution would be a public service, advertise the paper, and help to bring the county printing to the *Republican* office.

Elmer Bowers, who was local correspondent for the Danville papers, dropped in just in time to inspire further use of the idea.

"Want a story, Elmer?"

"Sure. Give me a long one. I get paid space rates."

I rewrote the charges against the courthouse gang. Bowers read the story carefully. "Well," he said, "I'm a Democrat, and I expect that if I send this out the boys will give me hell. But," he grinned, "this is news, and my duty is to send out the news."

Next day the Danville dailies, whose circulation in Fountain County exceeded the *Republican*'s, arrived with the dispatch in full:

Covington, Ind., Oct. 13. — (Commercial-News Special) Claims of the Fountain county Democratic administration that the affairs of the county have been administered in a business-like manner received a severe jolt Friday when the Covington *Republican* in a front page article showed figures taken from the auditor's office that revealed a decidedly unbusiness-like condition of affairs.

The figures, which were compiled carefully by Wheeler McMillen, the editor of the *Republican*, show that the Democratic county council has already appropriated $1,776.81 more than the revenue of the county for 1915 will be. The taxation receipts for 1915 were estimated by the auditor at $52,131.78. Revenues to be derived from the various county offices were estimated at $11,506.49, making a total of receipts of $62,638.27.

The appropriations for the 1915 budget, already made by the council at its September meeting, amounted to $64,415.08. Thus there has been appropriated $1,776.81 more than the total amount of the revenue in sight.

Basing the estimate on the amount of extra appropriations this year, it is plain that the county will have to spend next year between $1,500 and $2,000 more than the revenues will be.

Editor McMillen then points out that the lower levy this year is merely a trick by the democratic gang to deceive the people into believing that their taxes will be lower. The article shows that next year the county will have to borrow a big sum to keep the county going, and that then a much larger levy will be required the following year to meet the deficit and pay back the borrowed money.

A continuing barrage kept the Attica and Covington Democratic organs, as well as the party candidates, busy explaining and denying the charges. "When the infant editor of the *Covington Republican* emerges from his swaddling clothes," predicted the gentle editor of the Attica Democratic paper, "he will perhaps become better informed about county affairs that now seem completely beyond his understanding." Ignoring all explanations and denials, the *Republican* returned to the attack each week. Subscribers began to bring in tax receipts to prove how Democratic mismanagement had affected them.

A Wabash township farmer, J. A. "Gusta" Shaw, found himself in the midst of the controversy. The *Republican* reported that his taxes had grown from $64.07 in 1909 to $124.26 in 1914 and declared that this proved the extravagance of the courthouse gang. A three-column reply in the Fountain Warren *Democrat* of Attica declared in the headline that "Mr. McMillen, Editor of the *Covington Republican,* Is Either Ignorant or Purposely Intended to Deceive, or Both." The article conceded the increase in Shaw's taxes which were a matter of record. The rise had taken place, however, the detailed explanation said, because of larger township expenses which were administered by Dr. Coggins who was the trustee of Wabash township and also the Republican candidate for state representative; and because of the cost of new gravel roads, for which Mr. Shaw himself was partly responsible since his name appeared on petitions for four separate road improvements.

"Look at your tax receipts!" was the *Republican*'s answer. "See if they are not much larger now than when the Democrats took over the county. Vote Republican if you want lower taxes!"

Except for printing the cards which candidates passed out as they visited around the county and the bills which announced campaign meetings, the newspaper office derived little cash profit from the campaign's proceedings. But the excitement was enjoyable and the hope that the county printing business would improve the income buoyed up the effort.

The county chairman strolled into the office one evening wearing an unusually glum look. "Mac, we're in a fix," he said. "And I don't know what to do about it."

"What's the fix? Can't we get out of it?"

"I'll tell you. Here in Covington there are about thirty 'floaters' who always expect to be paid for voting. The state committee can't do anything for us. The Democrats have plenty and they are going to use it. We'll lose those votes. And we need 'em. Bad."

"How does anybody know how a man votes, even if he has been paid?" I asked.

"You don't know. If he is paid he is supposed to deliver."

"Seems to me that a man low enough to sell his vote might cheat in other ways. I'm glad we haven't got any money for such trash. We had better be beaten than to buy the election," I added, trying to be virtuous over our poverty.

"I hate it, too," Wilkey said; "but it's always been done to a certain extent."

We sat in silence for a few minutes. Suddenly Wilkey slapped his leg. "Bet you we can get those floaters yet! We'll pass the word around among these fellows that because we're fighting for clean politics the Republicans are not going to put out any money. Then we'll suggest to them that they might as well take the Democrat money — and then vote however they please!"

The town precinct committeemen scoffed at the idea but were persuaded to circulate the suggestion among the "floaters." The honor of the party was safe in view of our lack of cash resources.

At length came the day of decision and its night. In a few hours the results of the hard-fought campaign were to be known. Was the night to report triumph or failure? Was the county to have a new, business-like administration or not? And especially, was the *Republican* office to get the county printing and advertising?

The news came in with aggravating slowness. From a regularly Democratic precinct the first report arrived. It was discouraging. The precinct was still Democratic by a fair majority. Then someone produced the vote from the same precinct for the preceding election and pointed out that we had made a slight gain, especially for two or three of our stronger candidates. Could it indicate a trend? A big-enough trend?

By messenger and by telephone the figures trickled in from the villages and borders of the county. That our ticket had made a good race began to be clear, though the figures gave too much reason to fear that such cold comfort might have to suffice.

Finally, around three o'clock in the morning, weary messengers arrived with the full reports from the two remaining and determining townships. Their figures were eagerly added to those already reported. Columns were totaled in feverish haste. We had won!

Every Republican candidate except the aspirant for the treasurership had been elected. But by what majorities! Finis Drake had been elected county recorder by three votes. The highest margin of all was won by the candidate for sheriff, Harry Wertz. He had defeated his opponent by 152 votes. Most of the majorities were of less than a hundred.

I turned in that night reflecting that the county treasurer's office did not have much public advertising to dispense anyway.

In two years another campaign would come. I hoped that the "honest, business-like administration" slogan would still ring true then.

4

Personal Admissions

A WONDERFUL, a roaring, glorious, tingling time, that first year in Covington promised to be. A great year to be alive and twenty-one! Henry Ford had started to pay the least of his help five dollars a day. Common folks were buying automobiles. Though the marines were about to land at Vera Cruz, except for the brief victorious war with Spain, the country had known peace for nearly half a century. The first ships were soon to pass through the Panama Canal. No one dreamed that before the year had ended violent warfare would be thundering in Europe nor that before long Covington youths would go or be sent to fight overseas.

Here was I, a boy who thought he already was a man, at about the age when others were juniors or still sophomores in college. I owned a newspaper; I was the editor and proprietor. At least I had made a down payment and owned the title. In a new town in a new state, where no one had ever seen me before, I was free to make whatever character I chose. Away from home and with no supervisory eye upon me I could roister if I wished or set out to become a solid citizen. I was launched. The world, I thought, was mine to mold: the thought that the world might mold me instead was not to arrive until later.

That single year was to bring lessons in business and politics, in love and in the arts of leadership. Of course I aspired to financial success, to prestige, even to note beyond the nearby counties. I was sure that if I made the *Republican* good enough these rewards and more were certain to follow; and I was more than certain that I could make my paper the best weekly that Indiana had ever known. My opinion of my talents was not modest. There was much ahead to be learned by experience; the experience turned out to be full of adventures.

The first taste of "note" — or notoriety — came neither from a brilliant editorial nor from a creditable civic achievement. A dull day in news for Elmer Bowers, the Covington correspondent for out-of-town daily newspapers, was responsible. Bowers, a clever, genial gentleman, compelled by a childhood illness to walk with a crutch and cane, sent daily dispatches to two papers in Danville, the city of 30,000 across the Illinois line, and occasional items of wider than nearby interest to the Indianapolis *News*. The Covington newspaper owners in the past had given Bowers no assistance because his stories in the Danville dailies too often scooped the local weeklies. I had decided that since the Danville competition was a fact of existence, my best strategy was to print a quality of local news and comment that they could not supply; and, by helping Bowers occasionally, I figured he would be willing to quote the *Covington Republican* now and then, thus making them advertise my paper to prospective subscribers. It was easy to save Bowers some effort in obtaining for his Danville dispatches details that he would have gathered anyway.

As soon as spring had definitely come, I began going bareheaded as I had done for several summers. It was a surprise to find that in the informal atmosphere of Covington the habit stirred curiosity and attracted attention. "Where's your hat?" was a greeting I heard daily.

Then the Danville papers came to Covington with this dispatch:

Deputy County Clerk Vaun E. Flora, Wesley E. Blythe and Elmer Bowers, who are employed in the clerk's office, are trying to solve a mystery, but the plot thickens, and the mysterious disappearance of a box of fine imported Havana cigars from a private drawer remains unsolved. A gentleman with a heart as big as a Georgia watermelon left the boys the cigars, in remembrance of their courtesy in issuing a marriage license, but somebody in nosing around the clerk's desk discovered the cigars and gently appropriated them for his own consumption, being kind enough, however, to leave the box. Suspicion points to Ex-County Treasurer Will H. Thompson, County Assessor Charles Dochterman, or Sheriff Martin as being the guilty culprits.

A private detective has been placed on the case, and he is hot on a clue that connects Wheeler McMillen, the hatless editor of the *Republican,* with the disappearance of the cigars, as he was seen with a cigar stuck in his mouth that corresponds with the famous Havanas that are missing.

The "hatless editor" tag stuck. The Mexican border correspondent of the Indianapolis *News,* writing from the sunny Rio Grande about a shortage of headgear in one troop, reflected this curious notoriety in a comment: "It's all right to run around in Indiana bareheaded, like the editor of the Covington *Republican* does, but down here you must have a top piece, especially as most of the soldiers have shaved heads."

Friendly jibes from the press of nearby towns became common enough to establish the hatless legend. This ridiculous kind of prominence bothered me at first, until I realized that perhaps it could be more asset than liability. A sort of personal trade mark might become profitable. All references to the editor that appeared in other papers, whether favorable or unfavorable, were thereafter scrupulously reprinted, often with retorts, in a column of miscellaneous nonsense on the editorial page.

Amongst this nonsense was thrown occasionally a dash of doggerel, usually in the prose-rhyme style that had been made popular by Walt Mason in his nationally syndicated newspaper feature. The innovation prompted occasional sarcasms from the "brethren" of the state press: "The effect of spring," the Attica *Tribune* noted, "has finally worn out on the spirits of Editor McMillen of the *Covington Republican* and he has none of his handmade poetry in his paper this week."

With a boyish weakness for wordy alliteration, I sometimes let things appear in the "Editorial Effervescence" department that any sense of dignity might have excluded even from a column with that title. The Veedersburg *News* caught up one of these exuberant outrages:

Editor McMillen of the *Covington Republican* has gone dippy over the beautiful coloring of the autumn leaves and now being in the last stages of the "willies" is a sure-enough candidate for the madhouse. He has last been seen towering above the horse weed on the banks of the Wabash and as a parting word to his degenerate countrymen says: "And lost is he who cannot revel in the rainbow riot of royal refulgence, who cannot feel a stirring in his soul when he sees the sunkissed sepia and sanguine scenery of the enchantingly beautiful Baltimore Hills beyond where the wakeful waters of the waveless Wabash wash the willowy wildwood banks of Warren."

I was more serious in attempts to imitate the pithy one- or two-sentence semi-humorous editorial paragraph of the type that so long has been a standard feature of American newspaper journalism. These efforts ranged from comments on topics of current national interest to commonplace jibes at human frailties, with a sprinkling of exhortations to civic consciousness and of purely personal expressions. Examined now, when their allusions to the news are stale, the lines sound like flat space-fillers. But in 1914 I supposed that the tribute of wide reprinting certified their quality. If a line won quotation by a half-dozen of the country papers on the exchange list I felt that it was a fair hit; if the Indianapolis papers printed one, that was a kind of journalistic success, for then it spread to other dailies in important cities. A clipping bureau, in return for two copies of the *Republican,* mailed weekly whatever mentions of the *Covington Republican* or the editor were found in other papers. Simple comments upon human nature gained wider circulation, I found, than wisecracks upon the news in general. The Indianapolis *News* set afloat quips such as these:

The frost is on the pumpkin and the fodder's in the shock, and the Morris chair and davenport will soon bear the burdens of the two-passenger porch swing.

Another thing we never could understand is why the heroes in all the plays and moving pictures and magazine illustrations smoke cigarets instead of a corncob pipe, like editorial heroes do.

A few topics were regarded as standard, and every week I tried to invent a new turn to each of them. These included the current styles in the clothes of men and women, the corn cob pipe which I smoked, my fondness for mashed potatoes and gravy, the civic booster (who was always endorsed), the knocker (who was always condemned), and the Democrats.

Perhaps the reason they always hold the Fountain Warren Poultry Show in the winter is that then the hens are never so busy.

Neither did we ever hear of anyone getting ptomaine poison from eating mashed potatoes and gravy.

Some of the Democratic candidates who have staid up late nights to see the new comet, will stay up late two weeks from next Tuesday night and see stars without looking up.

A corn cob pipe may have its bad qualities, but it never masquerades under false pretenses.

A girl will be content to entertain her Covington beau at home, but if he is from Veedersburg or some other distant seaport she has to take him to the picture show and the ice cream parlor for the benefit of the other girls.

During the first weeks in Covington my acquaintance extended but slowly beyond the people who were in business around the square. I made assiduous effort to memorize and to associate faces and names. Names were not difficult; previous newspaper training had taught the imperative necessity of spelling them right. But to associate with so many new names all the new faces was harder. The problem was one-sided because, being one new man in town, my own name and face were soon remembered by the residents while I was confronted with the need to master hundreds of names and faces quickly.

People from remote corners of the county began to drop in to subscribe, or to renew subscriptions. Likely I might not see them again for a year, when the subscription would expire, and it was sure to be embarrassing then to have to ask their names again, and advantageous to be able to recall them correctly. Few were so helpful as to state their names at a second meeting without first waiting to see whether they were remembered. So I undertook to memorize the features and names together as people came along and found that the art could be acquired.

At the churches I began meeting people whom I had not encountered around the business district. Covington was abundantly supplied with churches — the Methodist Episcopal, the Presbyterian, the Roman Catholic, the Christian, commonly called the Disciple Church, a Baptist Church, and the "Little Brick." This latter was a small congregation of excellent and plain people who held to a particular doctrine locally described as an offshoot of the Christian denomination.

For two thousand people, plus a small number from nearby farms, seven separate church buildings had been erected. Each undertook to support a minister. Only about 300 people were available for each church; certainly fewer than one hundred families each, even if everyone took part in church affairs, which probably not more than half the people did. Excessive denominationalism left all the churches weak and ineffective.

Dr. H. K. Fox, minister of the Presbyterian church, a slight, dark, soft-voiced gentleman with a close-clipped mustache, entertained ideas of his pastoral duties that were somewhat in advance of those commonly accepted. He had installed in the basement of the church a table upon which a game resembling pool could be played. For this sacrilegious effort to make his church attractive to Covington boys, he had been well criticized. This he faced patiently, although he was disappointed because the young fellows had shown slight enthusiasm for the recreation room.

Fox challenged my special interest by extending an invitation to occupy his pulpit one Sunday evening. The occasion was to be the first of a series of "open forum" talks by local citizens.

On the Saturday before, handbills from the *Republican*'s job printing presses were scattered profusely around town. The text made it clear that an important event was impending:

PRESBYTERIAN CHURCH
SUNDAY NIGHT

An Address on Covington Matters by
WHEELER McMILLEN
Editor of the *Republican*

This will be a brief discussion of strictly home matters — concise, to the point, and maybe a little startling. It will be a straight from the shoulder talk on what is the matter with Covington, what it needs, what will make it a great home town where people will want to stay. The address will be of particular interest to young people and business men.

SUNDAY NIGHT 7:30 o'CLOCK

Sunday evening the church was packed to the doors, with every seat taken, men sitting in the windows and standing along the walls. There came, a woman said later, "the most people I ever saw in the Presbyterian church, except for a funeral."

I sat importantly in a high-backed pulpit chair and studied the audience during the preliminary services. Why had so many come, I wondered, and had to admit that most had come out of curiosity. For a layman to occupy a Covington pulpit was a novelty. The layman was very new to the town, and very young, and had threatened to say something startling; I thought that must be the explanation. Anyway, I was well pleased.

The speech appeared to come off creditably enough, though perhaps it is just as well that the text of this maiden address to Covington was not preserved. No doubt some paragraphs urged tolerance and friendliness and cooperation. That the physical beauty of Covington be enhanced with paint, planting, and cleaning up was certainly advocated. Confident words portrayed the opportunity by such means to lift Covington above the common run of small towns, and to make it distinguished amongst other Hoosier communities for being cleaner, more beautiful, friendlier. The weakness in my program was that human nature in Covington was no cleaner, no more beautiful, and no more friendly than in competing communities, so not much came of the speech. The listeners considered it a free show for a one-night stand.

The experience led to a closer friendship with the gentle, high-minded dominie who also had illusions about doing good for people here on earth. Between the hopeful preacher and the idealistic editor arose a bond of mutual esteem.

One day Fox said, "Why don't you become a member of our church?"

"I am not qualified," I protested. "I don't believe the necessary doctrines."

"What don't you believe?" I was all set to answer that at length, and did. Fox listened gravely to a glib elucidation of the mysteries of earth, life, and eternity.

"What do you believe?" he put in quietly.

"Well, I believe in the Golden Rule and the Sermon on the Mount. And the Ten Commandments."

"I think we can take you in on that — and trust that the fellowship will bring you around to whatever else is necessary. I shall take it up with the elders, just as a matter of form, and let you know."

A few weeks later I was made a member of the Presbyterian congregation. I insisted that I had joined Dr. Fox, rather than the church; nevertheless, as the churches were about the only institutions in town organized for good, it seemed more desirable to work inside with them than outside. Within a year I was to be engaged in a lively conflict against certain of the religious leaders.

For the first two months in Covington I had continued to occupy the little $1.50 a week room at Clifton's house. Then my classified advertisement brought an opportunity to rent a five-room cottage on Fifth street. The rent was twelve dollars a month, nearly twice as much as for the room, but the greater privacy and comfort of the house justified the extra cost. The need for cash to keep the office going was so insistent that money for furnishings was scant. I bought a small cot, a few strips of matting, a set of hickory porch furniture, and a Morris chair. I had a bookcase, and when winter came acquired a sheet iron stove. The privileges of sitting on my own front porch and looking into the quiet darkness on summer evenings and of reading through the long winter nights by the comfort of the sheet iron stove were rewarding after having spent most of three years in rooming houses and hall bedrooms.

The town gossips were disturbed that a young single man should rent a whole house for himself unless he planned to be married soon. If I appeared in public with one of the town girls there were suggestions that some distant fiancée was being deceived and that the Covington girls sooner or later would find themselves embarrassed. At the moment I had no plans except to enjoy the hours of quiet and privacy which the house afforded.

During the summer a congenial local doctor, my friend Dr. Wert, the city health officer, stopped at the office with a proposition. "Mrs. Wert and our little girl are up at Petoskey to stay until the hay fever season passes," he said. "While they're away I want to remodel my house. How about letting me move in with you until the house is ready?"

The prospect of Dr. Wert's pleasant company was agreeable and so was his suggestion to divide the cost. Cool weather returned and with it Mrs. Wert and Mary Virginia, their little girl, though the Wert remodeling job had not been finished. So room was made for the doctor's family for a few weeks.

To that circumstance I became indebted for a shocking revelation. I discovered that I was lacking in elementary common sense.

November had come, and one day Mrs. Wert asked if I hadn't been sleeping rather cold. I confessed that I had. "The other day I went over to Herzog's and bought two extra bed covers, and still I can't keep warm."

Mrs. Wert laughed. "Well," she said, "I think you will find your bed more comfortable tonight. I just happened to notice the way you had your bed made today, so I fixed it over. You have plenty of bed clothing, but you had it all on top of you except one thin blanket. No wonder you were cold!"

It was a small matter, but I was profoundly humiliated. Not to have had sense enough to make a comfortable and warm bed, so I could rest comfortably during the sleeping periods that occupied a third of my time, was disturbing. The realization that I knew so little was a blow.

Being twenty-one and apparently settled in business, I was not indifferent to the possibility that somewhere there might be a companionable young woman willing to share my future. I hardly expected that a small place like Covington could provide the "ideal," although I was not unwilling to look. Seeing the office lights ablaze one Saturday night as he was escorting two young ladies from a dance, Cooper Clifton brought them in for introductions. I was smudged with ink and not very presentable. Both the girls looked beautiful. I didn't catch their names, but when one of them passed the office a few days later I asked Cooper who she was. One of his high school classmates, he said, Edna Dorothy Doane. Meeting her shortly in the post office I was impressed by her gayety and charm and healthy beauty. She lived not far up the street from the *Republican* office. When she passed the office to go down town I began watching for her return. It was pleasant to drop work for half an hour and to walk up street with her, perhaps to stop for a while on the wide, shady porch of the Doane home. I learned that on certain evenings she played the piano at the picture show, and on those evenings made it my business to see that she had an escort home. One bright Sunday I hired for $3.00 a horse and buggy from Paddy McMahon's livery barn. We drove through the covered bridge over the Wabash and delightedly explored the river roads through the Baltimore hills in Warren county, finally discovering ourselves to be so far north that it seemed best to go on to the Attica bridge and return over more familiar highways. Stopping in Attica for supper, we were discovered by the Attica editor who in his next issue predicted a new outbreak of poetry in the *Covington Republican*.

When invited to nearby communities to speak at occasions such as the fall Home Coming at Osborn's Prairie, I was proud to have her companionship. Paddy McMahon's livery barn supplied a horse and sleigh for another memorable trip together. Belle Bantz and Nelson Galloway were getting married at the Bantz home, some miles out in the Salem neighborhood. Miss Doane was to sing. A heavy snowstorm had been followed by sub-zero weather, the coldest spell of the winter. Mrs. Doane heated bricks and flatirons to warm the sleigh. Upon seeing her daughter's escort appear in the usual hat with no protection for his ears, she insisted on wrapping those prominent appendages with an old-fashioned knitted fascinator. I submitted with some embarrassment to what I thought was an unnecessary protection.

The preacher in charge of the marriage ceremony that night was a new young man, who had come to minister to a "circuit" of four rural Methodist churches. The next year he was arrested for stealing the gas light tanks from automobiles of his parishioners while they were at church. He confessed the crime, and added that he had also stolen an automobile that was missing from Crawfordsville. After serving a term in the state reformatory, he was said to have settled in another state under a new name.

The wedding was on Thursday night, the night when I always worked late at the office to complete the make-up of the paper — placing the type in the forms and making everything ready for press early next morning. Returning from the cold sleigh ride I hurried to the office to finish the pages in time to catch the late night train for Indianapolis. Time was short. Without bothering to renew the fires, and too busy to realize how intense the cold was in the old building, I filled and locked up the forms and hurried to the train. In the hotel bathroom at Indianapolis next morning I was astonished to find that my ears, which had been quite warm and normal when I reached the office, were swollen to twice their normal size and one had literally burst. They had frozen in the cold office. Mrs. Doane had shown more sense than I had.

Dorothy and I had become engaged during the autumn. The problem of obtaining a suitable engagement ring loomed formidably when the time for that formality arrived. Diamonds were costly stones. I was barely able to count up enough money to furnish the house, even after pledging the future a little. A diamond really suitable for so magnificent a bride-to-be would cost hundreds. Finally an inspiration came. What could be more fitting for such a jewel of the Wabash than a fine pearl from that noble river? Albert Hegg, the principle pearl buyer, was cautiously asked what he would charge for a choice specimen. Pulling a tiny box from his vest pocket, he spread on the window sill of Loeb's store an assortment of iridescent beauties.

"Which one do you like best?" he inquired.

"What are their prices?" I countered.

"I want to know which one you like first," Hegg insisted.

Reluctantly I indicated a choice — not the largest but one that seemed more perfect than the others. Hegg quickly laid the pearl between two bits of soft cotton in another tiny box and pressed it into my hand.

"But I have to know how much it is!" I was fearful of being pushed into a transaction beyond my financial depth.

"Not a cent. It's yours now," smiled Hegg.

Hegg, I had reason to believe, entertained political ambitions and was taking advantage of an opportunity to place the publisher of the *Republican* under an obligation.

"Albert, I'm sorry, but this won't do. I appreciate your generosity, but I've got to pay you. How much is it?"

"Twenty-five cents, then."

The enticing beauty of the pearl and the firm refusal of Hegg to change his price overcame the scruples that may not have been justified since we were warm friends. The two-bit pearl, when set by a local jeweler, was accepted by the young lady as graciously as though it had been a costly diamond. She may have thought privately that a pearl was a curious engagement stone; probably she also feared that it came appropriately from a slightly peculiar young man, who would need a number of improvements later on.

Our personal plans brightened measurably on election night with the certainty that the county printing and advertising would come to the *Republican*. We celebrated the election on the next Friday night by taking the train to Danville for a Chinese supper and attending a performance by Harry Lauder. A week after her twentieth birthday, and four months after my twenty-second, we were married on May 28, 1915.

After the ceremony we went by train to Ohio to visit my father and mother and meet old friends. Then we returned to occupy the house in Fifth Street, which we had proudly furnished with a set of fumed oak furniture and the paraphernalia of housekeeping. Looking back, after many good years of congenial companionship, I could wish that my judgment had been as sound in all things as it had been in the choice of a life partner.

Dorothy made herself a welcome part-time hand at the newspaper office. She was wise enough not to get too deep into the arts of printing, but she gathered news, collected bills from sometimes reluctant payers, and pitched in for miscellaneous emergencies. She even learned the difficult art of flipping the big sheets of paper one by one into the grippers of the rumbling cylinder press.

One "miscellaneous emergency" arose every Friday morning following the final press run. After the bundles of papers had been hurried to the post office for the principal distribution points, the "single wraps" had to be hustled out. These single copies were folded, wrapped individually and addressed to scattered postoffices wherever in the country former Covingtonians lived and subscribed. Essential to the process was the liberal use of a printer's paste. This concoction of flour, water, and some other adhesive element was always available in a small bucket which, never completely emptied, was replenished on press day. It had a peculiarity. The leftover paste grew rank and rancid, and the mephitic emanation of this malodorous mixture, while hardly noticeable to those of us accustomed to the varied fragrances of a printing office, must have seemed highly foul and fetid to a sensitive nostril from the fresh outer air.

Dorothy not only had two sensitive nostrils, but as the months advanced the prospect that a third member was to join our family became evident. It is hardly necessary to add that, after a week or so when the morning sickness and the single wraps coincided, a decision had to be made as to whether to do without the deft assistance of the prospective mother or to begin the job with a clean bucket of paste.

As the ninth month turned up on the calendar I pronounced a stern warning. From Thursday noon until Friday noon of each week my presence at the office was indispensable while the paper was being put to press, printed and mailed. Under no circumstances could child-bearing be approved during this period as long as there were six other full days and nights available.

Happily a Saturday was chosen, Saturday the third of June, for our son to be born. In the early hours the doctor was called. He was Dr. James W. Aldridge, who had only recently opened his office in his home town. As an interne in Chicago he had delivered more than seven hundred babies. Our child was the first of his private practice — the first for which he was paid. His fee was $25.

Just at daybreak I was dispatched to bring Mrs. Paisley, the nurse. As I skipped along the walks the dawn of a perfect June day brightened. Robins were singing in every tree, it seemed, and song sparrows from every shrub. No hour before or since has brought quite the same spirit of elation. His mother named the boy Robert Doane. She devoted to his upbringing her remarkable taste and good sense, and inspired him with the sound qualities of her character. He, in turn, long since matured and carrying on his own responsibilities, has not only commanded our admiration but as well our love, and has never through all the years given either of us cause for a needless hour of worry. The elation of that June morning was fully justified.

The practical matter of making the paper pay a profit became, now that there were three instead of one to support, ever more urgent. To "do well" economically was an imperative more immediate than "doing good" ideally.

5

More Fun Than Profit

THE POLITICAL campaign had been fun and the outcome
indicated that it had been an investment of energy from
which practical dividends were to come. Meanwhile the
paper had to come out every week and the payroll had to
be met every Saturday afternoon. Paper supplies had to be
paid for, and while a single sheet had never appeared to
represent cash I discovered that when purchased by the ton
or hundredweight the cost of paper was substantial.

Most of the merchants were solicited weekly, but the
volume of advertising remained small. Even had it been
larger the rates were too low to have yielded a fair profit.
Each weekly issue contained eight pages of printed matter,
six columns to the page. The columns were twenty inches
long. At the established rate of ten cents per column inch
an advertiser could buy a whole column for two dollars; for
a dollar he could have a space two columns wide, five
inches deep. If he wanted to splurge for a whole page he
received a discount; the page rate was ten dollars. The
front page carried only news and editorial matter. Therefore the maximum weekly revenue from display advertising,
even had all the other seven pages of space been occupied
by advertisers, would have been eighty-four dollars, or if all
the customers bought full pages, seventy dollars. No such
bonanza issues appeared. No extra pages had to be printed.
The weekly income from display space seldom exceeded
fifty dollars.

Among the merchants who did advertise some might as
well have saved their money as to have paid for the kind of
copy they prepared. The customary rite, upon agreeing to

take space, was to tear off a strip of wrapping paper, lower the elbows to the counter, glance speculatively for a moment at the shelves, and quickly pencil off something like "FOR WALL PAPER, PAINTS AND VARNISHES, SEE GEORGE W. COGLEY, N. SIDE SQ., COVINGTON, INDIANA. We handle the Sherwin-Williams Line. A Square Deal to All."

After a time I learned that advertising revenue could be increased slightly if the busy and unliterary merchant were relieved from the vexatious travail of writing his own copy. Occasionally I could make a sale by sizing up the man's stock, preparing an attractive layout with a catchy phrase or so in about twice the size of space he ordinarily purchased. A persuasive lure was to black in his name with the largest letters the layout would permit.

This kind of effort to make advertising in the *Republican* more productive could also lead to reverse results. Mike Mayer, owner of the leading hardware store, one day wrote on the customary piece of brown wrapping paper this burning message: "JUST ARRIVED! CARLOAD OF FENCE . . . M. MAYER, HARDWARE, COVINGTON, IND."

Choosing a ten-inch space, to cost a dollar a week, Mike ordered that it run until he said to stop. After it had appeared for eight months I went over to the store and proposed a more timely wording.

"I guess I won't advertise any more for a while," said Mike. And for more than a year he didn't.

In one instance I acquired an advertiser by unexpected means. He was a merchant who had steadily declined to buy space. One day in Indianapolis I passed as he was entering a small hotel and gave him the cordial hail with which one Covingtonian normally saluted another on meeting away from home. Early next morning he appeared at the office carrying a piece of copy for which he asked the price. The smallest space into which it could be fitted was five column inches, costing fifty cents.

"Well, I've been thinking I ought to advertise more. Put it in this week, and I'll have a change every week or so."

I thanked him. He had more on his mind. "Don't say

anything about seeing me in Indianapolis yesterday," he said, with feeling. Only then did it dawn on me that the woman with him at the hotel entrance was not his wife. I promised not to mention it. He continued to advertise for several months.

The shopkeepers complained constantly because so much local money was spent out of town for merchandise which they could supply. Their two black beasts were the mail order houses and the more enterprising stores of Danville, Illinois, only fifteen miles away with thirty thousand population. Danville was a magnet that lured thousands of Covington dollars. The chain stores had not yet arrived but Danville stores could display more varied selections and offered frequent bargain attractions.

The *Republican* carried on a more or less continuous campaign against the mail order houses, hoping that in appreciation the local dealers would reciprocate with more liberal advertising orders. A typical blast was this:

THE LARGEST FEDERAL INCOME TAX PAYER IN CHICAGO IS JULIUS ROSENWALD.

- Did you get that?
- Julius had a NET PERSONAL INCOME last year of $1,320,000.
- One million, three hundred and twenty thousand dollars!
- Mr. Rosenwald paid $70,000 as his income tax.
- Rosenwald is but one member of the firm.
- His share of the profits of that mail order house, not counting what went to other stockholders, what went back into the business — his share net — was $1,320,-000.
- The country towns and the farms paid it.
- The country storekeepers lost the trade that went to Julius Rosenwald to give him a million dollar income and then some.
- Farmers and villagers and small city people of the country sent Julius the money.
- He got a million and more of it.

- A lot of it went to Julius from Covington.
- It will never come back.
- It will build us no streets.
- It will give us no municipal improvements.
- It will not improve our rural roads and rural schools.
- IT'S GONE.

As for evidence that such diatribes kept Covingtonians from continuing to send their checks and money orders to Chicago, none appeared. Nor did the merchants enlarge their advertising space in gratitude. The paper urged the home dealers to study the catalogues in order to offer competing bargains through its advertising columns. Some did follow the advice far enough to examine the catalogues and thereupon proceeded to order for their personal needs merchandise which they could have bought from other stores in Covington.

The tradesmen hated the Danville stores more bitterly than they viewed the mail order concerns. The only dislike which appeared to exceed their ill will toward Danville was the hatred they cherished for their competitors in Covington.

In contrast to the almost complete absence of cooperation among the Covington stores, the Danville merchants worked together to draw trade from the surrounding counties. Every now and then they advertised widely a "Dollar Day." On such days the Danville stores joined in featuring long lists of items marked down, and perhaps in some cases marked up, to one dollar. All efforts to prod the Covington storekeepers into competitive effort failed. A news paragraph which followed one Danville "Dollar Day" may not have been tactful:

Several hundred dollars of money from this territory were spent in Danville Thursday, attracted there by the sole power of newspaper advertising of a trade event. And many of the merchants of a town we might name had plenty of time to watch the people drive by, since they had no ads of their own in the local papers.

The indifference of the home-town merchants began to dull the editorial home-trade ardor. I let it be known in Danville that advertising space was for sale in the *Republican*. Weeks followed when most of the cash support for the buy-at-home editorials came from Danville stores' advertising. The next time "Dollar Day" came along the *Republican's* rasp was rougher.

Next Thursday is dollar day in Danville. Apparently the Covington merchants are willing for the people in this section to take advantage of this special trade and bargain event. Although several were solicited, they have taken no space in the *Republican* this week to state the advantages of trading with them. On the other hand, Danville merchants, without solicitation on our part, have taken ten columns to tell why they offer the best place to buy.

News stories from two successive issues of the *Republican* described a turn of events that, a little later, enlivened the home trade topic:

"Trade at Home" got a boost Wednesday when several Covington motorists were charged $14 for the privilege of driving over the streets entering Danville. Traffic officers stopped about every car with an Indiana number and haled the drivers before a Justice who fined them each $10 and costs, presumably for being Hoosiers.

A few drivers, more resourceful than others, talked the officers of justice out of doing anything that wasn't nice, but most of them paid the bill. One car that was stopped carried two young men and two girls, and the whole party was taken into the Justice's office. The driver paid the fine under an assumed name. Danville papers advertised the fact that Peter Smith of Covington was one of the men fined.

William Cline, the well known horseman, was picked up a few days ago charged with going too fast. Cline started to fight the case, feeling the injustice of the charge, but later decided to pay the assessment.

Motorists who have been annoyed by the Danville tactics are urging that the local police be given the necessary assistance and instructed to make a systematic catch of speeders here. At Danville officers were stationed well out on the road. The larger number of the local people who drive to Danville go there to shop or spend money otherwise. Little money is left here by the Danville people who scoot through at lawbreaking speed. There would be far more justification, it is argued, in arresting them.

The suggested retaliation was undertaken. The *Republican* echoed the mercantile chortles when one of the grasping Danville merchants fell into the Covington speed trap. "DANVILLE MERCHANT HOWLS LOUDLY WHEN FINED FOR SPEEDING," the headline read.

More than a dozen violators of traffic laws have been arrested by Lee Murray, special motorcycle policeman, and taken before Mayor McGeorge. Four or five have been fined. Among them were Adam Plaut, merchant of Danville, and Bob Kramer of Mudlavia. Plaut kicked like a peeved broncho at leaving in Covington $13.50 of the hundreds of dollars Covington people had spent in his store. He declared that he would never spend another cent in Covington, but he was told that since this was probably the first money he ever did spend here, local people would not be greatly offended. Doubtless he will not be too mad at folks here to accept their money hereafter when they buy of him.

Local drivers, knowing the motorcycle cop when they see him, are more careful, and none have fallen into the toils so far. However, no distinctions are being made, and violators whether from Covington or Hong Kong will be pulled when caught. "We are going to stop the speeding," says Mayor McGeorge.

Historical accuracy might require a footnote to the effect that few Covington drivers happened to be noticed exceeding the speed limits.

For one form of home trade the *Republican* never lost enthusiasm; that was trade with the home newspaper and printing shop. One year a hustling salesman for an outside printing concern snatched some school orders. The editorial feelings were expressed in a short paragraph, which I can't now say for sure was original. Anyway it came to be widely reprinted:

> Nothing could give the editor of a home paper a more delightful thrill than to receive an invitation (printed out of town) to see some sweet girl (gowned in out of town clothes) receive a diploma (printed out of town) at the commencement, and to have an opportunity to congratulate her father and mother (who subscribe to an out-of-town paper but to none in the home town) on their beautiful daughter's accomplishments, and then go to his office and write a column and a half congratulating the taxpayers of the town on the splendid achievements of the schools.

Although the business community did not rush to assure the *Republican*'s prosperity, I continued to believe that constructive efforts for the general good were part of a newspaper's function and that eventually they would pay off in larger revenues. Early in March of the second year an editorial paragraph offered a suggestion:

> Covington should have a Clean-up Week this year that will take the rubbish and trash out of sight for the summer and get the clean-up-all-the-time habit instilled into residents. If the City Council will set a Clean-up Week date we believe that a thorough scrubbing of the city can be obtained. A few dollars for teams to haul stuff away should be the only cost. Tell the Council about it if you agree.

The city health officer, Dr. Wert, immediately responded. "That's the best thing I've seen in a Covington paper in years," he said. "You write some more pieces and talk it up.

I'll see what can be done with the Council. They're pretty slow about such matters, but we can try."

A member of the Council was induced to move that the city should provide teams and men to haul away rubbish on the days that had been suggested. There wouldn't be much of it, he argued, and the Council should show its willingness to support civic improvement. Mort Steely, a saloonkeeper, who as chairman of the street committee would have to superintend the hauling, opposed the idea. With the endorsement of Mayor McGeorge the motion carried without enthusiasm.

Front-page publicity urged everyone to join in the Clean-up. A few merchants were cajoled into advertising brooms, paint, lawn and garden tools, and seeds. On the first of the Clean-up day mornings, Dr. Wert and I took a walk around town. Hundreds of piles of trash, baskets and boxes of rubbish, were set at the curbs along every street. I thought the evidence indicated that the *Republican* had been an influence for some good in the community.

The street cleaning department was overwhelmed. Several days elapsed before the hauling-away was finished. At the next Council meeting Mort Steely grumbingly reported that the work had been done, but complained bitterly that some residents had included brush from their shrubs in the rubbish piles.

"If I'd knowed that everybody in town was goin' to start clearin'," he growled, "I'd never have agreed to this thing." The Council, nevertheless, was proud of what had been done and complacently assented when Mayor McGeorge assumed the credit in behalf of the city administration.

When the agent for a Chautauqua company came to town he was directed to the *Republican* office. For $900 the company would agree to provide a five-day program of lectures, musical numbers, a play, and various entertainers — inspiration, instruction, and entertainment. With a little difficulty the agent and I obtained fifteen signatures to a contract to guarantee the $900. The entertainment turned out to be good; the audiences small. The guarantors were called upon to dig up four dollars each to make up for the deficiency in ticket sales, but signed another agreement for the next year anyway.

A Fourth of July celebration was sponsored by a group of citizens who had fallen in momentarily with the urge to make things happen in Covington. It helped. That week the *Republican* chronicled five accidents, the arrests of six celebrants for drunkenness and fighting, and concluded an account of the program by saying that "The editor of this palladium of liberty read the Declaration of Independence, and was highly complimented upon the excellent subject matter."

Anxious that Covington become known as a "live" town, whether it cared or not to be one, the paper relentlessly offered suggestions:

> Whoever complains that there is nothing doing in his own hometown is growling at himself. When there is nothing doing it is proper to start something. There are many things that could be started in Covington. Why not have an old-fashioned debating society? A spelling match once in a while? There is an abundance of musical talent in the city. Why not more public musical events? There is plenty to do if folks will do it. The trouble is that some one else is expected to do the doing.

No debating society was organized nor were any spelling matches arranged. Nearly every summer a band was talked about and in two or three years the matter went so far as to result in a few concerts in the courthouse yard on Wednesday nights. Sufficiently inspiring leadership to keep up the interest through the winter months never appeared.

Nothing that appeared in the editorial columns ever admitted that a small town could not provide everything essential to civilized American living. Avoiding any intimation that Covington itself might be a "tank town" an editorial spoke up in behalf of the lesser villages nearby:

> It is not unusual to hear villages of 200 to 700 inhabitants referred to as "tank towns." The sneer is not justified.

Fountain County has more than half a dozen villages of this size. They are among the most attractive and pleasant communities in the state. Their inhabitants are not provincial. In education, dress, business customs, wealth and knowledge of the world at large the citizens of these communities are more cosmopolitan than the average New Yorkers; even more so, we'll say, than the city bred Indianapolitan.

Newtown, for instance, is numerically a trifle and can't boast of a railroad. But it will average more college bred folks to the dozen than any other town in this section of Hoosierdom.

Kingman is no industrial center, but it has a library that for selection of good books and for patronage offers a record worth examining. Wallace is ten miles from steel rails, and it is building an institutional church that would credit any county seat. Cates is a wee burg, but two of its stores do business that averages $100 a day. Perrysville, across the river, is erecting a school building that will be a model for any community in the state.

The "tank town" is not to be sneered at. In these little villages is the real Americanism of the land, the genuine patriotism, the true wealth, the ideal democracy.

Moments came when I found room to doubt the usefulness of my exhortations. The moments were most likely to occur toward the close of a week when the gross income and the payroll figures stood uncomfortably discrepant. The rival paper, the *Friend*, appeared to make as much money, if not more. It didn't bother about trying to improve the town and its editor didn't work so hard. However, I didn't believe he had as much fun, either. I could usually convince myself that in the long run the efforts to be constructive would justify themselves in direct profit or in prestige. I clung to the hope of "waking up" the community and of leading it toward becoming a more profitable business center as well as a better place to live. Whenever an event or a cause appeared that promised benefit for the portion of the human race that inhabited Covington and its trade territory the *Republican* tried to help it along. Only now and then did a little honest cynicism break out, as in the paragraph that said: "This is a great world. The newspaper gives a worthy enterprise dollars' worth of advertising without charge and then the editor is asked to buy tickets besides."

I was not alone in believing that somehow Covington could be built into a more prosperous town. "If the business men only would pull together, something could be done," it was often said. "If we had a factory paying out wages every week things would be different."

Doubtful whether Covington's resources at that time afforded a sound basis for industrial development, my faith in the factory idea was small. We had a labor supply not fully employed but little else to offer that other localities could not excel. These doubts were not lessened by some slight knowledge of fly-by-night promoters who had accepted substantial "bonuses" from aspiring towns to establish factories, only to depart without maintaining a permanent business.

The community's latent agricultural possibilities offered more hope, I thought, than its industrial prospects. At first I saw little that an editor could do about them other than occasionally to throw out an idea. An editorial asked "Why Not Organize?"

Of the abundant crop of apples in Fountain county this year thousands of bushels are wasting for want of a market or a plan to get them to market. Why should the farmers lose this profit when a way to make his apples pay can be devised? Not every year will see as great a crop here, or elsewhere. But with proper attention, spraying and picking, Fountain county can always have apples to sell. Ben Brown of Shawnee township has sprayed for three years and in that time has harvested splendid apples from trees that never paid before. Hood river apples from Oregon are famous almost the world over. It is not because Hood river apples are superior, but because Hood river apple growers

are thoroughly organized. They own needed equipment.
They market together — have a secretary who watches
the markets everywhere, and their apples are sold together. Why couldn't Fountain county have "apple
rings" as well as threshing rings? The farmers of a
neighborhood could pool their apple interests, go together and buy spraying outfits, etc., and make money
from their orchards. For that matter the plan would
doubtless pay with the big crops as well. We should
like to see the experiment worked out.

Not long afterward an unexpected and important agricultural stimulus came to the county. It came in the person
of a lank, six-foot-six graduate of Ohio State Agricultural
College and in a new capacity, as a county agricultural
agent. He came, in a way, on an impetus created by Abraham Lincoln. Lincoln as President had signed the land-
grant college law. That in turn had led to creation of
the state agricultural experiment stations, the beginning
of organized agricultural research. The findings of the experiment stations were not widely used by farmers, partly
from lack of simple interpretation, partly from resistance to
new ideas. So the federal Congress had authorized a system
for the extension of agricultural knowledge and Gordon W.
Rosencrans was its first agent in Fountain county.

"Rosie" set up a desk in the courthouse in a corner of
Recorder Fine Drake's office. He was soon too busy to see
much of the desk. Although his instructions were that he
should never intrude his services or suggestions he never
needed to do so. The more progressive farmers quickly
realized his value and called for his expert aid. His knees
brushed the steering wheel of his Ford roadster as he rushed
around the county in response to requests for his presence
and advice.

Recalling an earlier experiment with a farm page, I soon
found Rosencrans a constant source of ready material for
such a page in the *Republican*. He appreciated the help
the publicity gave his work and every week had a budget
of notes I could use. A few headlines and summaries from
a typical page:

Web Metzger to try out Soy Bean crop. . . . Shawnee Farmers Club gets started. . . . Tomato growing
contest for boys. . . . Campaign is on for big corn
yield; 5-acre contest opens. . . . Richland farmers
have good session. . . . Corn cost here below average.
. . . Corn will be topic for talk at Cates. . . . Club
contests to close May 1. . . . Big farmers meet in Lodi
Tuesday. . . . Morris Young favors breeders Ass'n.
(interview advocating association to further pure-
breds). . . . Mace Davidson of southeast of Covington
has recently put up a woven wire fence along the road
by his farm, a considerable improvement to the appearance of his place.

Son of Will Ritchey paid $125 for 10 ewes, by end of
three years had sold $750 in lambs and wool.

When scoffers did raise their voices against the county
agent to flaunt the ancient scorn of book farming the *Republican*'s farm page refuted them with news:

J. E. Soey, who lives near Newtown, believes it pays
the farmers of Fountain county, who take advantage of
his services, to have a county agent. Mr. Soey has the
figures to prove his contention.

He sowed 66 acres of oats. One acre he sowed with
untreated seed. The other 65 he treated with formaldehyde as advised by Rosencrans. On the 65 acres he
had no smut at all. On the one acre there was 65%
smut. In other words, the treatment increased his yield
9 bushels to the acre, or 585 bushels on 65 acres. At
36 cents a bushel this means $210.60. His total expense
for treating was $20.

This was before the day of the Farm Bureau and well in
advance of the wave of cooperative marketing associations
that came several years later. The *Republican* hammered
away in behalf of the organization of agriculture:

Fountain County now has two Farmers' Clubs, one
at Newtown and one at Rob Roy. The building of

organizations such as these is well worth while. The interests of agriculture are the greatest in the nation. At the same time they are the most poorly organized.

Permanent practical farmers' clubs over the country will, in the end, mean not only better crops but better plans of marketing. The farmer today takes what he can get. Properly organized, the farmers of large communities will some time be able, in a measure, to set the prices for their products, as do most manufacturing establishments. And the farm is a factory; a plant, as Will Madigan puts it, where corn and oats, beef and pork, are manufactured. Farm organizations, such as have been launched in Fountain County, will open new avenues of interest for the young people. We hope the Farmers Clubs of this county will in time recognize junior auxiliaries, in which the boys and girls will take part. Under the capable management of County Agent Rosencrans, a worthy movement has been started, and we know the farmers of this county well enough to believe that they will do their part in perpetuating the work thus begun, for the good of their communities, themselves, and the farmers of the future.

"Rosie's" first popular project had been to demonstrate how to treat seed oats with a simple formaldehyde solution to prevent smut from reducing the yields. Neighborhood meetings were called. A few bushels of seed oats were spread on a barn floor. After showing how to spray on the formaldehyde he seized a scoop shovel and turned over a few bushels, then handed the shovel to a watcher who quickly discovered that the job was simple — just a little plain work. The farmers went to their own barns and repeated what they had seen. A year later we were still reporting results:

"Oats smut is the worst in years," County Agent Rosencrans said Thursday.

"I have found from 8 to 30 per cent of smut in fields in the county. The loss will be as high as 12 bushels per acre in some fields."

The oats smut campaign last year saved for farmers

in this county about $7,000. This year the saving will be more than $10,000. Fields where seed was treated show practically no smut. It costs only about three cents an acre to treat the seed.

The cash value of the county agent's organized work in the county is well illustrated in the oats smut matter. The savings on the oats crop is many times the cost of the county agent's office. The agent doesn't tell farmers much that they don't know, but he is able to get communities to working together to do the things they do know.

Better profits for farmers were likely to bring more new money into Covington. Impressed by the county agent's work I was anxious to see another step taken. Why should not agriculture be taught in the schools, taught to the prospective farmers of the generation that in a few years would control the farms? The Covington school board had declined an opportunity to install a teacher of agriculture:

That there is no instruction in agriculture in the Covington high school is to be regretted — and should be corrected. A very large percentage of the high school students come from farms, or expect to make the farm the scene of their life endeavors. If the public schools, especially the high school, of Covington are to fulfill their proper mission — that of preparing youths to make a living — it is imperative that an adequate course in the science of agriculture be introduced. It would be desirable to arrange in cooperation with the township trustee for an agricultural instructor to serve 12 months in the year, cooperating with the pupils in their homes where the most effective work can be done.

A year later, when the Covington school authorities still had done nothing, a half-column news story described the prospective opening of an agricultural course in the rival town of Veedersburg, only a few miles distant. Another longer article praised the exhibits of the boys' and girls' farm clubs at the county fair. With these went an editorial on "Fountain County's Best Investment":

The best investment Fountain county makes is that which is directed to the well being of the boys and girls. Money invested to guarantee the futures of our young folks will bring greater returns than any other expenditure. The vocational education work being conducted thru the boys' and girls' clubs in Fountain county costs some money. Some outlay is necessary to employ a county agent, to hire teachers in the schools, to buy equipment to teach agriculture and domestic science.

Few will question the integrity of the investment. Veedersburg is making a fine step forward in establishing a full four year high school course in agriculture. The usual academic high school course is very good in its way, but it fails utterly to equip the student for practical affairs. The agricultural course will. A few months of practical study of farm concrete work or animal husbandry is worth to the boy in this county who intends to farm a hundred times the value of four years of Latin.

Some day, perhaps, more schools in the agricultural communities will cease to cram students with useless lore of by-gone centuries, and begin to prepare them for the arduous task of making a living.

Covington school authorities continued to be happy to supervise a poor job of teaching Latin and algebra rather than any of the agricultural arts and sciences. The commencements were recurrent tragedies which launched the youngsters into life ill-prepared for anything. The more vigorous students, nevertheless, survived the poor instruction and went away from Covington usually to do well. Few of the better ones remained in the community.

The county agent's efforts brought visible improvements in farm methods that in a year or so could be noted in many neighborhoods of the county. Far distant a stimulus had gone to work that was even more potent for a while

at improving Fountain County farm incomes. The stimulus
was Mars across the seas. Fighting armies abroad demanded
supplies from Fountain County fields and prices began to
rise noticeably. A note on the farm page said:

> While waiting for the club meeting to begin at Rob
> Roy Thursday night, several men, Clint Florey among
> them, were holding down nail kegs in the store. Will
> Hushaw hesitated before coming in, saying, "Where
> are all the rigs?" "Hell, we're farmers," said Florey.
> "We came in automobiles."

The farm page also noted the inception of the power
farming age with a sentence that indicated no vision of the
significance of its news: "Among the farmers of the county
who have purchased tractors recently are Dan Young, Bud
Stucker, Frank Campbell, and Ben Martin." None of us
then dreamed that this was the beginning of a revolution.

The rising agricultural income did not alleviate my publishing problems. Outgo continued to press hard upon the
income. I sometimes wondered whether I was really competent to run a newspaper, aside from the editorial department. An apologetic complaint in one issue spoke a
good bit of truth: "Too much work in the job department
again this week has cut into the amount of local news in
the paper. We like to see the job department busy but
would rather it did not interfere with the newspaper business quite so much."

There were times when the belief that Covington was an
economic blind alley rose strongly; there were more times
when I wondered whether I was too poor as a salesman, or
whether some other deficiency of my own was preventing
the achievement of greater prosperity. I knew the world was
full of other interesting things to do. Yet a dim inner voice
cried out that here was life and experience and real education; that I should keep open my eyes and mind and miss
nothing. I hoped to squeeze more of the entertaining juice
of life out of the people and events that surrounded me.
The conquest of Covington had not yet been accomplished;
I determined to intensify the effort.

6

Wet or Dry

Two MONTHS after the county election had been won, another campaign had to be fought.

Under the state local option law, Indiana towns could vote saloons in or out after any two-year period. When a town voted dry the wets were obliged to wait two years before again putting the question before the people; when the wets had triumphed the drys were obliged to tolerate saloons for two years before another election. Ever since the local option law had been established, Covington had wavered biennially, first to one side and then to the other. For twenty-four months thirsty natives would be able to pickle their interiors within sight of the courthouse; then for one hundred and four weeks they would have to travel to Veedersburg, Attica, or Danville in order to lave a parched esophagus.

Covington had now been without saloons for nearly two years. Liquor advocates obtained enough signatures for a petition asking that an election be held in March. The county commissioners set the date.

Knowing the bitterness and ill-feeling usually engendered in local option campaigns, I had opposed holding the election. Also, I believed the saloons to be undesirable, injurious both to moral welfare and to business prosperity. Then, hardly had the election date been set when I found myself opposing churches as well as saloons.

After a week or so of delay, a committee met to plan the dry campaign. The members included the Rev. E. W. Strecker of the Methodist church, the Rev. H. K. Fox of the Presbyterian church, a lawyer, a dentist, a retired farmer, a garage owner, an insurance agent, an undertaker and furniture dealer, and the editor of the *Republican*.

The Rev. Mr. Strecker took the floor at the committee's first meeting to propose a union evangelistic campaign as the easiest and most certain route to a dry victory. "We will convert the sinners, and they will vote dry" was the essence of his simple plan. Responsibility for keeping saloons out of Covington was to be placed in the hands of an unknown evangelist and the Holy Ghost. The proposal was accepted by most of the committee members. They hesitated to oppose anything that bore a religious brand.

"You will make the opening of saloons here as certain as the coming of spring, if you undertake to bring an evangelist to Covington now," I asserted.

"Why do you say that?" the Rev. Strecker frowned.

"In the first place," I explained, "every previous election here has been carried by a very small margin. We have about 600 voters. The records show that from 250 to 275 vote dry at every election, and about the same number always vote wet. These are the men who do not shift from one side to the other.

"Your election depends wholly upon 50 or 100 men who change from wet to dry, or from dry to wet. These are the fellows whose votes we have to get. You know who they are. You certainly know that they are not of the sort likely to be converted by any evangelist — probably they will not even attend the meetings. If they do attend, they will be offended by the evangelist's diatribes against dancing, card playing, and theater going, the cardinal sins of the revivalists' catalogue.

"We can win this election by talking fairly and moderately with these few doubtful voters. We will lose it if we turn loose a fool evangelist to holler at people."

One committeeman shook his head at such blasphemy, and others looked uncomfortable. I felt sure of my argument: "We have just six weeks until the election. Strecker tells us that it will be two weeks before an evangelist can open meetings. Even granting that an evangelist could help us, which I deny, he would not have time to do the work."

"Not in four weeks?" someone inquired.

"No. I have watched Billy Sunday and Fenwick Reed and some of the other big experts in this line. One of Billy Sunday's press agents told me once how they do it. A skilled evangelist takes six weeks to work the hysteria up to a full climax. It would be two weeks after election before the tough nuts could be expected on the mourners' bench, if you got them at all."

The minister said he assumed that I would cooperate if an evangelist were obtained. I was stubborn enough to say, "I won't print a single line supporting an evangelistic campaign before election. I'll do everything I can to keep the saloons from coming back. If you want to save some souls later on, I will print any news you make, but right now I want to see this town stay dry."

The committee agreed that I didn't know Covington, having been there less than a year. They seemed embarrassed that a preacher should have been contradicted in their presence. On Sunday night, four weeks preceding the election, the ponderously pompous Rev. Mr. Augustus Dusenberg lifted his raucous voice from the First Methodist church pulpit. The combined church congregations of Covington listened.

"I have just closed a great meeting in Gas City," he blared. "Gas City is a clean town tonight because of my preaching. When I went there Gas City was a seething cauldron of iniquity. Card playing and dancing were rampant. Two damnable moving picture theaters were running. The cards have been burned. Dancing has ceased. I closed both the hellish movie shows."

He roared denunciation of the card players in Covington, of the dancers, and of that sink hole of evil, the lone little movie house. Knowing that nearly all the Methodist choir members on the platform belonged to the same 500 club, and that most of them attended the infrequent dances at the armory, I enjoyed listening.

More important, I learned two things about the Rev. Augustus Dusenberg — that the evangelist was very green at his trade and was a boastful liar. An experienced old-fashioned evangelist usually spent his first week or so denouncing the sins more peculiar to church people, and at assailing the churchgoers themselves. That brought in the sinners to enjoy hearing the church folks flayed, until the meetings acquired enough momentum that everybody could safely be hammered. Dusenberg started in on the outsiders first; they never did flock to the meetings.

That the evangelist was a liar appeared certain. For an evangelist to exert enough influence to put the last moving picture theater out of business in a town with 4,000 people, like Gas City, even in 1915, seemed conspicuously improbable.

A letter promptly was sent to the editor of a Gas City paper asking for the facts. Quite true, he replied, no picture theaters operated during the evangelist's engagement there. One establishment, which had been on its last legs, went out of business. The proprietor of the other closed his house during the meetings. He advertised the closing as a courtesy to the church people. Actually, knowing that business would be poor during the evangelistic competition, he was redecorating his theater, which reopened the first night after the revival closed. The letter ended, however, with a hearty endorsement of the evangelist's work, which "had done a great deal of good."

The Gas City editor sent the inquiry and a copy of his reply to Dusenberg in Covington. The Reverend learned that the scent of his trail was being followed by a nose for news. The *Republican* carried no advance mention of the meetings. The Methodist preacher had brought in an announcement, with a two-column cut of Dusenberg; I refused to print either. When the *Republican* came out on Friday of the first week of the meetings the columns were closely scanned to see what had been said about Dusenberg. Predictions had been made that I would publish an article removing the evangelist's pelt.

The town was disappointed after a first glance at the paper. No denunciation of Dusenberg could be found. A half column review of the progress of the local option campaign commented favorably on the general moderation displayed by both sides. In the middle of one paragraph a sentence was discovered that sent a gasp around the square: "The maudlin mouthings of an itinerant evangelist have sounded practically the only note of bitterness so far injected into the campaign," it said. There was no other reference to the ripsnorting hero of the blessed effort to make Covington dry by soul conversion. The irreverent chuckled. Dusenberg was furious at being dismissed with three contemptuous lines, in which not even his name was mentioned.

The Rev. Augustus blundered himself into more trouble when, during his sermon one night, he sniped at Dr. Fox, the Presbyterian minister. Covington had never had so strange a preacher as Dr. Fox, who actually believed that people could enjoy themselves without sinning. Covington people by a large majority believed in enjoying themselves without much regard to whether they were sinning or not, but they expected to do so without approval from the preachers.

"When a town gets so low that it will tolerate little dried up preachers who lug pool tables into their church basements, the time has come for that town to get down on its knees and pray for salvation," Dusenberg thundered.

The friendly, unassuming, broadminded Dr. Fox had not welcomed the effort to defeat the saloons with evangelism, but constrained by his position had cooperated with the other churches. Dusenberg's narrow intolerance pained the gentle dominie. Though he continued to support the evangelistic campaign even after this attack, his warmest friends lost interest.

Dusenberg complained that he needed a "tabernacle" in which penitents could "hit the sawdust trail." Led by the Methodist brethren, volunteers erected a frame barn on a vacant lot, from whose platform Augustus continued his battle against the evils of dancing, cards, and the movie house. One might have derived the impression that Jesus Christ was crucified in protest against these three cardinal sins.

The crowds grew no bigger in the tabernacle. Interest sagged. Dusenberg sent to Chicago for an assistant, the Rev. Mr. Sweezey.

The Rev. Mr. Sweezey brought his camera and a miscellaneous lot of lantern slides. The slides portrayed missionaries proselyting the heathen in Africa, pictured the evils of great cities, the white slave traffic, Biblical scenes, and the joys of salvation. With his camera he took pictures around Covington to be thrown on the tabernacle screen.

The *Republican* forms were being locked ready for the press one Friday morning when someone telephoned that Perley Myers had shot himself. Perley was a colorless young fellow who worked in Will Schma's livery barn. That had been the limit of his ambitions. He and his wife lived quietly in a little house owned by Mrs. Cora Doane, my mother-in-law. Why Myers killed himself no one ever learned. His unassuming presence in Covington had been so inconspicuous that people soon forgot to speculate over his motives. He had pulled the trigger of a shotgun with his toe. The discharge tore a horrible hole in the left side of his chest.

Mrs. Doane and her daughter hurried to the house to help look after Mrs. Myers and perform what other offices they might. A few other people were lingering about when Dusenberg and Sweezey bustled into the house. Without knocking or asking permission, they stumped into the room where Perley's body still lay against the wall, awaiting the coroner's coming. Sweezey was setting up his camera and Dusenberg was eyeing the horrible wound when Mrs. Doane faced them.

"Who are you and what are you doing here?" she demanded.

"We are the evangelists. We have come to photograph this sinful man's body. We're going to show this picture on the screen in our tabernacle. We will bring salvation to Covington by exhibiting the awful consequences of wickedness. This man was a drunkard and a gambler." Dusenberg did the talking.

Perley had undoubtedly taken part in seven-up games at the livery stable, and possibly had tasted liquor. He never had money enough to gamble and had never been seen drunk.

"You fellows pack up and get out of here," Mrs. Doane snapped, fire in her eyes and hands on her hips.

"What right have you to order us out?" Dusenberg's attitude turned belligerent.

"I own this house. Get out!" Making a "shooing" motion with her apron, Mrs. Doane stepped forward. The soul-savers hastily departed, Sweezey waiting until he reached the sidewalk before folding up his tripod.

The details of the incident were telephoned to me in time for a paragraph to be added to the suicide story:

> Two self-styled evangelists, Dusenberg and Sweezey, who are conducting a revival meeting in a tabernacle here, attempted to take a picture of the corpse with its ghastly wound, and announced their purpose to use the picture on the screen as a horrible example. They were put out of the house by friends of the widow.

Sweezey referred to the paragraph from his pulpit that afternoon. "That statement," he declared, "is a foul-mouthed lie, conceived in the maggoty head of this paper's sneakthief editor. That dirty young smart aleck ought to be tarred and feathered and rode out of Covington as an enemy of righteousness. Every decent-minded Christian here should stop his subscription to that lying, filthy sheet."

There was more language of the same general Christian character, according to a friend who came hotfooting to the printing office. I telephoned to Sweezey next morning, asking that he come to the office, which he did within an hour.

"I understand," I said to him, "that I was called a liar from your pulpit yesterday. That is a rather discourteous epithet. Did you have any particular reasons for it?" Sweezey seized a copy of the *Republican* from the counter, laid his finger on the last paragraph of the suicide story, and fiercely demanded to know if that were not reason enough.

"I should say it was no reason at all for calling me a liar."

"Why isn't it?" Sweezey demanded.

"Because that paragraph is a perfectly true account of what happened."

"It is not true. It is all false, every word of it."

"Didn't you and Dusenberg go to Perley Myers' house yesterday morning?"

"We did. It was our duty as ministers of God to visit the house of sorrow."

"Didn't you attempt to photograph the corpse?"

"We did not."

"I have the word of people who were present that you did."

"But I tell you we did not."

"Mr. Sweezey, these are people that I know. They have no reason to misinform me. I believe them, and I do not believe you."

Sweezey fairly danced with fury. "Do you mean, young man, that you would believe these common people around here and refuse to take the word of me, a man of God?"

"I certainly would believe them rather than you. I think that as a man of God you are a third-rate four-flusher."

"Young fellow, I suppose that if I were Billy Sunday I would pull off my coat and clean up on you for that!"

"There is a nail if you want to hang it up. Go ahead!"

Without a farewell the visiting saint departed and I saw him no more.

The revival gradually petered out. Dusenberg was too obviously insincere. He could denounce but could not persuade. The church people had agreed to pay all the expenses of the campaign from the nightly collections. Dusenberg was to pay the personal expenses for himself and his assistants. The last night's collection was to be his.

The collection to which he had long looked forward was disappointingly meagre. He packed his valise and departed on the midnight train, after assuring the landlord of the hotel that the local committees would take care of his bill. Eventually they did, after a number of meetings about which I was not told. Other bills incurred by Dusenberg for personal expenses were presented. He never sent his address to any of the good people who had entertained him in Covington.

In the meantime, the election had been held. The result was reported in the *Republican:*

Covington voted wet.

The majority was an even 30, contained in the third ward. The first ward was 11 dry, the second 7 wet, and the third 34 wet.

"The election passed without any noticeable excitement, and with less than the usual bustle on the day. Most of the campaign was less vitriolic than local option campaigns frequently are. Both sides worked earnestly for the last few weeks. The wets were well organized and had their lines of campaign well laid. The drys had an equally good organization, but had to drag the weight of some perhaps well meaning but fatal influences that cost heavily, as the result showed.

The saloons are to return. The *Republican* regrets the fact, believing that a saloonless town is a better town. However, postmortem examinations never cured a patient nor won a poker deal. We believe it is the duty of every citizen to go ahead just the same as ever, only more so, to boost Covington and to fight for the continued improvement of its every business interest. The saloons will take care of themselves. An effort will be made to see that no unqualified men are permitted licenses. We have here the material for a thriving, attractive town, and this is a time to keep on working.

Defeat in the local option campaign was discouraging. My wounded pride did receive a small application of balm when the moral defeat turned out to be a financial victory. The saloon men had been astonished to see an avowed enemy of their cause come out in print against the type of personal denunciation they expected to experience. By law they were required to publish notices of their applications for licenses, the cost of which at the legal advertising rate was $7.50. At a meeting the applicants resolved to favor the *Republican* with a majority of the notices, and instructed their attorneys to notify the editor that their decision was made in appreciation of the *Republican's* fairness. "We knew you were against us; we know you will be against us the next time. But you were fair, and not personal."

Their legal notices were accepted in the spirit intended, and the money gratefully deposited in a scanty bank account. Shortly after the saloons opened, the *Republican's* front page duly chronicled the consequences of licensed liquor selling:

> The first gun in the next campaign for a dry Covington was a brickbat — or several brickbats. An argument, started over a disreputable woman who had been circulating around the saloon section, broke out into a fight and the fight soon developed into a general picnic at the southwest corner of the square Saturday night.

The names of six persons who were arrested, with details of their trials and fines in police court, completed the account. An editorial in the same issue declared:

> We do not recollect that during the years Covington was dry there were any such young riots as occurred on the southwest corner of the square Saturday night. Such rumpuses are by-products of the saloon. If the men who voted wet believing that saloons would increase the business of the town consider that a brawl on the square will bring business to Covington, their viewpoint is rather unusual.

Not long afterward a paragraph in the editorial column undertook to be satirical: "Another nice thing about having licensed and orderly saloons in a town is that it is possible to work up a pretty good fight about once a week." Under the heading of "A Political Opportunity" an earlier editorial discussed the advance of the prohibition movement, closing with the statement:

> We would heartily favor a prohibition plank in the next Republican state platform. We believe it would insure the success of the ticket in the state, and bolster up every county ticket with additional strength. The

power of the brewery and distillery is waning. They
should never have been in state politics. Now is the
time to kick them permanently out from all parties.
Let the Republican party, with its magnificent record
of achievement, take the step now.

In consequence of the precipitate impatience of the dry
forces, and the poor sportsmanship of the wet centers, the
adoption of national prohibition not only set back the
temperance cause, but produced new kinds of crime. None
of this, however, was foreseen by an enthusiastic young
editor who, week after week, chronicled the rapid progress
of the anti-liquor movement. Gleefully he reported the
expulsion of saloons from Danville, Illinois, where, just
fifteen miles away, his neighbors who craved a drink had
gone whenever Covington was having a dry spell.

Covington and Fountain county will welcome the
news that Danville has purged herself of her 72 saloons,
and that after May 1 the curse of liquor will be re-
moved from our bigger sister city.

The women, aroused to their power as well as to their
civic obligations, helped to win for the temperance
forces. Another noteworthy feature of the big victory
was the fact that for the first time the drys had newspaper cooperation. The *Commercial-News*, after dwell-
ing in darkness for many years, finally discovered that
it is no longer popular to be classed as wet.

Danville will be better off dry. Covington will be
better off with Danville dry, and the time is not so far
distant when a thirsty citizen of these parts will have
to travel for some distance to lubricate his larynx or
to absorb sufficient liquid courage to give his family a
beating.

A few weeks afterward, the vote in the seat of the adjoin-
ing county, across the Wabash river, was announced:

History was made in Williamsport Tuesday when the
women of that city, their votes counting for the first

time in the history of Indiana, joined with the men in
ousting the booze traffic. Their vote was dry 310 to 15,
and the men voted dry 205 to 173. . . . This was a
history-making event for Williamsport, its women
having the proud distinction of being the very first in
the state to wield their newly acquired power of fran-
chise.

From another issue:

Twenty-three states and Alaska are now dry. Six
more were added to the list Nov. 7. Detroit, one of the
most rapidly growing cities in the nation, returned a
prohibition majority and noses out Seattle as the largest dry city in the hemisphere. Complete national prohibition, with the final abolition of the sale and manufacture of alcoholic liquor, is a matter of only a little
more time, a little more work. Indiana may be dry
within a year. Time for both rejoicing and work!

State-wide prohibition came to Indiana within a year, as
predicted, arriving just in time to save Covington the agony
of another local option election. The local option fights
and political campaigns were absorbing and instructing
intervals. The young editor felt that he had proved at
least one fundamental in endeavors to influence public
opinion. When in opposition, do not disparage personalities; fight the saloon, not the saloon keeper; fight the courthouse gang, fight with issues or denounce ideas, not their
individual proponents. These principles paid dividends for
years then uncharted.

Individuals and their personalities, nevertheless, provided ceaseless fascination. A human laboratory moved
constantly before the editor's eyes, and observation of the
actions and reactions built up a store of education which,
he was to believe in later decades, no Harvard or Yale
could have equalled.

7

Men About Town

THE HUMAN race in Covington provided the *Republican* with unending quantities of interesting "copy," even though the advertising was scanty. One could forget business problems in the ever delightful task of preparing the weekly news and editorials.

Of first importance were the "personal" columns where in paragraphs of a sentence or two the "simple annals" of each week were recorded. Astonishing events seldom occurred and if one did everyone soon heard all the details. Everyone knew everyone else. So, "names were news" upon any excuse. Each week from two to five columns were filled with items like these:

W. F. Gerhard of Mellott was a business visitor here Monday.

Walter Fink, head of the Cates schools, was among the teachers who took the examination here Saturday.

John Stevens is back from his Louisiana hunting trip bringing along as evidences of his prowess two deer hides, two big alligator hides, and other trophies.

Fred Kay, the well known Newtown meat merchant, dropped into the *Republican* office Wednesday in time to shove his subscription into the future another two years.

J. Wesley Whicker of Attica made a business trip to the blue grass region of Kentucky the first of the

week, returning home Wednesday night. He declares
that he saw no pretty girls nor fast horses and drank
no whiskey while there.

At best a half or more of such items each week had to be
colorless and uninteresting beyond the bare facts. The editor tried to put variety into the personal columns by adding
bits of color that, though trivial and far from newsworthy,
had some touch of human interest.

When it comes to downright nerve, there are a bunch
of men in Covington who are ready to take off their
bonnets to Rev. Howard. At the banquet Wednesday
night of local war workers, Rev. Howard walked right
out into the kitchen, during the addresses, and hushed
the good women of the church who in their discussion
of world politics or some other subject had allowed
their voices to grow loud enough to be heard in the
banquet room. Howard was publicly commended for
his bravery.

Bert Oyler, our capable and genial Mellott correspondent, was in the city Wednesday. Bert Saturday
celebrated the first annual anniversary of the day he
quit smoking. He acquired the habit at youthful age,
but decided it was doing him no good, and now uses
tobacco in no form. 'Tis said it is hard to quit the
weed, but Bert believes that the way to quit is to quit.

James J. Lewis of Fulton township was up Thursday
with his characteristic budget of fun. "Say," he said,
"this rain is awful hard on the poor. But, say, I don't
belong to that class — I sold a load of hogs yesterday.
I ain't poor but I ain't got any wife."

The item about James J. Lewis possessed interest to the
hundreds who knew him as a happy eccentric, who punctu-
ated his rapid speech with "say," and "yes, yes." From other
Lewises he was distinguished as "Yes, Yes" Lewis. In ap-

pearance and manner he was the perfect "Uncle Josh"; his conversation, sometimes none too delicate, was a machine gun monologue. One of his remarks was not considered suitable for quotation in the *Republican*: "Say, you ought to come down my way; yes, yes, you ought to. I ain't so bad off as I was, for, say, I've got a new housekeeper. Yes, yes! Great big double-breasted woman!"

No resident of Covington was too humble for his name to appear in the *Republican* if an excuse could be devised for printing it. To increase the number of names, and to add a news novelty, a short "What They Say" feature was initiated, where local people of various degrees of prominence were quoted with utterances that were usually inconsequential but seldom dull. (The identifications are added; in the paper they were not needed.)

WM. HAINES (restaurant man) : I don't believe all these flies in here belong to me. I am going to let some of them out.

KI CRUEA (professional fisherman) : No fishing this week. I had all I could do to save my trot lines when the river came up.

E. W. STRECKER (Methodist pastor) : That was a fine address by Mother Lake. It will make men treat their wives better.

MRS. R. H. MCKINNEY : This month marks our tin wedding anniversary. My husband bought a Ford for our present.

JIM SLIM : If you have something you can't use that I need, and I have something I don't need that you can use, we are both better off if we trade, regardless of value.

TULY MILLER (waiter in Shuler's restaurant) : When we get all the rest of the place cleaned up the old man says we can scour the fifty-cent pieces in the cash register.

FRANK VICKERY (*Republican* office devil) : It ain't always the biggest heads that have the most in 'em.

OLLIE HUTSON (drayman) : Ought to have a thing is one thing and havin' it is another.

Three of the men quoted above were conspicuous Covington "notables." So modest were their ordinary routines and activity that under customary definitions of news their names would not have been in print from New Years Day to New Years Eve, unless they were seriously ill, injured, or dead. These three were Ki Cruea, Jim Slim, and Ollie Hutson.

Ollie Hutson was a landmark. No one professed to know his age, but his years were many. In physical contours the town offered no counterpart. His shape was almost precisely that of a goose egg on legs. The legs were very short. His low waist was of spectacular girth; his body tapered upward to the head, which was of the same shape and sat close to his shoulders. He greatly resembled one of the pioneer cinema comedians, now nearly forgotten, the hilariously funny John Bunny.

Ollie drove a one-horse dray as he labored at his principal occupation, the delivery of packages from the express office at the depot. By a peculiar local arrangement, he was entitled to collect five cents for each delivery, though the parcel may have arrived prepaid. Daily he went about his rounds, lumbering into stores with his packages and boxes, ever repeating in a thin, falsetto voice his unvaried formula, "Gimme nick, gimme nick!"

"What do you mean, give you a nickel?" Ernest Goodman, a new storekeeper who had come down from Chicago, demanded one day of Ollie. Unfamiliar with the customary delivery charge, he bristled at what seemed to be an unjustified extortion. Ollie impatiently essayed an explanation which Goodman failed to grasp. A clerk who tried to make the matter clear only increased the new owner's determination not to pay a nickel without knowing why.

Ollie's way of emphasizing a remark was to repeat it. His "Gimme nick" phrase was always spoken twice. So were most of his observations. At the grain elevator where he bought feed for his horse, his regular request was "More stuffin's, more stuffin's." Once when the feed supply had been eaten sooner than he thought was proper, he expressed his exasperation to Walter Moore, the elevator proprietor, by saying, "All head, no horse; all head, no horse."

When Goodman's delay in paying the five cents had exhausted his patience, Ollie rose to the situation. Placing his hands flat on the merchant's desk he leaned over and in a fast sing-song closed the discussion by repeating "Gimme nick, gimme nick, gimme nick, gimme nick," until the merchant in despair paid the nickel.

One day I arranged with Dick Burnett, the tall photographer, to take a picture of Ollie sitting high on his dray. The picture, made without Ollie's knowledge, turned out to be a characteristic likeness. It appeared two columns wide on the front page of the paper with the following article:

We present herewith a picture of Covington's most prominent citizen.

There may be others who appear more often in public; others whose names are more often mentioned in the affairs of the city; but there is no citizen of Covington personally known to more people, young and old, rich and poor, than Ollie Hutson.

For years and years and years and years, back to when the memory of many men runneth not, Ollie Hutson and his dray have been notable of all the features of the streets of Covington. For all these years, with no interruptions but for an occasional illness, six days a week, has this quaint old man hitched up his horse and quietly gone about his daily tasks.

As a town's most prominent citizen should be, Ollie is a man of many and conspicuous virtues. Let us catalog a few of them:

He is industrious. He works right along, just as long as work lasts.

He attends to his own business and allows other folks to look after the affairs that belong to them.

He is thrifty. His bank account, the result of frugal living and quiet habits, might surprise many who see in him a subject for jibes.

He is temperate. Ollie even refuses to handle saloon drayage.

He is honest. He pays to the last cent, and collects the same way.

Why add more? He is a good citizen. Ollie sees the funny side of life, and has a joke for every call he makes. Rain or shine, cold or warm, he sees that his packages are delivered to their right places. He's a happy man, who performs his useful task well. Our salutations to Ollie Hutson! May he live many more years of joy and usefulness, in full possession of his title and position as Covington's most prominent citizen — a title he honors as well as deserves.

A half dozen copies of the *Republican* were laid aside for the prominent citizen's next visit to the office. I was eager to hear what Ollie would have to say. The next morning Ollie stumped in and tossed a five-cent piece on the counter.

"Gimme pape'," he demanded. "Gimme pape'."

The extra copies were handed over and the coin pushed back. "Here, Ollie, I thought you might want some extra copies, so I laid these back for you. They won't cost you anything."

"Jist one, jist one," Ollie declared, taking the top one and departing without further comment. He left the five cents, for his philosophy about paying was as rigid as it was about collecting. He never mentioned the matter again, nor did I ever find out what happened to the one extra copy. The *Republican* had been wrong about Ollie's bank account. He died in the county poor house.

As Ollie was obviously a model of industry, Ki Cruea — Hezekiah was his never-used full name — was regarded as an exponent of the lazy life. Ki was dean of the river men, the fellows who lived by fishing, trapping, and mussel gathering. Tall and gaunt, well past middle age, Ki appeared occasionally along the west or south sides of the square where the saloons and pool rooms were located. No one recalled ever having seen him in new clothes. Usually in summer he was barefoot. In spring and fall he wore rubber boots, and in winter felt boots. There was some speculation as to whether he ever bathed, even in the river.

Like the younger men who worked the river, he ran trot lines (heavy lines stretched across, or nearly across the river, to which short lines carrying baited hooks were suspended) in season, fished with hook and line, and dragged for mussels. Mussel shells were salable by the ton for manufacture into buttons. The gatherers dragged the river bottom with large hooks, upon which the live mussels closed their open shells and were brought to the surface. When a quantity had been gathered they were heated enough to cause the shells to open. The flesh, not considered edible, was always examined carefully for pearls. Pearls worth as much as several hundred dollars each had been found. An industrious mussel digger could make average day wages if he stuck steadily to the job, and he always could hope for the bonus of a good pearl.

Ki had three grown sons, Bill, Asa, and young Ki, who were industrious and well behaved fellows. All of them followed the river for a while, but eventually took up more conventional occupations.

Nicknames were common in Covington, with some of the more spectacular being attached to river men. "Taterbug" Hegg (pronounced Heck), had acquired his designation as a small boy by eating a potato beetle on a dare. One fellow was called "Greasy" Tittle, for some forgotten reason. "Crookneck" McDonald was so-called from a physical deformity. There were "Bogus" Thompson, "Cocky" Hendrix, "Ginger" Martin, "Turny" Hedges, "Farmer" McMahon, "Coon" Hutson, and "Commodore" Lowe.

The "commodore's" title was conferred by the *Republican*. One cold night fire destroyed the old wooden covered bridge over the Wabash. Lowe, an enterprising and alert retired farmer, remembered that upstream at Lafayette there had once been a ferry-boat, which he hurriedly purchased and floated down to Covington. Despite difficulties he rigged up engines and cables and set the boat to carrying traffic across the river, first charging tolls, and later operating it as a free ferry under contract with the county commissioners. The public service rendered was genuine, for the nearest bridges were several miles up and down the river. Without the ferry, Covington would have been cut off for months from the extensive trade territory that lay across the river in Warren and Vermillion counties, and an important east and west highway would have been out of use.

The ferry charges were widely believed to be making Lowe rich. Before long appreciation for the service he was performing was replaced by fear that he was making an undue amount of money. Lowe, a fun-loving, vigorous fellow who delighted in hoaxes and jokes, encouraged the belief. When charged with having a gold mine in the ferry, at the expense of the public, he cheerfully exaggerated the profits, which actually were disappointingly small.

One night during the winter while Lowe was running the ferry, the men of the Presbyterian church talked about staging a public entertainment to raise the funds that were needed for some goodly purpose. A mock trial was proposed.

"Whom shall we try, and what for?" was asked.

"Let's try Charley Lowe for burning the bridge, so he could get rich out of the ferry," I suggested. Lowe readily agreed. The trial in the county court room was almost as well attended as the "ax murder" trial years before. After two hours of hilarious testimony, the jury returned a verdict of guilty, which was immediately set aside by the prompt arrival of a "pardon" from the governor.

In advance notices of the trial, the *Republican* dubbed Lowe "Commodore" of the Wabash Boat Line. Not only did the title stick, but a belief became established in the minds of a few, who were dimly aware of the feeling about the ferry and did not clearly understand that the trial was a mere entertainment, that "Commodore" Lowe had actually burned the old bridge.

Jim Slim had only one connection with the river. He did not fish nor dig mussels, nor run a ferry, but he had undertaken once or twice to revive the steamboat industry. Whether Jim Slim was his real name Covington had ever been doubtful. Legend told that he had arrived in town many years before when still a young man and, for some pecadillo or perhaps for vagrancy, had been confined in the little town jail. During the night he made his escape through a stovepipe opening, so slender then was his body. When asked his name he had said, "You can call me Jim Slim," and as Jim Slim he was ever after known. He married and had two daughters who grew into handsome young women. Jim's interest in life was mainly the prevention of waste. As a dealer in junk and second hand goods, his establishment was always surrounded by an astonishing collection of miscellany. He would give from ten cents upward for almost anything offered, figuring any object ought to be worth at least a dime.

Jim was an original conversationalist whose view of the physical character of the earth was free from orthodoxy.

"The earth is flat," Jim told me during one of our Sunday afternoon discussions. "It is flat, surrounded by enormous walls of ice."

"But, Jim, doesn't circumnavigation prove that the earth is a globe?"

"Not at all. That is a fallacy that unfortunately is believed. The part of the earth's surface that is known to man is disk or dinner plate shaped. Now what is circumnavigation? Merely traveling around the world in one direction, say from east to west. What determines east and west? Why, right angles to north and south! Now, tie a toothpick to a string, and hold one end of the string down in the middle of a dinner plate. Straighten out the string. In whatever direction it lies, that direction is south or north. Push the toothpick around the plate — it always travels due east or west, or at right angles to north and south. All right, you see now how the geographers fool themselves. They think they are circumnavigating a globe, when actually they are merely describing a circle around the middle of a plate.

"Now, when ships travel to the outer edges of the earth, what do they find? Great walls of ice! Let me tell you! When the old continents of Asia and Europe and Africa which then constituted the known world became overcrowded with people, a Columbus was sent out and he discovered a new continent, with enough land to keep the human race busy for several centuries. When this American continent in turn becomes overcrowded, another Columbus will find his way through these walls of what we call polar ice, and beyond them will be new inhabitable lands. Thus nature has provided for the indefinite expansion of the population of the earth."

Jim's mechanical ability was directed in spare time to tinkering with the worn machinery he acquired. But at intervals he labored upon ideas for the wider benefit of mankind. At about the time the Wright brothers were experimenting with airplanes at Dayton and Kittyhawk, Jim had been constructing a flying machine in his junkyard at Covington. Some technical difficulties arose, however, and when the Wrights finally flew, he abandoned his efforts.

"They have learned how to fly. Why should I bother with a problem that has been solved?" he said.

Twice he began the construction of a steamboat to resume navigation of the Wabash. While the result of neither attempt ever navigated, one finally grew into a habitable houseboat which he occupied in the summertime.

Jim owned the last two-cylinder high-wheeled, buggy type of "horseless carriage" to survive in that part of the country. It worked intermittently, and when it did move the exhaust explosions could be heard for half a mile. Eight-cylinder Coles were gliding about the square before Jim finally gave up the old noise-maker. One day it stopped dead in the street in front of the First National Bank. Jim leaned back in his seat and laughed to himself.

"What's so funny, Jim?" Billy Dennis, the grocer, asked.

"I was just thinking what a lucky fellow I am," Jim replied. "I have so danged much trouble with this old two-cylinder bus. Ain't it lucky I ain't got an eight-cylinder car?"

The single exception in Covington to the rule that a prominent and able citizen should not be excessively addicted to liquor was a brilliant lawyer of delightful personality. This was "Judge" Oliver Perry Lewis whose enthusiasm for distilled spirits was said to have cost him at least one nomination for Congress and other political opportunities. I never heard Lewis express himself on the point but came to suspect that the gentleman did not regard a mere nomination for Congress worth giving up a drink.

Addressed by everyone as "Judge," Lewis had never held judicial office. The honorary title was said to have been derived from a temporary service on the bench as arbiter of some forgotten suit, although the view was expressed in Charley Bergdahl's tailor shop, the male gossip center, where the question was once raised, that it was held because Lewis was an excellent judge of liquor. However that may have been, Judge Lewis was universally admired in Covington. He had no enemies. A jovial, democratic man, he was well built and handsome of figure, with regular features, a clear skin that contrasted attractively with his thick black mustache, and an impressive bearing. He liked everybody, and would stop to chat with the lowliest citizen in the same manner he employed when exchanging views with the most prominent. As an orator he had no peer in all Fountain County. Upon the slightest or most momentous occasion, he could be depended upon to say the fitting and felicitous thing. The rich tones of his melodious voice, the grace of his gestures, and the flowing harmony of his language invariably delighted all hearers.

Even in commonplace conversational exchanges, Judge Lewis was the orator. He exuded magniloquence. Probably his reputation for legal brilliance was due more to his ready command of language than to judicial learning. He lived over Jesse Smith's grocery store at the southeast corner of the square, in a two-room apartment reached by an outside stairway. One room was used as his office, and shared by Evan Heath, a bachelor insurance agent.

One morning I greeted the distinguished lawyer as he appeared at the foot of his stair. "Nice morning, Judge!"

"Magnificent in the extreme!" was his reply, accompanied by an appropriately sweeping gesture toward the rising sun. Another morning we met in the post office. "How are you this morning, Judge?" I inquired.

"Sober, my dear friend, but the sun has not yet risen far above the horizon!"

Courtesy, verbal and actual, was an accentuated quality in the Judge. Nearly all Covington people were notable for their friendly courteousness, but none could make so courtly a rite of any commonplace occasion. Indeed, no one in

Fountain County could make an apology, or beg a pardon
with such polished ceremoniousness nor so diplomatically
present an unpleasant matter. His courtesy increased with
his alcoholic content. And that gives point to the story
that Covingtonians thought the best one about Judge Lewis.
The incident, which had taken place two or three years
before my arrival in town, involved the Judge and two other
actors.

Ed Mayer, wealthiest and gayest of the young men about
town, had naturally owned the first automobile. This was
a primitive car with seats for two in front, and at the rear
another little seat for one, facing backwards. Late one hot
and humid afternoon Ed invited Judge Lewis to drive over
to Danville after a glass of beer.

This was during one of Covington's saloonless intervals,
and cool beer was not to be had around the square. Also,
automobiles were so new that the fantastic and modern idea
of driving fifteen miles after so trifling albeit desirable an
object as a glass of beer appealed mightily to Judge Lewis's
imagination. "I am," he declared, "extremely delighted to
go and highly grateful for so extraordinarily happy an invitation; but, sir, since there is another seat, could not our
mutual friend, Senator Boord, who would also appreciate a
refreshing stein of amber ale, also be invited?"

The Senator, who will be described more fully, accepted
the invitation appreciatively. In less than an hour their
right feet were resting comfortably on the brass rail of the
Aetna house bar in Danville.

It soon became apparent that if such an expedition had
been well worthwhile for one glass of common lager, its
success would be all the greater if other potions followed
when an abundance behind the bar awaited their order.

Two hours had passed pleasantly when Ed Mayer jerked
out his watch and in the crisp manner of the business man
announced that they must start home. The Senator managed to elevate himself into the little back seat. After having
properly bowed his companions to their places, the Judge
sat with erect dignity beside the owner and driver. Down
Vermilion street they could see the Big Four evening train
just then leaving Danville for Covington.

"See that train pullin' out?" Ed asked. "I always aim to leave here just as she's leaving the station, so's I can beat 'er in to Covington. We'll pull up in front of the bank at home before the passenger gets stopped at the depot."

Out of Danville they rumbled, Ed driving with reckless skill. The Judge clung firmly to the cushion in a diligent effort to appear entirely at ease and unconcerned. Roads had not yet been paved. Over the rude macadam the little car bounced from side to side, bumping roughly over frequent chuckholes. As they whizzed past a familiar landmark that meant the state line had been crossed, it occurred to Judge Lewis to see how Senator Boord was coming along. He turned to look into the rear seat.

Eyes wide with horror, he almost toppled out of the careening car. He loosed his hold on the cushion, when another bump nearly threw him out. Taking a new grip, he was about to shout out when his instinct to do the right thing in the courteous way conquered his momentary impulse to be abrupt. He leaned over and tapped Ed gently on the shoulder.

"I beg your pardon, Sir," he said. "I hope I am not intruding, and that by speaking I will not hamper your efforts to guide this most admirable vehicle. But I fear, Sir, that we have lost the Senator!"

They found Senator Boord a mile or so back, serenely brushing the dust from his trousers.

"I thought for a minute that you fellows had decided to go on and leave me," he remarked in the voice of one whose feelings were, in spite of himself, slightly wounded.

Fountain County was rich in human individuality. Men dared to be their natural selves without trying to worm into the standard molds which the communication and mobility of ensuing years have tended to establish. Before I was well enough accepted as a Covingtonian to be admitted to personal confidences I had heard scores of the treasured tales that were told, in friendly humor rather than in malice, about the local "characters."

One such story concerned Senator Fred Boord, the third actor in the motor car yarn. Boord was fifty years old, a slight, spare man with heavy, dark hair. Several days' growth of sparse brown beard usually littered his pale face. He tottered and leaned on a cane, bearing the perpetual appearance of a person just emerged from long weeks of wasting illness.

While a very young man he had been elected a state senator through the influence of older politicians who liked him and thought he would be useful to them. He was a bright chap with a ready flow of words. They had encouraged him with predictions of a distinguished political career. But he had enjoyed being a senator too much. In the gaiety of a legislative session he had contracted an illness from which he suffered thereafter.

The story was told that during a recess in his first senate session he came home and was invited out to the Bend Chapel, a country church in the bend of the river above town, to speak on the afternoon program of an all-day meeting. He began his address in an impressively deep voice:

"I am very grateful to you my friends, for the invitation to address you this afternoon. I am indeed glad to be here. It always does me good to get out among the common people."

No one took offense. The Bend folks thought his reference to "common people" was funny, since they knew, and knew that Fred knew, that he had been one among these same common people all his life, except for the month or six weeks he had been at Indianapolis in the legislature.

How Fred managed an existence in his later years was a mystery. Although listed as a member of the bar, except for rare trifles he had no cases. Now and then he was called upon to draw a simple document or contract, or to help clear a title. Otherwise he had no apparent source of income. He lived in a house owned by his father, a Civil War veteran who drew a pension and perhaps gave Fred a little aid from his own meager means. He managed in some manner to obtain stimulants frequently. Unless someone gave him a cigar, he smoked a brown clay pipe with a yellow reed stem. Eventually his father died and the house was sold. For a time Fred slept in the powerhouse or by the

furnace in the Chamber of Commerce building. Even when
reduced to these extremities, he proudly refused to accept
the repeated offers of a prosperous half-brother to pay his
board and room in some comfortable home.

After surviving until past sixty he fell ill and died. I was
not in Covington at the time, but when I heard the news it
called to mind the tragic passing of the gifted Judge Lewis.
One cold Monday morning the winter after the saloons reopened, while on my way to the office, the news was repeated by a passerby that "they found Perry Lewis dead
this morning down in John Duncan's place." John Duncan
was a poor old printer who had a little job shop around
the corner from the *Republican* office, who was glad to be
hired at fifteen cents an hour when we needed extra help.
Hastening to the place, I found a little group of silent men
in a shabby, unswept room, gazing toward a cot at the ash-
white face and congealed form of Covington's most charming and gifted man. After a brief, horrified look, I hurried
around to the office wondering, as never before, how and
why men could let alcohol destroy them.

Bill Harden, the *Republican*'s shop foreman, maintained
a comprehensive and accurate knowledge of the quality and
character of almost everyone of the slightest consequence in
Covington. His contacts were few, for most of his waking
hours were spent either upstairs in his department of the
office or quietly at home. Yet he managed to know of everyone who lived in town nearly every fact of interest — a resource that would have profited his employer to have used
more freely.

His speech was blunt. "Bill, what do you know about
So-and-So?" I might ask regarding a person with whom
business dealings were contemplated.

"Make 'im pay cash," Bill would reply, barely hesitating
in his work. "He's crooked as a bucket of guts." Or, "He's
good as gold."

"He's a church worker — might be honest but the pre-
sumption is against him" was another of Bill's favorite
characterizations.

Religion in any form he viewed as a huge joke, except

for the single concession that it might be a comfort to simple-minded old ladies. The conception that amused him most was that of angels. He loved to speculate about the probable performances of well known local personages once they had adjusted their wings and set out to fly. Ollie Hutson, the spherical drayman, he thought would make a particularly interesting angel. He thought that heaven ought to be plentifully equipped with perches, because so many Covington people were in his estimation too lazy to do much flapping.

A strange aerial sound one afternoon brought Bill and me into the office backyard. It was the first airplane ever seen over Covington, an army plane traveling from Wright Field near Dayton to Rantoul, Illinois. When it had disappeared I asked Bill how he would like to be riding up there.

"No, Sir!" he replied emphatically. "When I go to heaven I want to go on my own wings."

Virtue, in his opinion, was dealt out sparsely to the human race. He believed that meanness, in one form or another, was the prevailing quality. Particularly he detested the unwillingness of other employes to toil with the same earnest enthusiasm that possessed him to get the most possible work completed every day. Not to do one's best for an employer was, he thought, downright dishonesty.

Never ill-natured under any circumstances, Bill delighted in the chaffing that became part of our daily routine. Public praise he denounced as an invasion of his modesty and privacy, but when I began writing about him in the paper he solemnly set up the copy, pretending that being only the foreman his duty was to submit to whatever abuse a high handed employer chose to shower upon his shrinking person. So it came that elaborate descriptions were written about Bill's fishing trips, and even a brief holiday visit to a relative was chronicled in big words:

Hon. W. B. Harden, Esq., presiding genius of the mechanical department of this palladium of liberty and engine of righteousness, shed his effulgent rays of sunshine and the beams of his scintillating and corruscating wit over the home of his brother, O. H. Harden, in Danville, Christmas.

One week an announcement appeared:

The editor of the *Republican* is going to take a vacation next week. . . . Our week off is to be a week free from all cares of duty. So we cannot write any editorial column. While we do not delude ourselves with any fancy that the column would be greatly missed, it would violate an office rule to issue a paper without an editorial column.

We have therefore conveyed, given, donated and handed over, free gratis, for nothing and without charge, for the period of one week, the sole and exclusive use of this column to the Hon. William B. Harden, Esq., the sweet angel who presides over the destinies of the mechanical department of this paper. Mr. Harden, in earlier days, say about the time of the exodus of the children of Israel, wielded a trenchant and very effective pen. His editorial paragraphs gave Julius Caesar and Mark Antony many a hearty laugh together, and Cleopatra in vain sought to induce him to start a paper in Egypt. He wrote her that he wouldn't live in Egypt, because he didn't like the way the women dressed. Later, when associated with the late Benjamin Franklin in the publication of Poor Richard's Almanack he wrote many of the clever proverbs and sayings that were generally accredited to Franklin. However, Mr. Harden doesn't mind being deprived of the credit for these maxims, as with more years of experience and observations he can now, as he says, write much better ones.

In recent years he has written but little. However, his eye is undimmed and his mind unclouded, and we anticipate that next week's issue of the *Republican* will carry the best editorial column of its history. We have authorized Mr. Harden to say what he pleases, about whom he pleases, in any manner he pleases. Order your extra copies early.

Bill brought out the paper full of news next week, and handled the editorial page problem without gloves:

We deny the Cleopatra charge as we were very careful of our reputation at that period, as we have been ever since.

No top line — no bottom line. Not much of anything except local news and plate — boiler plate of unusual interest. — Of course the editor is enjoying a week of rest — and so are our readers.

There won't be an editorial column this week.

I tried one year to persuade Bill to make his birthday a day of rest. The effort failed ignominiously because he insisted that too much work was on hand and had to be done. Since Bill refused to celebrate his own birthday, his employer determined to observe it for him. The lead article was the editor's celebration:

"Bill," said the editor of this palladium of righteousness this morning to the foreman, Hon. W. B. Harden, Esq., "If I had a picture of a man who weighed about 360 pounds I would run it in the paper this week and label it 'W. B. Harden, taken on his 66th birthday.' However, I would be forced to admit that 360 would be considerable exaggeration of you."

"Run a picture of a flying angel labelled me, and it would be more appropriate," replied the honorable.

"Why a flying angel, Bill?" we had to ask.

"Because, I will be one before long, flapping around in space. If I ever bump into Ollie Hutson there will be a shower of stars."

All of which is preliminary to saying that today, the 7th of September, marks the 66th birthday of William B. Harden, foreman of the *Republican* office from time immemorial. Sixty-six years ago today he arrived in this world and asked his mother where there was a good place to fish. The next morning he got up at three o'clock and fished till ten, catching one goggle-eye. When he started home he remarked that he believed this world could be improved materially in some respects, an opinion to which he still adheres.

To catalog Bill's interesting opinions would be a long task. He believes the world would be better off without churches, and has no objection to telling the preachers so. He believes strictly in personal liberty, and recognizes the right of others to think otherwise. But to catalog his opinions is outside the province of this little article. We just want to remind the readers of the *Republican* that every week Bill is working for them.

Faithfully, honestly, truly, bravely — for half a century and two years more, Bill has been a printer and a good one. Except for a few years of this time, he has been connected with this paper. As a printer he has made his living. To him, tho, the printshop is more than a living; it is a life work. At 66 he is working this morning with all the earnestness and enthusiasm of the craftsman who loves his task. He even refuses to celebrate his birthday with time off; too much in the office to do, he says. He refuses to be limited by hours; he does not depend on the whistle.

When 14 years old, Bill started to learn the printer's trade — and now he's 66. Fervently we hope that he may live to enjoy his work for a half century more (two centuries if he cares to) for in no place have we ever found a more faithful helper, nor a cheerier working companion, than he. His wit and unfailing good humour are constant antidotes for weariness and discouragement.

We have been trying for 17 weeks to get a picture of him to print in the paper this, his birthday issue, but he's too modest and too busy to have his picture taken. He is a pretty good looking man, too — height a little over or under five feet, weight a little over or under 100 pounds; head bald except where there is hair; never wears glasses except when he has a pair on; likes spittin' tobacco; wears a Grover Cleveland mustache, a twinkle in his eye, no coat, a vest buttoned with one lower button, usually in the wrong buttonhole; and some other clothes

If I knew of a higher tribute than this I would offer it — he is as True a Friend, and as Genuine an American Gentleman as I have ever known. W.McM.

"Must be hard up for news this week," was Bill's only comment when he laid proofs of the galley on my desk.

For thirty or more years Bill had been a widower. He lived with the family of his younger brother, Elmer, a plumber, and lavished affection upon the children of the household.

The gloomiest days in the office were illumined by Bill's faithful presence. Though he had toiled in printing offices since his fourteenth year, his hands and wits were as quick as ever. He was a good printer, but the virtues that stood out in his character were his attitude toward his job, and the unwavering cheerfulness that never presumed yet always made his presence felt. He calmly assumed that no matter how much work piled up, or how many difficulties arose, the work would be finished and the perplexities dissolved if only one kept persistently plugging away.

The thirty-hour week had never been heard of in Covington. Bill would have been a sturdy opponent of the idea on the ground that time would hang heavy on his hands. The ten-hour day was the standard, and the sixty-hour week. Workers were expected to start at seven o'clock in the morning, take an hour for lunch from twelve to one, and to finish at six in the afternoon. For his labors during these hours Bill had received for many years the extraordinary sum of eleven dollars a week. The new editor, upon taking over the office, had munificently raised Bill's wages to twelve dollars.

Bill's interpretation of the sixty-hour week was his own. He was supposed to see that the office was swept out and that fires were made each morning. This, to his mind, was not really work; work was something done in the composing or press rooms. Sweeping and making fires were mere chores. Invariably, winter and summer, he unlocked the office by six-thirty and got these tasks out of the way in time to begin his proper work at seven o'clock. Correcting the mailing list by changing addresses and crediting subscription payments was reserved for Sundays. Each Sunday morning he opened the office to do these jobs and such cleaning up and straightening around as he may have saved up for the seventh day. Summer Sundays were exceptions. Then he first took his rowboat to spend the forenoons fishing in the Wabash, and after his morning on the river looked after the office chores. I liked to go along with Bill on his Sunday expeditions. Occasionally during a week, when office duties were not pressing, an ideal fishing morning would come along, but Bill would never go then. An agnostic, who thought going to church on Sunday to be sinful, he believed with equal fervor that fishing on a weekday was equally reprehensible.

Bill's view of women was not exactly reverential. A young woman, who was our stenographer and bookkeeper for a while, worked at her job almost as faithfully as Bill did at his, but failed to capture his admiration. She was a tall, heavily-framed and liberally fleshed girl who might have been described as ponderous.

"Bill," I teased one day, "why don't you shine up to that girl and marry her? Her Dad's got 80 acres of good Wabash township land, and she's his only child!"

"Nope," Bill replied promptly and firmly. "That farm's too heavily encumbered."

8

Grist for the Paper

BIRTH AND death, marriage and making a living, were major concerns in Covington. They were highly important to the people immediately involved, and of personal interest to everyone else in the community. The parade of normalcy! The second marriage of Widow Blank was a far better news item for the *Republican* than was the second marriage of President Wilson and of incomparably greater interest than the passage of the Federal Reserve Act. The people knew the Widow Blank personally; and they hadn't much idea what the Federal Reserve business meant, except that probably it would not affect them much one way or another and, if so, not right away.

A truly trivial fact often made better copy than the second marriage of the Widow Blank. By the time the paper was in the post office Friday morning the details of the widow's wedding in print would only confirm or deny what the swift tendrils of the town grapevine already had spread. But in more trifling matters the paper might have a chance to scoop the gossips. For instance,

After a week of joyously anticipating the pleasures awaiting him, Luke McGeorge shined his shoes and arrayed his person gorgeously Thursday afternoon, preparing to grace with his presence the banquet of the Indiana Implement Dealers Association at Indianapolis that evening. His father is secretary of the association. Resplendently garbed for the occasion, Luke marched to the Big Four station to take the 3:36 train that would get him there just in time for the banquet. There

he learned that the train was late, and would leave a
little after six, and get into Indianapolis an hour or so
after the banquet was over. So Luke banquetted in
solemn and lonely state at Lonny's.

Not everyone in town knew about that, but everyone did
know Luke, who, in addition to being the mayor's eldest
son, was a wit and well on his way toward becoming one of
the town's "characters." A story about him had already become part of the local folklore. It seemed that when he was
a small boy, his favorite aunt one day entertained the upper
circle of Covington women. Luke was invited to assist, his
special assignment having been to carry a napkin and fingerbowl around to each guest after refreshments had been
served. This procedure was new to Luke and, as he viewed
it, not entirely necessary. He doubted whether the women
had soiled their hands enough to justify urging them to
clean up; indeed, they might resent the insinuation that they
ought to do so. Certainly not all of them would need the
attention, so he acted in what seemed to him to be the
simplest and most sensible manner possible. Napkin and
fingerbowl awkwardly in hand, he paused in the doorway of
the parlor and boomed out in his boyish bass: "Any of you
women here want to wash?"

Whether it was important or not, I found the news that
went into the *Republican* eternally fascinating. There was
drama in "the short and simple annals of the poor," human
interest, comedy and tragedy in each week's events. The
following item appeared in January:

"Widower of 11 Days is Wedded Again," the headline read.

Justice Asa Osborn Saturday morning performed a
ceremony uniting in marriage Albert Vyse and Mary
Henderson, both of this city. Vyse's wife died Jan. 4.
After a vain search for a home for his babe of 7 months,
he took the advice of friends and married again. Mrs.
Henderson was willing to look after the child under the
conditions. Vyse has been married twice before, and she
once before

It may be said that the condemnation of this proceeding by self righteous people, under the circumstances, is hardly to be concurred in. No one offered to make a home for the baby, and Mr. Vyse felt that any kind of a home would be better than an orphanage. The child will have some measure of care, and will doubtless be better off than in any institution, for the State as a mother is perhaps worse than a step mother. The child is the person most concerned of the three.

This one came out in May:

A divorce suit has been filed by Mary Vyse against Albert Vyse. It will be remembered that they were married Jan. 15 of this year, less than two weeks after Vyse's former wife had died. They separated April 14. She complains that he was unfaithful, is a habitual drunkard, failed to provide properly, and was cruel and inhuman in his treatment of her.

What happened to the baby? With poor newspaperwork, the *Republican* failed to report the answer.

Though names were news, an occasional item neglected to mention the names the editor knew:

A few Covington girls who don't object to a flirtation with a stranger were all dressed up for nothing a week or so ago. A motor load of local men drove to Terre Haute Monday, and from there sent a bunch of postal cards to girls here, each bearing a similar message: "Meet me on the south side of the square at 7 Tuesday evening." No names were signed. Tuesday evening found a committee of the men posted at vantage points — and also two or three of the girls, dressed up in their very finest, looking in vain for their unknown cavaliers. Several girls who got the cards ignored them. The father of one of the number got her card and tore it up at the post office.

The run of news was usually dashed off in whatever language appeared adequate to convey the facts. Now and then an item had to be produced that deserved something a little more than casual slapdash words. There was the obituary of little Mary Virginia Wert. The Werts were amongst my best friends, and their sunny, handicapped little girl who had been ill from birth was an unusual child personality. From Tuesday, when I heard the news of her death, until Thursday night when the paper was to be printed, I wondered what to say. Finally, while Bill stood ready to lock up the forms, I sat down before the linotype keyboard and tapped out a tribute:

Mary Virginia, five years old, the daughter of Dr. Charles C. and Mrs. Ethel Wert, peacefully closed her eyes in the bright sunshine of a summer morning, Tuesday, June 19, after a brief illness from bronchial pneumonia. Funeral services were held from the home Thursday at 10 a.m., conducted by Rev. O. W. McGaughey.

Brief, as the years are measured, was her conscious existence in this mysterious world where joys and heartaches dwell so close together. From out the unknown she came, an evanescent gleam of sunshine into the home; from the blessed innocence of infancy she unfolded into the sweet purity of babyhood and into the charming simplicity of childhood; and then, as an ephemeral vision of a rainbow's promise, the soul of her vanished into the unknown from whence she had come.

Her lovable sweetness, the charm of her quaint, bright manner, won for her a home in every heart. How profound, then, was the tie that bound her to those whom she loved best! None may ever know the unutterable anxiety, the untold sacrifice, of the father and mother who struggled unceasingly that her frail body might endure, that her voice might never be hushed into this eternal sleep.

There is no phrase that can assuage their pain or allay their grief. But they have treasured her a messenger from the unknown, who carried joy and happiness into their world; and, departing, on what mission we may not know, left in every heart she visited a new

love, and charity and tenderness; a circle of hearts,
better, purer, because she came into them — than which
no higher tribute can be laid at the shrine of mortal
being.

Mawkish and sentimental? Maybe the reader who didn't
know Covington, nor Dr. and Mrs. Wert, nor little Mary
Virginia, was right if he pronounced it so. But when Doc
Wert put out his hand and managed to say, "Thanks, Mac!
That was the most beautiful thing I ever read," I felt that I
had not failed the two readers that particular obituary
notice was exclusively for, a father and mother whose little
girl I too had loved.

When the misbehavior of people was flagrant enough to
bring them into conflict with the law, the obligation to
print the news made it necessary to chronicle the facts in the
Republican, although reasons were often enough found for
making exceptions. To advertise good deeds was more
agreeable, however, and just as easy. One of the satisfactions
of running a country newspaper was to be able to tell the
people that:

H. E. Rhodes, the efficient assistant road superintendent for Wabash township, found a Stringtown
resident hauling a heavy load of coal to Covington on
the gravel road that passes his house, with a narrow
tired wagon. He hailed the miner and informed him of
the law's provisions. The miner explained that he had
to have the money from the coal for family necessities.
Mr. Rhodes intended to enforce the law, and he did not
wish to inflict a hardship upon the man. So he just paid
the fellow for the coal and had it unloaded in his own
shed.

A twenty-word item about a well known individual was
on occasion the prize news of a week:

Henry Snyder has followed Tom Taggart's example
by shaving off his moustache, and now faces the March
winds with bared upper lip.

Tom Taggart was Indiana's Democratic boss and most famous politician. Henry Snyder was little and elderly, known all around the square as being fairly good at sweeping out and doing odd jobs if one bossed him a little. His friend and hero was Pete Harmon, who lived on Civil War memories and a Civil War pension. Admiration for Pete brought Henry to a tragic end.

One of Pete Harmon's war memories had once provided a story for the paper:

Peter Harmon says he wishes he were 20 years younger so he might enlist for Mexican services. Pete relates an interesting tale of meetings with General Grant. In 1861 he was employed on a farm just south of Springfield, Ill., owned by J. G. Luce. Luce told Pete to get three other teams and haul a rick of hay to the fairgrounds where it had been ordered for the soldiers. Mr. Harmon, then a youth, was on the head wagon as the loads entered the gates. With a rush the soldiers upset the wagon, with wheels flying in the air, and helped themselves liberally to the hay for their bunks. Pete demanded to see the "boss" and was directed to the tent of the commanding officer, who happened to be Grant. On hearing Harmon's grievance, Grant sent a lieutenant with orders that the boys should right the wagon, re-load the hay, then that the four loads should be distributed among the other soldiers, and if any should be left, the fellows who upset the wagon might have it.

Later in the war Harmon says he met General Grant on the streets of Memphis. Saluting, he called the general's attention to their meeting on the rainy afternoon in Springfield. "I knew you would be in the army soon," laughed the general. "I could see it in your eyes."

The great day of each year for old Pete was the Fourth of July. Then it was his function to fire the weathered Civil War cannon that stood in the courthouse yard. Pete loved to fire the old gun. On the morning of the Fourth he would be downtown at daylight, with his bags of powder, the swabs

and ramrod and wadding and whatever else he might need.
He would have examined the old gun carefully some days in
advance, to make sure that nothing was wrong.

No one then living in town could remember a Fourth of
July when old Pete had not fired the cannon. By what
authority he happened to be official high priest of the noisy
ceremony no one could recall. He always had done it; and
when his time to leave should come, it was tacitly assumed
that the roaring piece would forever after be silent. Such
the truth proved to be, though grievous tragedy was to
intervene.

Pete's friend and follower, Henry Snyder, after many
years of devotion had worked himself up to such a high
point in the old soldier's affection and confidence that he
was permitted to act as cannoneer's assistant on the Fourth
of July. At first, of course, he was allowed to do little more
than to help polish the barrel, or hand Pete the ramrod. In
time Pete thought he could trust Henry to pick up the
powder and hand that over. As the years crept up on the
old veteran, Henry asked for greater responsibility.

On the Fourth of July in 1917, when his country was at
war, Pete had fired the cannon with new fervor, regretting
only that the weapon was not located where Germans would
die and fall back at its every discharge. About two months
later, when the first group of draft men were to leave
Covington for training camp, Pete resolved that their departure must be celebrated with the highest military honor
the county was capable of conferring. Admitting that after
the strenuous efforts of the recent Fourth, he would have to
give up some of the heavy work, he instructed Henry in new
and more important duties. Perhaps he hoped Henry would
turn out to be good enough an artilleryman that in the
years to come, after Pete had gone, Henry would shoot the
old piece on the Fourth of July so well that people would
say, "Look! He's almost as good at it as Pete Harmon was;
but, of course, *nobody* could be expected to shoot this
cannon quite as well as Pete always did."

On the day of the big sendoff for the drafted boys, Henry
Snyder, for the first time, was allowed to use the ramrod,
to slide the bag of powder down the cannon's throat, and

to tamp the wadding after it until all was tight and firm.
Pete stood by, giving directions. He, as always, was to pull
the string.

Exactly what happened that morning was never discovered. The draft boys, already atingle with the prospect
of tremendous adventure, were probably startled when the
cannonading began at break of dawn. Four shots had been
heard; then a fifth — and then no more. Early risers found
in front of the old cannon the pierced body of Henry
Snyder, with the bloody ramrod lying a little distance away,
and old Pete, weeping and groaning, saying to himself over
and over, "Poor Henry! I oughtn't to have trusted him with
so much. I told him to stand away. He must have rushed
up to give 'er another tamp. Poor Henry! He didn't have
much experience with cannon!"

The next Fourth of July the valiant old gun was silent.
Five weeks before, on Memorial day, a new little flag and a
new metal G. A. R. emblem had marked one more grave in
Mt. Hope cemetery, where Peter Harmon had been laid to
rest.

He was not forgotten. When the German Bertha dropped
shells into Paris from a base seventy miles away, Covington
read the account with tremendous interest.

"Wouldn't old Pete Harmon have loved just one chance
to pull Big Bertha's string?" came to mind all over town.

The itinerant population of the United States, even in
those pre-war days that were also pre-hitch-hiker and pre-
unemployment, must have been numerous. Every day or
so Covington was visited by wanderers, footloose with whatever excuse would provide a living. Evidently, too, the
well-rooted homefolks of such towns could always spare
enough change to keep the traveler moving on his way. The
tramp printers came directly to the printing office. Most of
this species were poor workmen, little disposed to do more
than enough to make a dollar or two, and few were interesting enough even to spin entertaining lies.

The devices for separating the natives from money were
mostly standard schemes that had stood the tests of many
years and many towns. One that had the virtue of being
slightly different was a Missourian:

Clifford Lewis, of Jefferson City, Mo., a roving personage, dropped in to Covington last week with the announcement that Sunday afternoon he would dive from the top of the railroad bridge into the Wabash river. A big crowd gathered in the bottoms to see him make the drop. He took up a collection before his act, and raked in about $8. The dive was made without accident, although he got a little wet. "Speedy," as he calls himself, may be satisfied with what little change he can get that way, but it appears to us that his nickname is a misnomer. If he hasn't speed enough about him to make a living by working for it he might about as well dive off the bridge and forget to come up.

The "Tom show" made its appearance at intervals, and never failed to draw something of a crowd. An advertisement, embellished with a photograph of the impressario, announced the

SIXTH SUCCESSFUL SEASON of Mort Steece's Uncle Tom's Cabin Co. "The Play that never grows old," produced by a company of celebrated artists appearing in a large tented theater.   40 people — prices 25¢ and 35¢ . . . 20 colored singers and dancers. Special Music. Band and Orchestra. Monster Street Parade. Saturday, July 31.

I attended the show, and sat in a reserved seat with my feet in the July grass. The next issue contained a plaintive paragraph:

We wish we could invent some kind of an itch that would attack chiggers.

Amongst the more interesting itinerants were the medicine show men, who always had tales to tell. One old fellow, whose yarn could not be disproved by close questioning, provided an interview of a historical quality to match Pete Harmon's story about General Grant.

F. D. King, the veteran showman and military man,
who entertained a crowd on the street corner here Monday night, was a personal acquaintance of Abraham
Lincoln. King, who will soon celebrate his 93rd birthday, fought in the Mexican war in Jefferson Davis's
Tennessee Company under Zachary Taylor. In the
Civil War he was in the secret service.

"After the Mexican War," he said Monday, "I began
my long career in the show business. I was in Springfield in charge of a gang of bill posters. We came to
the office of a lawyer, Abraham Lincoln, in a building
with an outside stairway to the office above. I could
not find the owner to get permission to paste the bills
on the building, so I told the boys to go ahead, and I
would fix it up afterwards. We had finished when a boy
said, 'There comes Old Abe now.' A tall figure came
shambling down the street. 'Is this Mr. Lincoln,' I
asked. He said it was. 'I tried to find you a bit ago,'
I said, 'to get permission to bill your building, but
couldn't find you.' 'Well, smiled Mr. Lincoln, 'I see
you got 'em up all right.' 'Yes,' I said, 'And we make
it a rule to give tickets to the show in return for such
courtesies. How many are there in your family?' 'O,'
he said, with a twinkle in his eyes, 'Give me one for the
boy and one for the old woman, and if I want to go I
will take some other girl. I gave him four tickets and
completely forgot the incident. A few years later, after
the rebellion had begun, I was summoned to the
White House to receive dispatches to be carried through
extremely dangerous territory, in Virginia. When I
took the papers, I said, 'I will get these papers through
if I can.' The president said, 'Well, if you have as much
perseverance at carrying dispatches as you have post-
ing show bills, you will get there all right.'

City papers have long delighted to quote in ridicule the
homely news paragraphs of the country press. The point of
ridicule usually impinges upon either the naïvete of expression or upon the paltry triviality of the "news." I believed that almost no incident could take place that was too

slight to make a news item, if tied to a personality, or to another well known fact. Further, I thought that the ordinary matter-of-fact treatment of small news, in imitation of the "who, what, when, where and why" policy of the metropolitan press, made a newspaper dull and tiresome. So from time to time I tried innovations designed to make good use of the very slightest of incidents. One of these was the KOVINGTON KALEIDOSCOPE, a column in imitation of the style of writing at which so much fun had been directed by the city press. The names used were real and the facts true. A few excerpts from the Kaleidoscope:

Zeke Evans announces that the neighbor's chickens must not pick his tomatoes this summer, but we don't know whether Zeke is prepared to enforce his ultimatum or merely intends to write a note.

Summer's sweet presence was announced Tuesday when Morris Herzog, our hustling merchant, got his arm chair out in the middle of the sidewalk where he could survey the progress of events about the square.

Councilman Albert Hegg was hoeing potatoes before breakfast Tuesday morning, which as he says is hard work for a Dutchman.

Two large parties from here visited Turkey Run Sunday, one being composed of 8 men and the other of Chauncey Vickery.

The exceedingly high winds which blew Wednesday afternoon and the presence of so many Attica men in Covington were regarded by several of our citizens as more than a mere coincidence.

Editor Baker of the *Veedersburg News* was in town Monday looking very smiling and happy, saying that his wife is on her vacation.

The other day Manford Livengood, our co. sup., took a bundle of teachers' exam papers to the P.O. to mail to the state board. P. M. Schwin asked him if it was a second class package. Manford said he didn't know, he hadn't looked at 'em yet.

We had quite a fire in town Tuesday night, but the Kaleidoscope doesn't aim to print particulars of such happenings as everybody knows all about them anyhow or else thinks they do.

Arista Livengood, president of our genial school board, appeared here in our midst last Thursday evening wearing a light palm beach suit in which he looks mighty comfortable.

Leland Moore has entered the champion mouse-trapper contest with a record of mouse-trapping three of the unsuspecting but ferocious rodents in ten minutes in the same trap.

In a similar mood, news was found — at least names — in the horseshoe pitching contests that were among the relaxations on summer Sunday afternoons:

The horseshoe game in our back yard, long sanctioned from an educational standpoint by the participation of County School Sup't Manford Livengood, has now been approved from a health standpoint, County Health Officer C. C. Wert having been an active and successful pitcher in Sunday's contests. Incidentally the doughty doctor helped snatch some laurels from the co. sup't's brow — for it will be remembered that the sup't is the man who pitched ringers in the dark. The doc. and ye ed. were playing against the co. sup't and Shorty Lape, and skunked them in a fair and open game. Charley Bergdahl and Harry Voltz, out taking their Sunday stroll, appeared on the scene long enough for Charley and his walking cane to wonder what the Indiana *Daily Times* and the Chicago papers would have to say about the skunking episode. Walter Moore shoved his mark a little higher by pitching five ringers in succession, twice in pairs, while in the closing game Leland Moore entered the lists as a chip off the old block by pitching a few ringers. Asa Osborne, LaFayette L. Burress, and other horsehoe luminaries appeared on the scene with demonstrations of skill. Last, but not least, came Capt. W. B. Gray, who could not be prevailed upon to participate in a contest though promising to do so later.

A little friendly "kidding" of citizens whose names were well enough known was always in order, enjoyed by the victims as much as by their friends:

Horace Peyton is nursing a mighty sore shin as a result of a mishap at his home Sunday. A rumor reached his ears that the family cat had grabbed the family canary with malicious intent aforethought. Peyton leaped to the rescue and in the fracas the door of the kitchen range took sides with the cat and thrust itself in front of him. The fact, later discovered, that the cat didn't have the canary after all, failed to alleviate the condition of the injured shin.

Charley Cheney has been pestering us for a week with tall sounding exaggerations about the great sport of fox hunting. Charley has fox hunted for a hundred and fourteen years and never caught a fox in his life. He tries to defend his utter failure at fox hunting by saying that it is not to catch the fox he goes, but just for the race of Reynard and the canines and to hear the dogs howl! Shucks! In the night he doesn't see the race, and he could get the howling by putting his foot on the hound's tail. With a little turpentine he could get both results with a brace of pups in his back yard at home. What a record! Years of fox hunting and never caught a fox.

Even a tin cup, if it were a prominent tin cup, could make news:

Pursuant to a state board of health order, the public drinking cup at the court house yard pump must be used no more. Agitation for a sanitary fountain there is brewing, and may crystallize into something definite before long.

Two weeks later:

The common drinking cup, which was abolished from the pump in the court house yard and other sections of Indiana by order of the state Board of Health, refuses to stay abolished. In fact, while there used to be only one tin cup hanging on the court house pump, there were most of this week two, in which were lurking feral and viciously ferocious microbes awaiting their opportunity to dash into some innocent mouth. However, the common council of Covington, in solemn session Monday night, authorized City Health Officer Wert to expend not more than $25 on an improvement by which the well can be used in a sanitary manner, and the dangerous cups permanently eliminated.

No couple could be married around Covington without the barbarous custom of the charivari (pronounced shiver-ee) or "belling" being inflicted. A party of friends would descend upon them, armed with whatever handy noise-making equipment might be picked up. Tin pans, wash boilers, and shotguns were amongst the favored devices. After an interval of din the newly married couple was expected to appear and provide refreshments for the callers. A wedding was almost always an occasion for crude jokes. If the bride and bridegroom could be made a public spectacle, their friends considered the occasion a delightful entertainment. The *Republican* thought these folkways might stand a little civilizing, and either ignored the rough-housing in narratives of weddings, or undertook to describe such matters as it saw them:

Displaying marked originality, Attica friends of Mr. and Mrs. Clarence McDonald and Mr. and Mrs. Elvin

Farmer, just wedded, decided to have a tremendous joke on the brides and bridegrooms. They did. Bubbling over with enthusiasm for the brilliantly clever and novel idea, they loaded the two couples on a truck, hitched the truck by a strap to the rear of an automobile, and started out at a great rate. The strap broke. Mrs. Farmer's wrist was broken, and the charivari was declared an unqualified success.

9

Good Time Had by All

THE WEEKLY columns of the *Republican* reflected, though perhaps faintly and a little flatly, the never languishing buzz of social activity in Covington. Sociability was so conspicuously the town's dominant characteristic as to be quite inseparable from the regular pursuits of the day. Customers chatted with clerks and merchants, depositors with cashiers, everyone with everyone else in the course of routine encounter. Conversation was the town's major output.

The more formally organized social groups fell into overlapping strata whose doings were impartially chronicled. The newspaper welcomed organizations. They made news, even if it might not be very interesting, and better, gave occasion for printing names. It printed complete lists of the participants in public entertainments and of guests at parties; the names of pupils in the classes at school; the memberships of different organizations. Had it been convenient to obtain them, it would probably have printed the names of the people who attended each church on Sundays.

Naturally, women were most conspicuous. The principal organizations were theirs, although they made occasions at intervals to drag out their husbands. The aristocracy of Covington society, if such a term might be used at all in reference to so democratic a community, included the families represented in the Daughters of the American Revolution, the Woman's Club, the Booklovers Club, the Matinee Musicale, and the Tri Kappa. These represented most of the culture, except for the few shy or aloof individualists who preferred to take their culture privately.

The Republican files afford a glimpse of the Daughters

of the American Revolution being patriotic and merry with
the presence of husbands and guests:

Patriotism and fun were intermingled Wednesday
evening when the Daughters of the American Revolution
entertained at their annual Washington party in the
parlors of the M.E. church. Seventy-five were present.

A reproduction of an old-fashioned country school,
with Miss Hazel Martin as schoolmarm, was a feature
of the entertainment. The school's session proved to
be a merry succession of comic occurrences, winding up
with a holiday program. Those who took part were Miss
Hazel Martin, Mesdames C. W. Dice, H. G. Ost, Fred
Johnk, and Wheeler McMillen, who comprised the entertainment committee for the evening; and Misses
Blossom Boord, Berenice Livengood, and Mrs. Louise
Bilsland. At the close O. M. Livengood, in the character of a visiting patron of the school, gave a patriotic
song, "The Old Flag Never Touched the Ground," that
was heartily encored. Mrs. C. L. Myers was accompanist. After the dismissal of school, Mrs. Alma Rogers
presented an appropriate song, with Mrs. M. Mayer
as accompanist. In response to insistent applause, she
gave a preparedness reading of up-to-the-minute sentiment.

A supper was served by the Methodist ladies. Considerable amusement was derived from a series of biographies of persons present, read by Miss Martin.

The prime object of the D.A.R. is the fostering of
patriotism, loyalty to country, and good citizenship.
The membership is limited to direct descendants of soldiers in the American Revolution.

A paragraph extracted from a column article about the
annual banquet of the Woman's Club avers that

Mrs. Michael Mayer, president of the club, put
everyone at ease by the charming manner of her address. She reviewed the club's activities for the year,

mentioning the participation of the club in the purchase of Turkey Run, in the City Beautiful movement, in aiding the endowment fund for the Pioneer Mothers memorial, and the Belgian fund.

The Tri Kappa membership approved of patriotism and culture, but the organization had a more direct purpose. The Red Cross was not yet prepared to aid the suffering in every hamlet; it was still an organization that functioned in earthquakes, floods, and wars. Relief for the unfortunate had not yet been accepted as a governmental responsibility. So the Tri Kappa girls were the Good Samaritans, who sought out the needy and tried as gracefully as possible to be of substantial help. The members were mostly mature young women, under middle age, married and single, drawn together by congeniality and a mutual desire to be of use outside their homes. Their aims were highly respected in the town. When a situation required greater resources than the girls themselves could supply, they seldom had difficulty in raising the funds they wanted. Nonetheless they went in for their share of happy fun, as a routine report of one of their meetings reveals:

The Tri Kappa members were entertained Monday evening by Mrs. H. G. Ost in a most delightful manner. A feature of the evening was the drawing of two exceptionally handsome quilts, which went to Mrs. Mary Coffing and Mrs. Irene Kerr. The manner of drawing was unique; two miniature quilts were concealed in walnut shells within popcorn balls and were found there by the winners.

Most democratic of the major women's groups was the Matinee Musicale, to which any respectable female, regardless of age, financial or social position, might be admitted if she had an interest in music. If she were known to be skilled at the piano or with violin or vocal chords, she had difficulty in keeping out, for the society was ever scouting for new talent. Besides full programs of music at each meeting, plus the inevitable "dainty refreshments," the Matinee Musicale now and then organized a public entertainment of more than a little pretentiousness:

> Under the direction of Miss Verna Glascock, rehearsals are well under way for the presentation of the noted oratorio, *Queen Esther,* to be given here under the auspices of the Matinee Musicale, assisted by a large number of male singers. The production has been widely given, and promises to be a notable musical event for Covington. Local soloists will have all the various roles. Mrs. Wm. Walker is to be the accompanist.

In due time the oratorio was presented. According to the column account of the event, all the singers fell no whit short of perfection. I had only a moderate private enthusiasm for the public infliction of amateur music, but felt that aspiration ought to be encouraged; moreover, to have told the plain truth might have made continued residence in the community impracticable. So the reviews were based on the tacit assumption that everyone knew that the standards of amateur performance were the basis of criticism.

Self-improvement was a serious purpose with the members of the Musicale, of the Woman's Club, and of the Booklovers. The latter two each year laid out a definite course of study. Few topics were too difficult to be assigned for the meeting day programs:

> The Woman's Club will meet Friday, March 22, with Mrs. Rogers. The work for the afternoon is from "America in Ferment." Mrs. Sangster will discuss "Big Business, Competition or Combination"; Mrs. Nebeker, "Proposed Remedies for the Concentration of Wealth." Election of officers will take place at the meeting.

The choicer adjectives were summoned into the newspaper office when the important yearly dinners of such groups as the D.A.R. and the Booklovers were to be described:

Covers were laid for 57 guests Wednesday evening when the Booklovers Club members entertained at their annual guest night, at the commodious and tastefully appointed home of Mr. and Mrs. Manford A. Livengood. Mrs. Livengood is president of the club. . . .

A salient feature of the evening was the presentation of a delightfully amusing farce, "The Kleptomaniacs," in the spacious library that had been arranged as a miniature theater. The "taking" ways and funny costumes proved to afford a rollicking entertainment.

Mrs. Livengood delivered the prologue to the play, and spoke the club's welcome to its guests.

Mrs. William Walker, as a fascinating widow from gay Paree; Mrs. Wm. A. Davis, the manicurist; Mrs. M. Schesley, the modiste; Mrs. M. F. Livengood, the colored maid; Miss Winifred Graham, the Irish maid; Mrs. Graham; Mrs. Virginia Boord; Mrs. Scott Hiigel; and Mrs. Elmer Leas comprised the cast, and displayed histrionic talent that was highly commended.

The spirit of St. Valentine's day was manifested in the decorations of garlands, designs in darts and hearts, and graceful festoons, and in the menu, an appetizing three-course dinner served by the ladies of the Presbyterian church at 7:30.

The Booklovers Club has done remarkable work within its membership in the study of dramatic literature and art. The products of modern dramatists have been studied with an enthusiasm that has proved of great benefit to the members. The club has a serious purpose in self-improvement that distinguishes it as one of the most valuable organizations of its kind in Covington.

No tongue pressed the editorial cheek when these fulsome accounts were written. The events were being described as they were viewed by the participants.

Around the churches another well organized phase of Covington social life centered. Each denomination had its Sunday school, its Christian Endeavor Society or Epworth League, the Wednesday night prayer meeting, the Missionary Society or Ladies' Aid, and undertook to keep alive a Men's Brotherhood. The town as a whole was not aggressively Christian. The number of citizens who attended church or participated in any organized religious activity was probably less than a majority. Covington tolerated human frailty, and looked calmly upon the minor weaknesses of the race. A man might drink a glass of beer every day, play cards Saturday night, attend a dance at the armory, go to the theater if he had a chance, and yet be considered pure and upright enough to pass the plate at both morning and evening services on Sunday. After intimate acquaintance with Covington and other country town communities of the corn belt, it was puzzling in later years to read the fiction which depicted such villages either as puritanical or as sinks of meanness and immorality.

Apart from the self-improvement and religious groups, much other sociability was evident. Women who didn't care either about the modern drama, big business combinations, or the unfortunate state of the heathen on distant continents, enjoyed frequent gatherings where sewing and gossip provided satisfaction for their gregarious instincts. Loosely organized as the "Thimble Club" or the "Good Humour Club," they met for no other purpose than to meet, to talk, and to eat. Equally informal were the few card clubs, where "Five Hundred" was yet to be succeeded by bridge.

Plain, neighborly dinners and suppers, where congenial friends met around the table, were too commonplace even to rate a paragraph in the *Republican*. The presence of a cherished visitor from another town was usually celebrated by inviting in a favorite neighbor family for Sunday dinner or a week-night supper. The hostess customarily was also maid, cook, and waitress. Such dinners were, in most homes, marked by the outward amenities of convention, though so strongly ingrained were habits of being natural that family contentions now and then exposed themselves.

An embarrassing moment at one of these week-night dinners required that I display an ability which I would not otherwise have acknowledged even had I suspected that I

possessed it. The custom of carving a fowl or roast at the
table I had regarded as a barbarous survival of the middle
ages, when the knight indicated the measure of his favor by
the selection and size of the portions served. Perhaps because I felt unequal to performing the art acceptably, I had
insisted that it was scullery work which should be performed
in privacy outside the dining room. Conceding to my stub-
borness on the point, my persuasive wife had been good
enough not to make it an issue at home.

We were guests one evening of a young couple who, recently moved to Covington, had been accepted in a friendly
circle of young married people. The wife was a vivaciously
handsome, olive-skinned brunette; the husband, an energetic, crew-cut traveling salesman with a few crudities of
manner that were overlooked in favor of his friendly qualities and his wife's undeniable charm.

Roast wild duck was the main piece of the dinner. Mrs. Y.
placed the platter before her husband and, with a gleam of
determination in her flashing dark eyes, laid down the
carving implements.

Mr. Y. clearly shared my sentiments. Forgetting momentarily that others were present, he shouted, "Here, for
Christ's sake take this out in the kitchen and cut it up. I'm
not going to do it."

Mrs. Y. snatched the platter away and triumphantly
placed it in front of me. "Well," she said, her voice quiver-
ing with anger, "if you are not man enough to carve a duck,
Mr. McMillen will do it. He's a gentleman."

There was no retreat for the distressed guest. Conscious
of the triumphant amusement sparkling in the eyes of his
own wife, he took up the carving knife and awkwardly
slashed the ducks. Between him and Mr. Y. a new bond of
sympathy arose.

Few were the weeks when a birthday, an engagement, an
approaching marriage or accouchement, a wedding anniversary, or the presence of an out-of-town visitor to be honored,
did not provide the occasion for a party. "Shower" parties,
with gifts for the prospective bride or mother, were so
popular as to become a rite whenever a wedding or a birth

was in the offing. No golden wedding day passed without an elaborate dinner and a great gathering of relatives and friends.

Miss Fern Flora, with the help of the telephone girls, gave a shower at her home for Miss Helen Geiger Monday evening. The house was prettily decorated in red and white, the color scheme being carried out in the refreshments. The bride-to-be received many presents and wishes of goodwill. Her marriage to Lloyd Brown took place Wednesday.

Thus, with a list of the guests, ran a typical account of a bridal "shower." After a few years a girl who had carried gifts to the showers for all her set was doubtless tempted to advertise for a husband in order to recoup for the contributions she had made to new households. A popular bride might receive several showers, but sooner or later she paid in gifts for others.

The Y.P.S.C.E. of the First Church of Christ observed the annual Christian Endeavor Day Sunday night by a very appropriate service, consisting of special music, a missionary sketch, and readings. The service was organized in behalf of the Boy's Orphanage at Damoh, India, for which a very liberal offering was received. Those taking part, etc.

A statistical record of the amount of money that went annually from Covington for distant charities would have been illuminating. The church pastors, who themselves could have been better paid, passed on the appeals of "good causes," and forwarded the pennies and nickels. The actual total may not have been impressive, but one wondered whether humanity might have been as well served had the money been wisely used in Covington.

Miss Emma G. Lemen, of Indianapolis, who has taken part in Sunday School work in this county, will be the state speaker for the annual tour of the Fountain

County Sunday School Association, which takes place this week. She will be assisted on the program by local county workers.

The Sunday Schools were better attended in Covington than the church services. Few parents neglected to insist that the children don their best clothes and go to hear the golden text and the lesson, with a penny or a nickel to be nursed until the collection basket took over its custody. Just why the Sunday School children failed to grow up into church workers was a puzzle to some of the elders and deacons who pondered the problem. I thought that the reason was obvious enough. The youngsters usually were compelled to go to Sunday School up to about high school age. Compulsion by that time ceased to be effective, and the religious workers failed to devise activities of sufficient interest to draw the young people churchward thereafter. Whenever an incident occurred that might make this point evident, an editorial was likely to appear:

A Covington business man appeared unexpectedly at his place of business Sunday afternoon. In a back room he found six boys gathered around a table, playing cards, some smoking cigarettes. They had been admitted by a lad employed in the place.

The boys are not seriously to be blamed for what might seem to be a serious offense. In the first place, their homes do not appear to be made pleasant places for them to gather in. In the second place, the community offers them no place where they may enjoy harmless games and amusements at any time of the week, much less on Sundays when they have much leisure. The library is available for some of their week day spare time, and many of them use it.

Both parents and the community are remiss in not offering better facilities for the boys, who have a right to demand more provision for their entertainment. We happen to know that this crowd of boys has tried unsuccessfully to rent, at their own expense, a room where they might gather in spare hours. Nothing being

done for them, they cannot be blamed for meeting where
they can, and indulging in amusements as reprehensible
as cards and cigarettes.

Give these boys more privileges, — even if they help
pay for them — and we do not believe they will abuse
the opportunities. In summer they will have plenty to
do out of doors. But here is a chance for some one to
do a big thing for the community before next winter
comes.

The suggestion fell on deaf ears. Doubtless the boys in
time became expert card players and cigarette smokers, as
well as good citizens who stayed home Sunday mornings,
relentlessly insisted that their own youngsters go to Sunday
school, and gave money to convert the heathens.

The men of Covington were not so anxious about self-
improvement as were their wives and daughters. Their
energies found sufficient outlet in the employments of the
week, though such might be no more strenuous than sitting
in the store waiting for a customer to saunter in with a bit
of coin and a fragment of news. Possibly they were satisfied
that no self-improvement was necessary, or at least not
worth the effort.

Nevertheless, few topics of local, state, national, or in-
ternational importance escaped masculine discussion. The
talk was not organized, nor were formal programs planned
in advance. Gathered in the drug stores, in Bergdahl's tailor
shop, in courthouse offices, in Gordon Ost's "Sanitary Soda
Shop" and making Gordon's work of sanitation more difficult, the males debated the topics and problems of the day.
If the debaters were often ill-informed, and even sometimes
totally ignorant of underlying facts and principles, the discussions were nevertheless earnest and animated.

Nearly every man in town belonged to one or another of
the "lodges." The Masons, the Knights of Pythias, the Odd
Fellows, the Redmen, and the Woodmen met regularly in
their various halls, where the officers donned the regalia of
their stations and pronounced the rituals of the respective
orders. The Knights of Pythias were the most active and

numerous; their tenets of brotherhood and friendship were held in high regard. Leadership in lodge work was looked upon as a highway to prominence. One citizen was regarded as particularly eminent because he had worked up to the high office of brigadier-general in the Uniform Rank of the Knights of Pythias. The brigadier-general was William B. Gray, who had been county auditor before the Republican victory, and who later owned successively a general store and a machine shop. General Gray's Pythian prominence won him a nomination for auditor of the state of Indiana in a year that, unfortunately for him, found the Hoosier majority unsympathetic to Democratic candidates.

The proceedings of the lodges were always conducted in full secrecy, under the guard of inner and outer doorkeepers. The initiation ceremonies, known as "riding the goat," were popularly supposed to be rough-house occasions for the humiliation of the candidate and the boisterous joy of the members, although the pomp and solemnity of the ritual with its high sounding injunctions to the incorrigible virtues were more conspicuous. Despite the oath of inviolable secrecy, a story leaked out of the Knights of Pythias meeting once that became fixed as one of Covington's humorous legends.

The story concerned Peter Anderson, a thrifty, industrious Dane who as a youth had located in Covington. Proud of his Pythian membership as an evidence of his Americanization and acceptance in the community, he took an active part in lodge work. When the new hall had been furnished, his labors were bent to see that everything was done properly and at the least possible expense.

One night the secretary announced that a bill was due to the state lodge for thirty-one dollars for the "per capita tax." Peter, whose English was still a little fuzzy immediately jumped to his feet to protest.

"Ve got wery fine hall here," he said, "an' nice furniture, an' mighty fine carpet on the floor. But, broders, Ay t'ank t'irty-von dollars bane too motch fer carpet tacks!"

The fraternal spirit extended far beyond the borders of the town. Visits were exchanged with the lodges of neighboring towns, while county, district, and state meetings came frequently enough to give the brothers excuses to get away from home.

The Redmen initiated a class of new members last night. The work was done by the Mellott degree team.

Hillsboro is making ready for a big fraternal event Monday evening, Feb. 26, when the Pythians of the county will gather there. Several are expected to go from Covington. Robert A. Brown, grand keeper of the records and seals, who spoke here a few weeks ago, will be one of the speakers, with the grand chancellor and others.

The women, too, had a hand in the lodges. Although not admitted to the august proceedings of their lords, auxiliary organizations were composed of wives and relatives of the lodge members — the Eastern Star of the Masons, the Rebekahs of the Odd Fellows, and so on.

Unorganized social and amusement activity filled in the gaps left by the clubs and fraternal groups, so that anyone with a hermit's disposition found the town little to his taste. A fair summer afternoon usually set a ball game going at the fair grounds, either between town teams or with players from a neighboring village. In winter the high school basket ball contests drew crowds that taxed the seating capacity of the little high school gymnasium. One never had to go far during the warm months to get up a horseshoe game. The river always awaited the fisherman, although he needed plenty of patience for the fish were either few or too well fed to be tempted easily by bait. The poolroom was considered to be a little below the standard of the better citizen, but Charlie Crane's place never lacked patronage, either at the pool tables or the card tables. It was said to be one of the most profitable enterprises around the square. Now and then an itinerant entrepreneur set up a bowling alley or a shooting gallery that would be well patronized for a few months until the novelty wore away.

On Saturday nights practically the entire population of

the town and of the farms for miles around crowded the sidewalks and stores. A former resident who wished to see all his old acquaintances needed only to move around the square between seven and ten o'clock on Saturday night. He would see, or hear about, every person he ever knew.

At the moving picture theater a new film flickered every night. Each issue of the *Republican* carried an advertisement that listed forthcoming attractions:

LYRIC THEATER
COVINGTON'S BRIGHTEST SPOT.

Friday
Bessie Barriscale in "Honor's Altar."
Saturday
Charles Murray in "His Hereafter," and "Fido's Fate," comedy.
Sunday
Douglas Fairbanks in "His Picture in the Papers," comedy.
Monday
Fanny Ward in "A Gutter Magdalene."
Tuesday
Ralph Kellard and Dorothy Green in "Her Mother's Secret."
Wednesday
Pauline Frederick in "Sold."
Thursday
Frank Losee and Grace Valentine, in "The Evil Thereof."

Coming
Billie Burke in "Peggy."

A number of annual events could be depended upon to stir the town. Memorial Day was a ceremonious occasion, marked with exercises and a speech that preceded the parade to Mt. Hope cemetery where trim graves were decorated with flags to mark the last bivouac of all who had worn the nation's uniform. The closing of school brought the senior play and commencement.

The high spot was the county fair, always the week before Labor Day. Merry-go-round! Ferris Wheel! Race horses! Balloon squawkers! Doll racks and cane racks! Freaks! Girly-girly shows! Nickel catchers galore, crowds, dust, noise, bloodstirring excitement! And the exhibits, of course; the hogs and sheep, cattle and chickens, rabbits, quilts, pumpkins, fruit, pickles, fancywork! The latest farm and home machinery on display! And people, old friends, old acquaintances, folks one hadn't seen since the last fair. Maybe they were only from Veedersburg or Danville; maybe from Akron or Detroit. No matter where a loyal Covingtonian had gone, his hope was to be back home for fair week, with a new suit and money in the pockets to impress the stay-at-home folks.

Fair week had notable nights, too. After the exhibit halls were closed and the last squawker had burst, there was the big show up town. The Guy Stock Company came to Covington as regularly as fair week rolled around, pitched its tent on a handy vacant lot, set up a stage and a battery of seats — reserved seats ten cents extra — and delighted the town with expositions of the drama. Here no Little Theater experiments were billed; only the tried and true vehicles, whether *East Lynne, Uncle Tom's Cabin,* or the famous Broadway success of three years previous. Worse drama, much worse acting, has indeed been found on Broadway. Guy and his company knew what rural Hoosiers preferred and the customers got what they liked.

Seldom did a summer pass without the appearance of a street carnival, an itinerant aggregation of cheap amusements, grifts, and gaudy entertainments that combined the worst features of the county fair with none of the good ones. On a back street the carnival people were permitted to pitch their rows of wheels, exhibits, and merry-go-round. Dismally tawdry by daylight, after dark under the glow of strings of electric lights and the blaze of torches the street assumed an air of mock gaiety. The bellowing barkers, the grinding tunes of the merry-go-round, and the tum-tum of drums coaxing folks to step closer, sought to keep up an appearance of lively goings-on. Few regrets were heard when the tents were folded and the crews had moved on with whatever small coin they had been able to inveigle from the least sophisticated or most bored of the towns-people.

Rain was the enemy of the carnival. An editorial in the *Republican,* referring apparently to the downpours that soaked the tents, spoke the publisher's mind about carnivals in general and some forgotten disagreeable incident:

We rather fancy that Covington's recent experience with a street carnival will be of material weight in curing the town of the carnival habit. From year to year these aggregations of nickel grabbers with their dime devils come in, stay a week, and leave the town poorer and worse for having been here. The recent sad affair was facing a lot of misfortune, and the promoter is to be credited highly with having refused to permit any immoral shows to exhibit. With most carnivals these are the worst features. The increased street crowds may bring a few dollars more to the tills of some shops in town, but other dollars are taken away from other tills. As a business proposition it is a stand-off. The amusement feature of the carnival is slight -- in fact, they are rather boresome affairs even to the most easily amused. As educational or inspirational institutions they are less than nil. So why have a carnival, anyway?

On the other hand, Covington is soon to have a chautauqua. There will be five days of programs rich in entertainment and inspiration. There will be music of the very finest kind. Clean, healthful, entertainers will appear. There will be lectures that will amuse, instruct, and uplift. Which is worth most to the town, carnival or chautauqua?

The chautauquas were seldom more successful than the rainy week carnivals. I cherished a naive idea that in a perfect community, all the people would prefer chautauquas to carnivals. I fulminated at the indifference of the people to what I thought would be good for them. Amongst the cultural affairs of the winter seasons was always a lecture

course, sponsored by the Epworth League or the high school.
After a small crowd turned out for a "lecture" on community building, the editorial column burst forth with this:

> It is a reflection on Covington that fewer than 150
> persons heard Preston Bradley's wonderfully eloquent
> address at the high school building Friday night. The
> coming to Covington of a man like that, with a message
> like his, is an event. As we looked over the people there
> we noted a fair sprinkling of high school students, a
> large number of the intelligent women of the town, and
> just enough business and professional men to say they
> were represented. A bunch of our so-called leading citi-
> zens, who are presumed to be strong forces in the com-
> munity, were absent from this splendid opportunity,
> not only to hear one of the nation's most eloquent ora-
> tors, but to hear many a mighty practical thought.
> Keeping up a lecture course in a town where the most
> prominent citizens refuse to be interested or to attend
> is rather a discouraging game. A lecture like Bradley's
> is often the inspiration that sets a young man to the
> determination to make his life count for something. We
> can't get too many such men here, for the future of
> Covington, and it is a mighty short-sighted and selfish
> policy that withholds support from such movements.

Covington had a good time. The club ladies studied economics and the drama, the carnival-minded tried the sucker
games to win dolls and blankets, the lodge members enjoyed
their high-sounding rituals, and the sports played cards in
the poolroom — each to his choice. The *Republican*'s exhortations were ignored; each group and strata followed
the preference that was natural. That this way, and not
his way, was the way of the world a young editor might
learn in time.

Few were those who would have accorded to Covington
the popular encomium, "a live town." The weekly flow of
events was placid. Yet episodes, curious, comic and at times
dramatic came to the editor's notice; not all of them suitable
material for the *Republican* to print.

10

Comedies and Drama

JEHU MARTIN, the dean of Covington painters and paper-hangers, advertised in the *Republican* for eleven weeks, and then suddenly closed his account.

How a man with such a tremendous beard could be a successful paperhanger was a mystery which I had occasionally pondered. The question was how Jehu could keep the paste out of his whiskers.

Jehu was a thoroughly fine and admirable man. Though pleasant, he was not given to undue jocosity. Physically he was short and stocky, particularly short to wear such long whiskers. His body seemed to be about the right length, but either his arms were too long or his legs were too short. This did not make him look funny, just a trifle unusual.

The beard that Jehu wore began to spurt out just below his eyes and flowed with masculine vigor and determination down to within an inch of his belt. A half-inch longer and it would have been arch-patriarchial; an inch shorter, and it wouldn't have fitted Jehu. Nor was it the kind of a beard that weakened in the lower reaches. It was as thick and lively and silvery in the last inch as amidwhiskers. There was no better beard in Covington, if even in Indiana.

Jehu appeared to ignore his fine beard altogether. He seldom stroked it, never spoke of it, and apparently was oblivious of its very existence. Yet he must have been proud of it. Now and then someone who thought whiskers were funny would make a joke at Jehu, whereupon he would become furiously silent and would never speak to the offender again unless called upon for painting or paperhanging.

Jehu and I had become friends for no particular reason, although the old paperhanger may have sensed my admiration for his fine beard. I respected the old gentleman's sterling qualities. He subscribed faithfully to the *Republican* and never complained about having to pay cash in advance. Childless, he and his excellent wife adopted a boy and girl who had been left as orphans when some distant relative had died. They raised and loved these children as their own. The girl married a good man, and the boy became a prosperous dry cleaner in a larger town a hundred miles away. Jehu and his wife were deeply in love with their grandchildren, and were devotedly loved in return.

One day when Jehu stopped at the office, he remarked that business was not very good.

"For fifty years I have always had all the work I could do," he declared, "until just lately. Now why do you suppose that is? I have never cheated on materials or time. For fifty years I have painted the finest houses in Covington, and have papered the parlors of the most particular people, and not one has ever complained. I can always be proud of my record, anyway."

"Maybe," I suggested, "maybe the younger generation doesn't know so much about you. A good many new people have moved into town, and young folks have come along and have homes of their own." Jehu weighed the thought for a moment.

"That's probably just what's the matter with my business," he agreed. "I just kept on thinking everybody around here would know Jehu Martin. Come to think of it, three people I saw around town this forenoon that I couldn't call their names."

After further reflection, he asked, "Suppose I ought to advertise?"

I explained that for a dollar a week he could buy a space two columns wide and five inches deep, pointing out such a space in the paper on the counter.

"All right, put one in for me," he ordered. "Get your pencil and write down what I say." Without a pause he dictated his copy:

TO ALL IT MAY CONCERN

City of Covington, State of Indiana, 1915.

I AM PROUD OF MY RECORD

For having done painting that gives satisfaction. If you want painting done right, and with good quality, I will be glad to refer you to any of my past customers. I have a reputation for good painting, based on a business record of forty-nine years and forty-four of the forty-nine years' experience at Covington. I guarantee all my work to give satisfaction.

Jehu D. Martin,
Cor. Eighth and Pearl Streets.

"That'll be a dollar a week you say. All right. Run it until I say stop, and let me know whenever you want your money. Put my name in big type, and put 'I am Proud of My Record' in the biggest type."

For eleven weeks the *Republican* flaunted Jehu Martin's announcement that he was proud of his record. The first week the paper carried a little feature story about his having been nearly half a century at the same trade in Covington, challenging other persons to present equally remarkable records.

Then one week there came bad news about Jehu. He had again fallen victim to an unfortunate liking for liquor that for many years had caused him occasional embarrassment. Two years often elapsed between drinks for him, but once started, the result was always the same. He would take another drink.

When the effects began to be perceptible, Jehu would decide that he might as well do the thing thoroughly, and at a certain point in the process, he became bellicose. When he arrived at the state of belligerence, instead of proceeding to get soused completely, he would suspend further drinking and start in accumulating grudges. In a few minutes he would be hating everybody, and positive that everyone in town was regarding him with malign intents. Indeed, he became sure that the town was mobilizing to slay him, and that self-preservation demanded that he act first. At this stage he would seize whatever weapons were available and go forth on a vigorous campaign of self-protection.

The usual procedure at this point was for some one to notify his lawyer brother, John B. Martin. John B. would first threaten Jehu with the penitentiary, and then get his sympathy by telling how it would wound the feelings of their long dead mother to look down from heaven upon one of her sons in a penal institution. Jehu, who was afraid of John B. when drunk but rarely spoke to him at any other time, would then weep into his long beard, go to sleep, and wake up eventually more or less his natural self.

This time John B. had been out of town. The city authorities were unsympathetic and happened that week to be enforcing the law. The result was arrest and a sentence of twenty days in the local jail for Jehu.

I printed nothing about the arrest. Upon asking the sheriff how Jehu was getting along at the jail I was told that the old man was pining about something. His sentence was to end the next day at noon.

The following day about five minutes after noon, Jehu pounded on the counter at the *Republican* office. "Paper gone to press yet?" he demanded. It had not.

"Well, don't put my ad in again. I'll pay you soon as I can go home."

He darted out the door, and in a short time returned with eleven dollars. After laying down the money he read the advertisement over to himself. Tears trickled down into the marvelous beard.

"I suppose you heard what they done to me. Arrested me and put me in jail. I've been painting and paperhanging and getting drunk in this town for fifty years, and this is the first time I ever was put in jail. I've worried about this ad ever since I found myself in the calaboose. To think that they would put a stain like that on a man's record, at my age!"

More humorous stories were told about Morris Herzog, owner of The Leader, than about any other man in Covington. Morris was in most respects a genuine Hoosier, despite the fact that he was a Jewish emigrant from Germany. He was a good citizen and good businessman, respected as a man of his word, and liked for his joviality and fine human qualities.

The Leader, Morris's store, occupied one of Covington's three three-story structures. The upper story of the brick building was leased to the Knights of Pythias; Morris used the other two floors and the basement. His store was up-to-date, and so were some of his merchandising methods, though he relied more upon his own well known personality to attract trade than upon sales schemes. His son, Marx, and son-in-law, Frank Faust, were in charge respectively of the men's side of the store, where suits and shoes were sold, and of the women's side where dresses and dry goods were stocked. A "trimmer" was hired from Indianapolis for the spring and fall millinery seasons, to supplement the staff of clerks.

Morris himself, in the summertime, usually spent most of the days sitting in a large wicker armchair on the sidewalk in front of his store. Here he collected and dispensed the gossip of all the surrounding country. His acquaintance was immense as his memory was tenacious. He interspersed his chat with verbal advertisements of his wares. In appearance, Morris lacked but one feature to have been a perfect replica of the old-fashioned Hebrew comedian of burlesque and vaudeville. He had the big stomach — his was enormous — the close-trimmed chin whiskers, the dialect, and needed only the crock-over-the-head style of square haircut.

On a summer day his voice could be heard calling to some acquaintance he may have spied a half-block or more distant. "Hey! Charley! Charley! I got somet'ing to tell you."

Charley would approach and the colloquy would proceed.
"Hello, Morris!"
"Hello, Charley! I'm glad to see you. How're the folks?"
"They're fine."
"That's good. Charley, did you hear that Jake Benefield lost his black mare? She got overheated when they vas making hay."
"Yeah? Is that so?"

"You know, Charley, I thought maybe you could sell Jake your sorrel horse. He'll need one for fall plowing, and he ain't bought one yet."

"Well, much obliged, Morris. I'll drop over and see him." Charley would start to go and Morris would perhaps tell him goodbye.

"Oh, vait a minute, Charley! I shust happened to remember. Ve got a new order in of them socks you always like. And tell your vife ve're goin' to have a sale on pillow cases next veek." If Charley got away without buying at least one pair of socks his resistance was exceptional. Like as not he would also sell his sorrel horse before the week was over. In future encounters Morris would find means tactfully to remind Charley of his own part in the horse deal. "I like to do things for my friends," he would say, and he genuinely did. That he was shrewd enough to turn his kindnesses sometimes to business account was simply an additional good fortune. He believed in having friends.

One time a young man whom Morris failed to recognize walked into the store and asked to be shown a suit of clothes. Something about the youth's features struck Morris as being familiar, and he quickly set out to ascertain the caller's identity.

"Vell, how's things in your part of the county?"

"Oh, not so bad, Mr. Herzog."

This reply revealed to Morris that the young man knew him and was probably the son of some farmer acquaintance.

"Pretty dry, ain't it?"

"Yeah, it sure is. They had a good rain south of Hillsboro Monday night, but we didn't get any of it."

This gave Morris a clue to the neighborhood, and he was guessing close to the family by this time.

"How's my friend Duly Frazier down there?"

"Oh, Uncle Duly's pretty good. He's better'n he was."

"Did your father sow that field in alfalfa he vas talkin' about?"

"Yeah, but it ain't doin' much yet, on account it's so dry."

By this time Morris knew the young fellow was Virgil Frazier's son and was ready to proceed with the main business in hand.

"Vell, I'm certainly glad to see a boy of Virgil Frazier's come to me for a suit of clothes. I bet your father told you to come here."

"Yeah, he said you had a pretty good stock."

"Sure. I knowed your father now it must be forty years. He's a fine man. Vat he says he'll do, he does do. Him and me, ve've always been good friends."

Morris's grammar would not always pass a purity test, but his Teutonic accent, while conspicuous, was not gross except for his "w's," and in moments when he was excited.

"I bet I sold your father t'ousands of dollars vorth of goods. I paid him t'ousands of dollars, too, for the vool I bought. And ve never had a bad vord between us. I tell you, he's a fine man. Your mother, she's a fine voman, too; and a good housekeeper. I alvays hear good vords about her.

"Your grandfadder, I knowed him, too; him and me vas very good friends. He vas one of the first men in Cain township I bought vool from, and he never vould sell to anyvun else.

"Now, your suit! How you like this von? Or this?"

Carrying the conversation along, Morris watched closely while the young man narrowed his choice to two patterns.

"You know, I don't vait on trade any more, myself. The boys do that. But for you! Ven your father, and your mother, and your grandfadder, they vas all my friends! Sure, I vait on you myself, because you and I are friends, too. Ven you need a friend, think of Morris Herzog! You can count on me!"

"How much is this brown suit, Morris?"

"Eighteen dollars; and a bargain. You pay twenty-two fifty for a suit shust like it in Danville."

"Eighteen dollars? That's a little more than I wanted to lay out for a suit of clothes just now. Can't you make it a little cheaper?"

"I tell you! That suit, it'll vear like iron. Suits like that I have sold for thirty dollars. I vouldn't tell you if it wasn't so — not ven all your family and me has been such good friends."

"Couldn't let me have that suit for sixteen dollars, could you?"

"Sixteen dollars? My, no! I vouldn't make any money on a price like that."

"Well, Morris! You've been talking about what good friends our folks have been, and what good friends you and I are going to be. Now, you wouldn't want to make money off of your friends, would you?"

The youth was keener than Morris had expected. But the old fellow could not be cornered that way. Seizing young Frazier by the lapel and drawing him close, Morris lowered his voice and with a jovial twinkle in his eye, said: "Listen! You're a smart fellow. I tell you a secret for success. I haf to make my money off my friends; because mein enemies, dey von't trade vit me!"

With the offer of a free pair of suspenders the sale was closed at eighteen dollars. Quick thinking in a pinch was Morris's specialty, and the basis of most of the tales that were told about him. His fame for ready replies at times when most men would be too embarrassed for words had spread far and wide. One favorite yarn had to do with an incident that had occurred years before, when he sold groceries and dealt in produce in addition to wearing apparel.

A woman who lived several miles south of Covington came to town every Friday afternoon, and was a regular customer at Herzog's. Her husband ran a large farm. Besides nine children, the household included two or more hired men. Home consumption being so large, she usually had only a dozen or so eggs and a small amount of butter as surplus to trade in at the store, while her purchases were considerable. Her butter was notoriously poor. But since she never offered more than two or three pounds, Morris always accepted it at the current price and threw it out, knowing that he would make up the loss on her voluminous purchases. One day, after he had received the woman's butter and carried it back to the garbage can, he was busily engaged in filling her list of wants.

At this moment Mrs. Nebeker, one of his most fastidious and best town customers, stepped inside the door.

"Have you any good country butter today, Morris?" she called.

"No, Mrs. Nebeker, I'm sorry; none good enough for you. But I'll send up the first real good butter that comes in."

"Why, Mr. Herzog!" said the farm woman indignantly, "I just brought you my butter!"

Morris was not bothered for an instant. "Sh-h!" he whispered, leaning over the counter. "I safe *your* butter for mein own use!"

Morris's outstanding weakness was his habit of boasting, after an event was all over, what he would have done if he had been there. The favorite story bearing on this dated back to a time not long after Morris had established his store. He had soon made his name well known by an advertising slogan which, painted on fences and signs for miles around, was familiar to everyone.

I BUY EVERYTHING. I SELL EVERYTHING.
M. HERZOG,

it read.

One snowy November day a half dozen men were sitting around the stove, telling of having shot so many rabbits while hunting that they could neither eat, sell, nor give away their entire kill.

"Vy didn't you bring 'em to me?" Morris demanded. "You know, I sell everyt'ing, I buy everyt'ing. If you'd brought 'em here, I voud haf gife you ten cents apiece for all you fetch."

This inspired the loafers with an idea. The next morning they organized a rabbit drive. Shortly after dusk they drove up in front of Morris's store with a wagon box half filled with rabbits, and in a few minutes had stacked armloads of dead bunnies on the front counter. Morris, who had been in the back room measuring out kerosene, heard the door opening and closing. Hurrying out, he saw the rabbits corded high on his counter, and men bringing more. He dashed out to peep over the sideboards of the wagon at the scores of rabbits still to be unloaded.

"Vat's this?" he exclaimed. "Vat you fetching all these rabbits for in my store?"

"Why, Morris," gravely explained the leader of the practical jokers. "You said you would give us a dime apiece for all the rabbits we brought you."

"Sure! Yes! I know I did," Morris sputtered. "But I vanted 'em alive!"

Herzog's first establishment in Indiana had been a little store at Wingate, a small village about twenty miles east of Covington. While in business there he had entered into a partnership with a man from Mellott, another hamlet six miles away across the county line, to buy and ship live-stock. Morris and his partner fell into a dispute that terminated in a lawsuit before the justice of the peace at Mellott.

Morris was fearful of getting the worst of it because he was not familiar with the intricacies of American law. So he urged several of the Wingate friends who loafed around his store in the evenings to accompany him to the trial. He felt that their presence would at least lend moral support, and might be helpful if he got into a tight place. Several said they might go. When the day came the weather was cold and sleety and raw, with a January blizzard threatening. None of his friends cared to undertake the freezing six-mile drive in buggies through such weather. One pleaded that he had to help his wife do the washing, another had an attack of lumbago, and others found excuses as convenient. Morris had to go alone.

All were quite able, however, to be at the store that evening after supper to hear Morris's report of the trial. The clock struck eight before he came stamping in. The blizzard had started in earnest just before dark, and Morris was cold. He hurried up to the stove, shaking snow from his coat and cap, pulling icicles out of his beard, and rubbing his hands before the red hot stove. For minutes no one uttered a word. Morris, usually the first to speak and always the most voluble, angrily said nothing.

"How'd ye come out?" one finally inquired.

"Come out, noddings!" Morris snorted. "I didn't haf no chance. They made me shvear first."

To get ahead of Morris in a contest of wits was no mean achievement. Once I managed to come even with him although the triumph was won with a blow that may have fallen a little below the merchant's expansive belt line.

Business for the *Republican* had been extremely poor all summer. A prolonged drouth had discouraged the farmers, and the storekeepers in turn were in low spirits. For issue after issue through June and July the advertising revenue had been less than the payroll.

On Monday morning I set forth, grimly determined to extract enough advertising from the merchants to break even with August expenses, at least. Morris was not a regular advertiser, nor were any of his competitors, but when he advertised at all he was accustomed to take a fairly large space. I decided to solicit him first.

When I asked him to use a half page for that week, Morris made me stand and listen to a diatribe about how little advertising in either Covington paper was worth. He never got any return from his advertising, he averred. The expenditure was really a waste of money, when everybody for thirty miles around knew about him and his store. To prove his case, he told how once he had inserted a coupon good for a five-cent spool of cotton thread, free. Only seven coupons had been returned. Evidence enough, he declared, that advertising in the local papers sold no goods, when it didn't even help him to give away perfectly good thread. "Clark's O.N.T., it was." He vehemently assured me that nobody read the *Republican*.

"I vould never advertise at all," he asserted, "except that I t'ink you're a good, ambitious young fellow, and I vant to help you out a liddle."

The suggestion that the dignified editor of the only Republican newspaper in Fountain County was an object of charity was bad enough; the assertion that no one read the paper was infuriating. I stomped out, inwardly vowing to find a revenge that would make Morris eat his words without salt or sauce. For the moment I forgot the more urgent need to sell advertising.

Back at the office, I slumped into the springless revolving chair and lifted my feet to a comfortable position on the exchange table. "What," I asked myself, "is that damned old rascal's tenderest spot?"

The Faust boys! Even more than of his fine store and of his business success, Morris was inordinately proud of those

two stalwart grandsons. One was returning in September
to Indiana University, where he had already won honors in
both athletics and scholarship. The younger was entering
the same school with every prospect of doing as well.

The remainder of the morning was spent in compiling a
list of Covington young people who were going away to
college. A half-column article was prepared, in which names
of boys and girls were given, the names of parents, the
names of colleges the students planned to attend, the courses
they were taking or contemplating, the distinctions already
won in high school or college, along with friendly individual
comment for each.

The morning after the paper came out, Morris was waiting in front of the post office when I came down town at
seven o'clock. Seizing my coat lapel and pulling on that
while he pushed forward his protruding stomach — an in-
variable procedure when he wished to speak with serious
emphasis — Morris began:

"Mac! I read your piece about the boys and girls going
avay to college. That vas a nice piece. It vas nice for you
to say such fine t'ings about all of them. I appreciate your
doing that. And it vas shust like you to t'ink of such a nice
t'ing — shust the kind of t'ing ve have learnt to expect from
you." Morris said all this with gripping, low-voiced earnestness, while tightening his hold on the editorial lapel. "But,"
he hissed, spraying the editorial shirt front as he pulled
closer, "you forgot to mention my boys, my grandsons!
They vasn't in the piece. You know they both go to the
state — " His voice turned tremulous and actual tears welled
into the shrewd, hard eyes.

"Yes," I interrupted, backing away, "I know they are
both going to Bloomington. And I didn't forget them. I
left them out intentionally."

"Vat?" Morris exclaimed, loosening his hold in his in-
credulous amazement. "On purpose you left out my boys'
names!"

"You told me Monday morning that nobody read my
paper, that it wasn't worth advertising in. So I thought
likely you would rather that I didn't mention your boys
in it."

His hands dropped and his chin sagged. Then he grabbed the lapel again. "Mac, you come over this afternoon. I told Marx yesterday he should write a page ad for next veek, a whole page. It ain't quite ready yet."

The whole page advertisement was not even started yet, I knew full well, but it was ready that afternoon. And on the front page of the paper the next week was a nice paragraph about Morris's grandsons going to the state university.

PERHAPS IN a modern metropolitan tabloid newspaper, all the dramatic incidents that accompanied and followed the arrival of a son to Ben and Muriel would have been told at the time, with photographs. For good and sufficient reasons, the only announcement that appeared in the *Republican* was a routine two-line item.

Ben was a friendly, good natured, active-minded young fellow whose father some years before had left him heir to what was, for Covington, a considerable sum of money. His marriage to Muriel, the pleasant daughter of a good family, had been approved by the community as an appropriate match. Ben's devotion to his young wife was notable in a neighborhood where conjugal affection was taken for granted. He purchased a good home, furnished it lavishly, and seemed always alert to do whatever might add to his wife's happiness.

When he discovered that he was to become a father, Ben's concern over Muriel's comfort redoubled. He engaged a physician long in advance to watch over her progress. Two weeks before the event was expected he installed her in the best quarters a Danville hospital could provide. Their child was probably the first from Covington to be born in a hospital; so expensive an entrance into the world was beyond the usual means.

In spite of Ben's lavish preparations, Muriel suffered a terrible and painful ordeal. Their baby son died within an hour after birth.

Ben was frantic. He was positive that Muriel would die, too, when she found that her first-born son had not lived.

"We must substitute another boy," he declared. "She will die when she finds out the truth. We must not let her die too!"

In vain the doctor and his colleagues tried to assure him that Muriel would soon get well, and that nothing had happened to prevent the normal birth of another child to them later on. Ben would not be persuaded. He insisted that Muriel would die from shock on learning that her baby was dead.

He shoved the doctor out of the hospital into his automobile, and started toward Covington with the accelerator pushed to the floor.

"A fast train leaves here for Chicago in an hour," he shouted into the doctor's ear. "We'll be back in time to catch it. We're going to Chicago after a baby. We'll not let Muriel die that way."

They reached Covington safely. Ben leaped out of the car, to reappear in a few minutes stuffing a roll of several hundred dollars into his pocket. Full speed again he urged the car over the rough pike toward Danville. Two miles from the city the car ran out of gas.

"Come on, Doc!" Ben cried. Without stopping to look for the trouble, he began a dog trot toward the railroad station. Another automobile came along and carried them to the depot in time for the train.

Ben had no plan whatever in mind, except to get to the big city of Chicago where he was sure babies were being born every few minutes. Out of the thousands there had to be one that he could obtain. Over a supper in the dining car they discussed the problem. The doctor felt that the quest might be made to succeed, but neither of them was well enough acquainted in Chicago to know what to do after they reached the city.

A gentleman who had been dining across the aisle stepped over.

"I have heard your conversation," he said. "I have an adopted son myself, from a foundlings' home. Probably I can help you."

The stranger gave them the name and address of a woman who managed a society for the care and adoption of motherless babies. Although the train reached Chicago late that night, they telephoned the woman immediately from the railroad station. Her home was in a suburb twenty miles out. She said nothing could be done during the night, but promised to see them at her office at nine o'clock next morning.

Ben and the doctor were waiting when she came. She looked at Ben in blank amazement when he bluntly stated his mission:

"Madam, our train leaves here in an hour and forty minutes. We must have a very young boy baby in time to catch that train."

The woman made them sit down to explain the situation. Finally she said:

"We have a boy baby that is exactly what you want. He is the son of a university student and a respectable office girl. His parents forbade their marriage, and she could not take care of the child.

"But I don't know you. I can't turn this baby over to you without full credentials."

The doctor interceded. He referred her to a dozen prominent physicians in Indianapolis, and at his medical college, urging that she telephone anyone or all of them. Ben eagerly offered to pay the telephone charges. She called in an officer of the society, and the doctor talked to him. The man's face seemed familiar to the doctor. He identified the officer as a former member of the Indiana State Board of Health, and described a trip they had taken together in the doctor's buggy during an epidemic. The man remembered him. Rising, he said to the woman, "Give Dr. Blank anything he wants and don't stop a minute for any legal formalities. I'll guarantee that he will take care of those later."

The baby was being cared for by a widow in a nearby part of Chicago. Armed with the necessary papers and instructions, Ben hustled the doctor into a taxicab and ordered the driver to speed.

"Five dollars extra if you get us back for our train at ten-forty! I will pay all your fines."

The widow was abruptly told to prepare to travel, and shown the papers. The doctor dressed the baby and fixed a bottle of milk while she changed her clothes. They made the train by a minute.

At three o'clock that afternoon the widow carried the baby into the hospital. A nurse laid him in Muriel's arms. She smiled proudly and pulled him to her. The happy mother in a surprisingly short time was entirely well again, and at home. They named the baby Benjamin.

When little Bennie was about a year old, Ben went to the Doctor again.

"Doc," he said, "we can't fairly deceive Muriel any longer. You'll have to tell her. I can't."

The doctor found Muriel singing and sewing in a little rocker near the bed where the baby was comfortably playing with his toes. He talked an hour or so, about every topic he could bring to mind except the object of his call. Muriel no doubt wondered why a busy physician, who was usually rushing around from one patient to another, should be sitting half an afternoon visiting with her. Finally he managed to hint that he had come especially to tell her something, and then he had to go through with it. He explained that everything that had been done had been for the love of her and for her own good, and at last blurted out:

"Muriel, that lovely baby boy there on the bed is not your own. Your baby didn't live."

She fell across the bed beside the child. Clutching him against her heart, she sobbed:

"You are my baby now, Bennie. It doesn't matter how you came. They shan't take you away."

Little Bennie was formally adopted, and grew into a strong, sturdy, lovable youngster. When he was about three, a daughter was born to Ben and Muriel.

Then the war was declared. Ben hurried away to an officer's training camp, and came out with a captain's bars. Proud of her soldier husband, Muriel found time from her children to lead in the local war activities. Ben was not sent to France, but was assigned duties in an Eastern camp.

The story of Ben and Muriel ought to end at this point, but there is more.

Ben became infatuated with a canteen worker at his camp. He came home and persuaded Muriel to divorce him.

After marrying the other woman, he entered business in a Western city. When he returned to visit Covington, he always seemed interested in Muriel and her welfare. After some years he divorced the second wife. His third marriage was to a much younger girl from Covington, where he came to live a few years before going away again. The last news of Ben was that he was living apart from the third wife.

If this were fiction, the loose ends would all be picked up and everything explained. But this is fact, which is seldom complete and sometimes mysterious. And Muriel has been twice remarried.

11

Youngsters Make
Their Choices

O LD MAN Waterman thought that his son-in-law, Peter
Ost the grocer, was wasting money by sending Gordon
away to school. Gordon came back from the business college
in due course, determined that he could find as pleasant a
future in Covington as elsewhere. He purchased a corn-
popping and peanut-roasting machine, and launched his
business career.

His grandfather, who dimly supposed that one learned
Latin and Greek in all colleges, was further aghast. The
short, chunky old gentleman proclaimed his unfavorable
opinion around the square to whomever would listen.

Hand cupped behind his ear and his spade beard wag-
ging, he shouted in his shrill voice:

"Pete, he send Gordon away to college." Then, in one
breath of uprushing crescendo that was meant to carry a
full load of irony he would add, "Gordon, he come home
and run a peanut stand!" Shaking his head, he would
walk on to repeat to someone else the humiliatingly funny
event that had transpired in his posterity. A grandson of
his had had the magnificent advantage of a college education, yet chose to set up a sidewalk peanut roaster in Covington.

The deaf old gentleman lived to see that the young man
was not making fools of his family, after all. The peanut
roaster was followed after a few thrifty years by a small,
neat confectionery shop with an ice cream counter in one
of the cheaper frame buildings on the north side of the

square. That, in the course of time, gave way to the Ost
Sanitary Soda Shop, with an ornate new fountain, booths
along the walls, wire-legged tables and chairs on the floor,
plate glass display counters for candy and cigars, expensive
wall decorations, and a complicated mechanical musical
machine that played a violin when encouraged by a nickel
in the slot. The proceeds of this establishment bought its
owner one of the town's better homes and sent old man
Waterman's great grandson through the state university for
a full four-year course.

Only a few of the abler young people followed the Ost
pattern of building successful lives in Covington. From
month to month, with disturbing frequency, the *Republican*
carried items like these:

> Frank Little has obtained a position with the Pack-
> ard Co. in Detroit, and likes the outlook very much.
> Several Covington boys now have places in the noted
> Michigan city and all are making good.

> Roger McMahon and Gene Ryan left Sunday for
> Detroit where they expect to find positions in one of
> the automobile factories. Michigan has 86 car fac-
> tories, and is drawing within her borders hundreds of
> the active and ambitious young men of the country.
> McMahon and Ryan both have a turn for mechanics,
> and doubtless will soon climb into responsible positions.

"Whose Move Is It Next?" the editorial column demanded.

> The departure of one of Covington's young men to
> a large city gives rise to the eternal question, what
> must the small town do to keep its young men and
> young women?

> It appears to us that there is nothing more im-
> portant than to give them jobs. Home ties are not
> severed readily. But every red-blooded boy and ambi-
> tious girl wants to make a living and acquire a com-
> petence. If Covington offers no opportunity, we can

expect nothing else than that they will seek their opportunities elsewhere. And generally it is the best who
go. The slothful and lazy, those with little ambition
for their futures, little pride in themselves and their
city, will be the ones who remain to make our citizenship
unless the abler ones can find or make opportunities
here at home.

The small towns must fight for their existence. And
cities are calling for our manhood, our girlhood, and
our cash — not merely calling but coming after them.
We of small towns must fight our own battles. And if
we don't start to fighting pretty soon, not enough of
us will be left to fight.

How to fight or what to fight never seemed to become
clear enough that any course of action could be prescribed
for the retention in Covington of all the promising youth.
Though few local boys had become rich or famous in any
quarter of the earth, the lure of high wages in Detroit, Indianapolis, Chicago, and Akron kept drawing more of them
away. The only contemporaneous Covingtonian really to
achieve fame had been Eugene Savage, a talented fellow
who went away to win the Prix de Rome and acquire note
as a figure, portrait, mural, and landscape artist. Great
museums hung his pictures; Yale University made him pro-
fessor of painting. Covington knew little of his distinction,
for he almost never came back to visit; of his art, it knew
only his vivid portrait of Miss Olive Coffeen, a teacher who
had inspired and encouraged him in boyhood. The picture
was hung in the public library, as his gift. Miss Coffeen
lived into her nineties, after more than half a century of
laborious teaching in Covington's public schools.

Boys sometimes went to Indianapolis or Chicago for a
fling at the larger world, only to decide eventually that
Covington offered more of genuine satisfactions. One of
these was clever Harry Shuler, who became an advertising
artist in Indianapolis, following a term behind the counter
of his father's restaurant.

After a horse sale one chilly February afternoon at Mc-
Mahon's livery barn, a crowd of the buyers went together to

Shuler's restaurant for refreshments. Harry, a close observer of the course of business, had expected them and was prepared. He had quartered several pies and placed the cuts on plates, ready for the quick service that he prided himself on giving. The men ranged themselves on the stools by the long counter. With a practiced eye Harry chose the most influential one and said, "Piece of pie?"

The man nodded. All the others agreed on pie, as Harry had anticipated. In no time the pie plates were spinning along the board. Each customer found his order before him almost at once, with a fork at its side. Nearly all the triangles had been reduced to crumbs, when Harry noticed that one man had not yet begun eating.

"What's matter, don't you like that pie?"

"Don't know yit," came the plaintive reply. "You didn't give me no knife."

Harry returned from his Indianapolis experience to marry his little blonde childhood sweetheart, Irene Richeson, and set up a grocery business with his father. Jim Martin graduated from a dental college and returned to share and enlarge his father's practice. Charley Belles, the druggist's son, after preparing for an educational career, headed the schools in other towns and became superintendent for Fountain County. Oscar Kerr built up a furniture and undertaking business in Covington that later he sold to move to a larger Ohio town, where he prospered pleasantly. After an intensive medical training and war experience overseas, Jim Aldridge came home to build up the largest professional practice in Covington.

Frost Harden shined shoes, worked in a barber shop, became owner of the best shop in town, took over the Ford agency, and eventually captured the postmastership, with an interval during which he traveled the eastern United States for an automobile finance company. Three of his brothers owned separate Ford agencies in nearby Illinois towns.

Frost and the hometown girl he married, Cecil Murray, raised a fine son who became a doctor in LaFayette. Cecil became interested in Republican politics. She was in turn precinct committeewoman, county vice-chairman, state vice-chairman and national committeewoman for Indiana, and then went on to serve five terms in the national House of Representatives as Indiana's first Republican woman member of Congress.

Among the boys who went elsewhere there were a trolley conductor in Indianapolis, a chain store manager in Missouri, a detective in Chicago, a mining engineer in Arizona, a saxophone player in a Chicago jazz orchestra, a drug clerk in LaFayette, a high school teacher in Pittsburgh, a homesteader in New Mexico, a soda fountain clerk in some other town, a real estate salesman in Gary. Sometimes the forays abroad were brief, but the lads who once ventured away usually came home only for occasional visits.

Girls, too, found jobs in Indianapolis and Chicago, where they enjoyed the thrills of city life and carried on unrelenting and usually successful searches for husbands. One girl got as far away as Washington for a civil service clerkship. Another, who found a husband in a nearby state, eventually shot him. The most spectacular feminine achievement, however, was by a girl who stayed in the home town.

Dark-eyed Lura Ward, pleasant and competent, had been a clerk in the county auditor's office until her Democratic employer was succeeded by a Republican. Then she found a job in the Citizens Bank. One scorching afternoon, when the heat waves shimmered over the brick pavements and the August somnolence had reduced business to a minimum, the bank was deserted for a few minutes except for the presence of Polk Gray, the septuagenarian cashier. Two bandits, who had been sitting under a shade tree in the courthouse square, saw Lura leave for the post office. Their moment had come. Walking swiftly into the bank, one slugged Gray with a blackjack while the other rapidly stuffed his pockets with the money that was in sight on the counters.

Lura, returning quickly, stepped into the front door in time to see the two men moving toward the side exit at the rear. With a scream she started after them. In his haste the man with the money snagged his coat pocket on the door catch as he dashed out the alley door. Bills spilled and fluttered while the handsome girl in determined pursuit snatched them up in handfuls. The men outdistanced her, but within a few hours, aided by a posse that was more frightened than the fugitives, captured them in the woods south of town.

An immediate check-up of the bank's funds revealed that eight hundred dollars was taken from the counter. Lura had picked up nine hundred and seventy dollars in the alley. The robbers, who found themselves out of pocket a hundred and seventy dollars in the transaction, were sentenced to the penitentiary within twenty-four hours.

The heroine's picture was printed in scores of newspapers. The bank gave her a diamond ring and the insurance company sent a substantial cash reward. If the publicity brought her any proposals of marriage, she declined them to stay in the banking business.

Youth's triumphs were pridefully reported in the *Republican,* and drawn upon for pointing an occasional moral in the editorial column:

> It was an achievement that counts for something for Glen Newton, Van Buren township school boy, to make the highest grade of 207 Fountain county boys and girls in the eighth grade examinations. That grade, 96 3/4, revealed that there is a boy with ability and industry, a lad who cherishes the value of time, who is ambitious to make his life count for something. We hope this young man will keep up his speed. In his school at Sterling he has learned that great opportunities are offered right here in Fountain county. We hope he will stay here to realize these opportunities and make himself one of the citizens that in the future we will be proud of.

The headline was "A Comer." Glen Newton when last heard from was practicing corporation law in California.

Convincing evidence that youth was unduly aflame in town must have prompted the violation of all the rules of "Who, What, When, Where, and Why" in a brief article one week.

Two or three little "house parties" have been held in these parts in recent weeks that could as well be dispensed with. This kind of social affair really is not fashionable, and did the public know, it would not approve. In fact, parties of this brand never were strictly au fait in the most stylish circles.

In the first place, gin, according to the *Ladies Home Journal* and other authorities, is not this year in good form as a drink for young ladies. Even beer is somewhat passe. And, in the second place, Beatrice Fairface, and other accepted arbiters of good manners, insist that young women should not permit any undue familiarities from young men, especially if the young men are from Danville. This also holds true if the young men have wives in Danville who want divorces and are watching for evidence. Other dicta of the aforementioned authorities are interpreted to mean that it is in just as poor taste to hold such social gatherings at Lyons as in the city of Covington or nearby, particularly when the participants come from respectable families with reputations to uphold. There is also danger when these frolicsome evening affairs become too frequent that the names of the guests will get into the public prints on the society page. While advertising is effective, it is also sometimes embarrassing.

The editor may have been trying to be funny, or else had suffered a lapse of his customary tolerance with regard to strictly personal affairs. And, again, the apparently foolish piece may have averted a public scandal.

The fervor for "home trade" brought down an editorial lecture upon a high school superintendent and a graduating class one year:

A high school education is not in any way complete unless the boys and girls are taught their obligations to their own home town. The boys and girls have the advantage of twelve years of public schooling, wholly at the expense of the taxpayers. They should not be allowed to forget this.

The high school superintendent and faculty should in particular direct the attention of some of the members of the Covington Class of 1917 to the fact that this city has provided them with a splendid school and liberally paid teachers, and that, in return, they should not overlook any opportunity to repay the obligation.

Led by certain pupils, and with the tacit encouragement of the superintendent, the senior class purchased its class rings of an outside concern; photographs of the class are being made in a Danville studio; the invitations and cards have been engraved by out of town concerns. The local jeweler, photographers, and newspaper printing shops are taxpayers — their money helps to make possible the graduation of this class.

The superintendent and faculty should take matters such as this in hand and see to it that home institutions are patronized by the schools. The instructors who neglect this important phase of education are very seriously remiss in their duty; and if they persist, or have persisted, in such neglect, the plain duty of the board of education is to employ some one who can see in better light.

The merchants of Covington were probably better pleased with that outburst than with one that had appeared a few weeks earlier:

It will be but a very few weeks until the commencement and graduation season will be open full blast.

Every year in Indiana hundreds of families sacrifice from their savings or incur debt, to equip their daughters with as much finery as the daughters of their neighbors, or to enable their sons to splurge as liberally as anyone.

Annually after it is over a howl goes up about the foolishness of the procedure.

Why not start the howl now? Why allow commencement customs to destroy the work of many months of school?

Schools are supposed to prepare students to make a

living, and to live. When school customs demand an outrageously extravagant finale, an expenditure for display that can ill be afforded by many, those customs should be eliminated.

We should like to see at least one school in Fountain-co. hold a sensible graduation week this year.

No record appears to indicate that the suggestion was followed.

The town gave its young folks an average public school education, and maintained a fair Carnegie library that was open for those who cared to borrow the books. The churches announced Sunday School weekly services that were patterned after the programs of the year before and the years before that. Otherwise, so far as community responsibility was concerned, no attempt was made to do more. If a boy or girl was ingenious or fortunate enough to find a way to make a living in the home town, a welcome was extended; a welcome to get what could be taken, and no more. Others stayed because they were too dull, too fearful, or had too little ambition to venture into more fruitful fields. The pull of the cities then still had an economic justification. The preceding census had recorded 2,069 people in Covington; the next one found only 1,945.

A postscript referring to youth may here be allowable. To compare Covington with the other town I knew best never seemed quite fair. Ada, Ohio, my earlier home, enjoyed advantages arising from the presence of the university, advantages which attracted and tended to develop a high average type of citizenship. Ada was larger by five hundred. Looking back upon the two towns from this later period, when teen-age behavior and juvenile delinquency are so much discussed, the sharp contrast merits remark. In Covington an able, ambitious youngster who showed signs of striving to rise above his environment was likely to hear that he was "getting too big for his pants." In Ada his faults may have been noted but his excellences were applauded and encouraged. Covington appeared to find malicious delight in dissecting the young people's foibles and in exaggerating their gravity. The youngsters tended in turn to exaggerate their foibles. Ada exerted a gentle, almost impalpable pressure in expectation that girls would grow into ladies and boys into gentlemen. The youngsters responded as a rule by becoming creditable and often outstanding citizens.

12

Indiana's Favorite Sport

THE PRECINCT committeeman from Jackson township came in one day to renew his subscription. "Well," he said, "won't be long now till we'll have another election. Campaign and election is about the best sport we have down our way."

He meant exactly that. Political campaigns furnished stir and excitement and controversy. For a month or so in each election year every voting citizen was called upon by important men; his opinions were invited, and he had something besides weather and crops to discuss.

To an idealistic young editor the elections were more than an entertaining diversion. In them, I felt, the intimate processes of popular government were revealed. I saw each individual citizen determining as he dropped a vote in the ballot box — to the measure of some fraction of a million — the destiny of the national republic and in a larger measure the history of the state, county, and township. In every public question and in every selection of candidates I saw definite choices between right and wrong. By vigorous advocacy of the right, an "influence for good" could be a factor in the decisions of the electorate, and thus the function of a journalist would be fulfilled. After more experience I came to doubt whether the lines between right and wrong could always be so sharply drawn.

In 1916 the number of Indiana's political entertainments was doubled by the institution of primary elections to designate party candidates. The convention system for long years had been in vogue in all the political units. The party nominees for county offices were chosen by county conventions, to which each voting precinct sent delegates. Counties sent delegates to Indianapolis where in state conventions platforms were adopted and candidates nominated for the state offices. Every two years came a district convention when delegates from seven or eight counties assembled to pick a nominee for Congress. These events were exciting and interesting to the active politicians and "insiders." The voting public was granted its participation after, rather than before, the nominations. Usually, though not always, a few skillful and not wholly disinterested men ran the conventions and were able to influence the delegates to support the candidates whom they had agreed upon well in advance.

The primary was designed to permit all the members of the party to express their preferences as to who should run for offices in the general elections. Bosses, corrupt or otherwise, would then have to bend to the popular will; none but virtuous candidates would win the nominations, and nothing but the best of government would follow. The primary was a simple extension of democracy. These arguments seemed irrefutable.

The *Republican* a year later printed an editorial entitled "About the Primary."

This editorial is being written Wednesday morning when but very scattering returns from the state and county are available. Looking at the proposition from this time, when only a few precincts indicate who will be nominated, it appears that the primary in this particular instance is not worth the cost. Indications are that the nominees are to be about the same that might have been expected from the old convention system. About the same men have voted at the primary who usually participate in the choice of delegates for conventions. Perhaps, with lessons learned from this, at another primary the people will be more awake to their opportunity and a different tale will be told.

The next week another paragraph said,

The cost of the primary in Fountain county was approximately a dollar a vote. The total vote of all parties was about 2150. The election expense, including room rents, fuel, supplies, pay of officials, printing and other items, was about $2,000. It may therefore be appropriate to ask if you got your dollar's worth.

The primary system of nominating candidates proved to be no sounder than the electorate. The necessity for a candidate for Congress, for governor or senator to finance two campaigns, one for the primary and one for the election, has prevented hundreds of highminded, able men from entering public service. The procession of millionaires, demagogues, and lesser successful clowns in the primary parade tended in time to make an older idealist wonder whether a little old-fashioned convention corruption could have done worse. But whatever is new appears to youth to have virtue for being new; or, being untried, the apparent advantages shine more conspicuously than the drawbacks. The editor of the *Republican* favored the new things.

"Prohibition and a new constitution have been won. Woman's suffrage next, and Indiana will step into the very front rank," the editorial column proclaimed.

Soon afterwards the right to vote was granted to Hoosier women. An instantaneous effect was noted under the title "Circumstances Alter Cases":

Last year when the women of the City Beautiful Committee sought to get assistance from the city council, they were refused bluntly even the small request for an appropriation for one laborer for one week. This year the council covered itself with glory by generously and chivalrously donating one hundred dollars — not out of their own pockets, understand.

Let's see, how many women voters are there in Covington?

On a small, local scale, here was noted the inevitable result of the "reform" efforts to place the last possible bit of power directly in the hands of voters. As the reckless appropriations for pensions, subsidies, and doles in later years were to show, the officeholders' temptation to purchase re-elections with public funds was to become irresistible.

Jubilation over the prospect of a new constitution for Indiana ran high amongst the forward lookers. The great grandfathers of the state, back in 1851, had in their solemn wisdom adopted an admirable constitution for their time, with the proviso that it might be amended or changed by a majority of all votes cast at any general election. Constitutional questions when placed on the ballots had regularly been ignored by so many of the voters that no such majority had ever been obtained. Finally a legislature took the bit in its teeth, called a constitutional convention and provided for the election of delegates.

This opened a delightful field for constructive suggestions. The Democratic state chairman had proposed that his committee, and the Republican state committee should together pick the fifteen candidates for delegates-at-large to the constitutional convention. The *Covington Republican* came forward with its own idea:

> The meeting of Republicans in Indianapolis Tuesday did well to reject the proposition of Bernard Korbly, state democratic chairman, that the parties join in the nomination of fifteen candidates for delegates-at-large to the constitutional convention, that candidacies of the best possible men for the places might be assured.
>
> The objective point aimed at in the proposal was commendable, to be sure; but, as the Republicans decided, the method was impractical. From every standpoint it is better by far that the political parties should not constitute themselves as the agencies for the selection or endorsement of candidates to this convention.
>
> However, it is extremely important that pressure be brought to bear upon some of the state's most notably capable citizens to induce them to become candidates for the fifteen places. It would not be a bad idea if voters of Fountain county would take it upon themselves to write to men whom they consider most fit, urging that they become candidates.

We are not ready to undertake to name the fifteen who, we believe, would be the fifteen in the state best qualified to sit in the convention. However, here are a few suggestions:

Charles W. Fairbanks, former vice-president of the United States, than whom no better man could be suggested to preside over the convention.

Samuel M. Ralston, former governor, whose recent knowledge of the state government and its needs would be invaluable.

Albert J. Beveridge, former senator, one of the world's keen students of constitutions.

John W. Kern, former United States Senator, whose abilities would indeed be useful.

J. Frank Hanly, former governor, who, while of late devoted solely to the prohibition fight, is by no means a one idea man.

Will H. Hays, whose notable political achievements as Republican state chairman have led some to class him as only a politician, but who has remarkable abilities that would make him, as a delegate, most useful to the people of the state.

Arthur R. Robinson, of Indianapolis, floor leader of the senate in two sessions of the general assembly, a capable leader with a profound practical knowledge of many of the questions to be faced by the convention.

Judge W. H. Eichorn of Bluffton, George W. Stoutt, James H. McGill, George B. Lockwood, John B. Stoll.

There you have a dozen suggestions. This is no matter to be left to chance. Enough amateur statesmen will get into the convention from the districts without allowing them to "run at large."

The list was intended to advance the names of the state's fittest constitution makers, from among the most eminent of its citizens. I wrote letters to the men I had mentioned, urging that they agree to stand for the convention. Not long before I had stood beside Fairbanks at an Old Settlers picnic dinner table, and had found the tall, thin ex-vice-president a friendly, human gentleman, "common as an old shoe," with creditable capacity for consuming fried chicken. The reply to the letter, however, stated coolly in a single sentence that Fairbanks had "no desire to become a candidate for any office whatever." Ralston, then just out of the governor's office, who was to escape a presidential nomination in 1924 only by firm refusal because he knew that death waited a few months ahead, answered in a long letter explaining that he had resumed law practice in the imperative necessity to provide for his family and old age, and felt that he could ill afford to sit in the convention. Albert J. Beveridge made no reply at all. John W. Kern, a former U. S. Senator who had been Bryan's running mate in 1908, wrote from a sick bed that the convention was so important that no citizen could properly decline if his services were demanded.

The new constitution proved to be a short-lived mirage. The legislature had exceeded its authority, the supreme court decreed. No convention was held for another decade and Indiana made do with the obsolete charter of the eighteen fifties.

Participation in the excitement of elections was not to be limited to the weekly printed pages. "How about putting your name down for our speakers' bureau?" the Republican state chairman, Will H. Hays — he who was to become national chairman, postmaster-general, and "czar" of the moving pictures — asked one day in Indianapolis.

A voluminous stream of instruction and suggestions to party orators poured from headquarters. Assuming that, being an inconspicuous small town publisher, my services would not be called upon until the campaign's closing weeks when meetings were held in every hamlet, not much attention was paid to the material. Then a telegram came one morning in late August, asking me to go next day to open the Wabash county campaign.

There was just time to put the paper on the press before catching the train. With a copy of the Republican campaign textbook and a dependable memory for jokes, the speech was outlined en route. The formula was simple — a fact (or an alleged fact) taken from the textbook, application of the fact to prove a Democratic weakness or mistake,

and a joke to reinforce the argument; formula to be repeated until either the time allotted or the crowd began to
give out.

No committee met me at the train in Wabash, as had
been promised. Locating the proper persons later, I was
not complimented when the chairman said: "We met the
train, but didn't see anyone get off that looked like a
speaker, so we came away." A momentarily injured personal
pride was assuaged by the further remark that "We saw you
walking up and down the platform, but you didn't have a
hat so we supposed you were just a Pullman passenger
stretching his legs."

A sheepskin band escorted the speaker to the hall in a
village called Somerset where, according to next day's Wabash *Plain Dealer* (Republican),

> [he] made a masterful address. Being an orator of no
> meager talent and a man well informed on the issues of
> the present campaign, he laid forth convincing argu-
> ments in a clear, forcible and interesting manner. He
> . . . arraigned the present Democratic administration
> for their extravagance in handling the state funds . . .
> pointed out the gross inconsistency of President Wilson
> . . . lauded the various Republican candidates for the
> national and state offices and closed his remarks by
> predicting a big G.O.P. victory at the polls next No-
> vember.

No other record of the occasion remains, but clearly the
speech was in the full traditional form; both state and national Democratic administrations had been thoroughly
denounced, the Republican candidates had been suitably
praised, and a smashing victory had been predicted.

After so glowing a newspaper report, and full of self-
satisfaction over having held an audience for an hour, I expected that this auspicious venture into campaign eloquence
would be followed by insistent demands for more important
appearances. A rising star amongst Republican orators,
who might even get on the paid list! To be ready for the
next summons, I prepared carefully, drafting paragraphs

that should have withered the staunchest Democrat, and passages designed to hold breathless crowds agape until came the climax, when the applause should crash like cymbals while the artist drew breath.

Nothing more happened for weeks, not until the middle of October, when directions came to go to Jasper county for two meetings. Here no sheepskin band was provided. Whether for that reason or not, the first of the two speeches was an utter failure. The springs of eloquence would not flow. The fire and fury would not light up. After a half hour of pedestrian utterance, undistinguished by a single flight into higher phraseological regions, I sat down, a humiliated and disappointed speaker who knew all too well that his audience was equally glad the speech had ended.

Next day the *Rensselaer Republican,* the county seat daily, carried a column about the meeting, which quoted accurately several points but kindly avoided reference to the manner of their delivery. That night at Gifford, with more trepidation than I had experienced before an audience in years, I went laboriously and painfully through about the same kind of performance. The newspaper report said that "Mr. McMillen's address was better than the one given at Fair Oaks on Monday night by him"; and that was lavish praise.

Putting aside dreams of eminence as a political orator, I returned to concentrate on the campaign in Fountain county. The election resulted in fulfillment of the party's hope for complete control of the courthouse with every office in Republican hands. The voters had approved the promised "honest, businesslike administration."

A few years previously, the county commissioners had been persuaded to buy, on the installment plan, a set of voting machines for the county. Their justification was that much economy would result, since the cost of printed ballots would be avoided. As owner of the *Republican,* to which now came all county printing, I was not displeased to find that the state law which permitted the use of mechanical voting devices also required that a full set of Australian ballots be printed and held in reserve in case the machines failed to function.

When the time came to put in a bill for the election printing, I had no idea how much to charge. The task had, truly, been an onerous one in the amount of labor and worry involved. I consulted previous records to find what had been paid to printers in other elections. Too much, I thought; no printing job could bring that much. One or two friends, who were asked for advice, suggested that the *Republican* did a great deal of unpaid boosting for the county for which partial payment might very properly be collected by way of public printing. That argument seemed plausible to a young man deeply in debt who was not making much money. Elmer Wilkey, the astute county chairman, happened along, but refused any advice except "make it enough so you won't lose." Finally, on the last day for filing such bills, I made one out for a hundred dollars higher than the printing charge for the previous election. "There was considerable extra work this time," I explained, and the bill was paid without comment. I deposited the check cheerfully and the county chairman borrowed ten dollars of it.

The matter would not be put out of mind, however. As an exponent of civic virtue, I hated to believe that I might have overcharged the county. Finally I asked a friend who estimated printing prices for a union labor plant in Danville what the job would have cost in his shop. The report was that the Danville company, on their cost-accounting basis, would have charged a hundred and fifty dollars more than my bill had been. My moral apprehensions gave way to regret that I had charged too little.

On an earlier occasion I had been perplexed by another conflict between an ethical propriety and financial exigency. This had been when the annual contract was to be let for the county printing. The unsophisticated editor had blithely assumed that the paper which had supported the winning ticket automatically got the job. I was pained to learn that the contract went to the lowest bidder. "Alarm smote his vitals," for I needed that income and needed it badly, but how could I make sure of being the lowest bidder? And might I be in danger of bidding so low that if I won it there would be no profit in the contract? Besides, I was not very efficient at estimating printing costs, especially for complicated jobs. The problem appeared desperately complex.

The law, I learned, required that the county officers should make advance requisitions in full for all the stationery, blank books, and other printed material they expected to use for the full year. These lists set forth complete specifications for the information of printers; then bidders were required to quote prices on each item. The contract had to be let to the bidder whose price for the total list of requisitions was lowest. The statute's provisions appeared, on their face, to be admirably suited to assuring the county cheap printing while offering little help to a deserving party printer.

Bill Harden came to the rescue. I had confided my worry about getting the county contract.

"Why, don't you know how that's done?" asked Bill, his eyes wide in amazement as such innocence.

"No, I don't."

"Well, you go over to the courthouse and get the auditor and clerk, and maybe one or two others that you can depend on, to requisition four or five of them big leather-bound record books that they know they won't need. And make 'em promise not to order 'em. Books like that come to sixty or eighty dollars apiece. All right! They requisition the books, but they'll know they dassent order 'em. You know which books they are not to order. You put them books in your bid at ten cents apiece. Anybody else bidding don't know, so they have to put in a regular price. Then your total bid is the lowest, and nobody not on the inside can get under you. Nobody else is on the inside, so you get the contract. If anybody else did happen to get it, then your courthouse friends would go ahead and order them books. See?"

"I see, Bill, but it doesn't sound honest to me."

"Mac, it's a time-honored Indiana custom and you should show respect for its antiquity. Don't violate it. Besides, editors and printers have got to live."

The *Republican* was awarded the county printing. The contract prices actually were little if any higher than regular commercial prices. The volume, however, helped materially to sustain the business.

The abandonment of the party conventions was regretted by those who had enjoyed their picturesqueness, the excited wire-pulling and log-rolling, and all the phenomena that a century of party government had made traditional. The institution of the primary, however, offered no discouragement to candidates. The number increased; men who knew they would have no chance in conventions were convinced that the people at large would recognize their merits.

The state offices were still in possession of the Democrats. With the fading of the Bull Moose, the Indiana outlook for a 1916 Republican victory was bright. This prospect, combined with the primary, brought a proliferation of candidates for every office from United States senator and governor down to state statistician. The latter office was then actually elective!

Up to this time I had worked in continuous harmony with the county leaders. Nevertheless I hated and feared the possibility of coming to be regarded as a party hack. I wanted to oppose the local organization on some issue or candidate, preferably one important enough to attract considerable attention but not so vital as to cause enduring discord. The primary contest for nominations to the United States Senate provided what promised to be an admirable opportunity.

Two prominent candidates were pursuing the Republican nomination, Harry S. New, long identified with state political affairs, and the inimitable James Eli Watson. That the county organization men, including the courthouse officials, would heartily favor one or the other of these candidates was certain.

A young Indianapolis lawyer, then a state senator, had also announced his candidacy. He admitted to friends that he had no expectation of winning that year, but declared that since boyhood his ambition had been to sit in the Senate of the United States, and he wanted to acquire a statewide political reputation. His name was Arthur R. Robinson. He was a graduate of Ohio Northern University where I had attended briefly; alone of the senatorial candidates, he had declared himself in favor of statewide prohibition. I selected Robinson as the medium for my declaration of political independence.

That a lively reaction would follow this decision was indicated by an earlier incident. Not long after purchasing the *Republican,* I had published an article praising an old hometown personal friend, Frank B. Willis, who had just been inaugurated as governor of Ohio. The headline over a two-column picture of Willis read

"FOR PRESIDENT, FRANK B. WILLIS."

Promptly by word of mouth from an influential member of the state political organization had come the message, "Lay off of that 'Willis for President' stuff. Indiana is for Fairbanks." A return message was sent by the same grapevine route: "You ask that fellow who he thinks owns the *Covington Republican* and tell him to go to hell." When we met for the first time a little later the politician reported that he had received the reply, but had not yet got around to following the advice.

The first step in the independence program was to come out against one of the favored candidates. This was done in an editorial:

James E. Watson has announced his candidacy for the United States Senate. He has a perfect right to be a candidate. He has many excellent qualifications for the elevated position. Among them are a vast reputation and experience in national affairs; a vast acquaintance over the country; and a brilliant ability as orator. We should have preferred however, that Mr. Watson should not have become a candidate. He has been of signal service to the Republican party, notwithstanding his participation in affairs that acted to the disadvantage of the party in 1912. But twelve years in congress is some reward for party service. Notwithstanding his ability and service there is a legion of voters in Indiana who will find Watson's name on the Republican ticket an obstacle to their loyalty to the old party. We believe that in this instance he should re-

strain his personal ambition for the sake of the party
he professes to love well — that he should not embarrass
his friends by becoming a candidate."

As expected, the editorial was reprinted in Republican
papers whose editors endorsed the sentiment, and in Democratic papers whose editors saw future campaign ammuni-
tion if Watson were to be nominated. Each week the
Republican printed more reasons for opposing Watson.
Editorials against New were added, and finally a vigorous
endorsement of Arthur R. Robinson appeared.

One morning a distinguished looking gentleman appeared
at the newspaper's office counter.

"Good morning! Are you Mr. McMillen? My name is
Watson, Jim Watson!"

Was this the orator whose brilliant eloquence was famed
from coast to coast? The astute politician who by twelve
years in the national Congress had risen to high power, and
who had been floor manager for President Taft in the 1912
convention? There was no mistake. The fine figure, the
commanding, magnetic presence could be none other than
the distinguished statesman — whom the *Covington Republican* in its puny columns week after week had been con-
demning as undesirable for further public service.

The great man accepted a chair and in a moment was in-
quiring with every evidence of completely absorbed interest
into the life story of the young man before him. He in-
timated that very frequently he had been told that up in
Covington there was a bright young editor in charge of the
Republican paper. Fortunately, an engagement in a nearby
city that evening gave him opportunity to fulfill a long-
cherished desire to drop in and get acquainted with so
desirable an addition to the citizenship of Indiana.

I was thoroughly flattered. Watson genially told stories
of his public experiences, answered questions about famous
men whom he knew, drew me out to talk more about myself
and ambitions. As noontime drew near he expressed a wish
to be guided to a barber shop where, after introductions to
the barbers, we parted to meet at lunch. At no time during
the morning, during the lunch, nor during the afternoon

when we walked around town for the visitor to greet various Covington citizens did Watson by word or inference refer to the fact that he was a candidate for anything.

Here, in Jim Watson, was a man who knew thoroughly the experiences of political life. He had tasted victory and office and fame and knew the satisfactions of intimate friendship with the nation's great. He had known the sting of defeat, twice for Congress and once for governor. What did he really think about a political life? Here was a chance to learn something.

"Mr. Watson, I want to ask you a hypothetical question," I said. "Suppose you knew a young man, a young man with the responsibility of a family; suppose he owned a small business that yielded a very modest living. Suppose he thought he might have some capacity for public service. Suppose he was rather attracted by political life. Suppose he believed that, if he made the effort, he could become a state senator in a few years. Suppose he also knew that if he won that place, he probably wouldn't be satisfied until he had also run for Congress, or governor, or some other office. Suppose that, much as he might like to follow such a career, he wondered whether without an established income, he could afford to do it; knowing that if honest he would always be hard up, and if not honest he would always be ashamed of himself.

"What advice would you give a young man in such a situation?"

Watson hesitated, as though deliberating carefully before undertaking to make an answer. Finally it came:

"No one can assume the responsibility of saying what another person ought to do with his life. I would answer your question by saying that if I were back where I was when I accepted my first nomination for Congress, and could know then what I know now, I would stay in the practice of law in Rushville.

"The main thing that keeps men in politics is the fight of it. In Congress I have known men who had their districts sewed up in their vest pockets to resign in the middle of a term and go home. But if some young whippersnapper back there had started up in opposition, nothing on earth could have kept those men from campaigning for reelection, just to show the world they could win. Yes, it's the fight. No man likes to have it said that he is politically dead."

Watson's fabulous ability to remember faces and names was part of his national repute. Personal interest in that problem prompted me to ask his secret. From a file I produced a clipping of a Sunday newspaper article which credited Watson's memory to a system of associating names and facial expressions with animal similarities, such as "Mr. Fox has a fox-like expression," etc.

Watson laughed over the clipping and asked to be allowed to take it. "I have a trunk full of lies about me," he said. There was no explanation, he declared "except that I am just interested in people, and remember them."

The late afternoon train carried the interesting visitor away, still no reference having been made to the immediate political campaign. The next issue of the paper carried another vigorous article on the race for the United States senatorship. It warmly advocated the nomination of Arthur R. Robinson.

Again in the campaign I was to cross paths with the fascinating Watson. A congressional district rally at Lebanon brought a huge crowd of Republicans to meet and see what promised to be an almost equally huge swarm of candidates. So many aspirants for state offices were present that the chairman of the meeting announced time limits of two minutes for each candidate for the minor state offices, and five minutes for each candidate for United States senator and governor. Watson was seated conspicuously on the stage. When the five-minute limit was announced his face fell. Soon called upon to speak, he shook back his mane, squared his shoulders, thrust his hands deep into the slash pockets at the front of his trousers, and waited for the ovation to subside. Then, in the velvet voice that could still any Republican audience, he began slowly and deliberately:

"My fellow Republicans: If I could plant a pumpkin seed at seven o'clock in the morning . . . and could enjoy for my lunch that very day a pumpkin pie made from the fruit of that selfsame seed . . . I might — I might — be able to make a Republican speech in five minutes."

When the votes were counted after the statewide primary, Watson was defeated. Robinson, my candidate, was barely in the running, but our local politicos had been made to understand that the paper did not take orders. Robinson did, in fact, get several hundred votes in Fountain county which, when compared with his score elsewhere, testified that the *Republican* had some influence.

Harry S. New had captured the senatorial nomination. Then a Democratic incumbent, Benjamin F. Shively, died in office. The Republican state committee immediately designated Watson as candidate for Shively's unexpired term. A state convention assembled to adopt a platform and to ratify Watson's nomination.

New, as nominee for the long term, was introduced to the convention. He received a cordial though less than enthusiastic reception from the audience, and spoke briefly in his pedestrian fashion. Then Watson was introduced.

The delegates, hungry for a little old-fashioned political oratory, tore their throats in a wild tribute to a long-time favorite, even though he had been lately rejected by the rank and file. The ovation produced its reward. With his superb manner and magnetic presence, his experienced skill in playing upon political passions and prejudices, and an audience eager for something and someone to be enthusiastic about, Watson soon had the delegates roaring with applause and rocking with laughter at his broad sallies against the Democratic administrations. I marveled and thrilled at the man's lordly mastery of that crowd. One moment they sat in spellbound silence, listening as his rich voice carried a paean of patriotism to a resounding climax that set them pounding and shouting. A quick jibe at the mistakes of Democrats threw the mass into seemingly uncontrollable laughter from which, with the majestic turn of a hand, he brought them again to silent, open-mouthed attention. Grateful, he said, for their support and confidence, he appeared about to close, when a gray-haired delegate leaped to his chair and literally screamed, "Go on, Jim! Don't stop! This is the first pleasure I've had in ten years!"

"Go on, Jim!" came the unanimous shout from three thousand throats, and again the matchless orator caught them up and played them at his will. The convention was enjoying itself to the hilt, and so was Jim Watson. The nations of Europe were fighting then; war terminology was beginning to creep into popular speech. Closing a devastating enumeration of Democratic deficiencies, Watson raised his index finger high above his head, and as his hand lowered in one tremendous smashing spiral gesture he shouted in tones measured as though he were scanning a bit of blank verse, "Gentlemen of the convention! . . . It is just . . . as necessary . . . for a Republican administration . . . to follow a Democratic administration . . . *as it is for an ambulance to follow an army!"*

And once more there was chaos.

Watson and New were elected to the Senate. New served as Postmaster General in the cabinet of Calvin Coolidge, and Watson was to enjoy his senatorial eminence for sixteen years. Ten years afterward, Arthur Robinson became Indiana's junior senator by appointment to fill out an unexpired term. I met Robinson in the Capitol soon after he went to Washington. He was overwhelmingly cordial and recalled gratefully the support I had given him in 1916. Over the bean soup in the Senate restaurant he said in the deep and pompous voice that contrasted with his slight physique:

"Now, Wheeler, what can I do for you?"

"Not a thing, Arthur, nothing. I've just been curious to know whether your toga feels as comfortable as you thought it would?"

"Wheeler, you know my story. You know that since I was an orphan lad eight years old, selling newspapers on cold street corners to support my widowed mother, my ambition has been to sit in the Senate of the United States. Well, Wheeler, I am here. I am a senator, after all these years of hope and work. And, Wheeler, it's a dog's life. I wish I was back in Indianapolis, practicing law."

A shadow of suspicion prompted another question.

"Will you run for election next year?"

"Oh, yes! I must vindicate the judgment of our Governor in appointing me!"

13

Humbled, Arrested and Convicted

O NE MORNING late in my third Covington winter a paragraph in the Danville *Press* brought a flush to the tips
of my ears. Elmer Bowers, the town correspondent for the
Danville papers, had written a story forecasting the course
of the mayoralty campaign in Covington. The disturbing
paragraph read:

> The Republicans are not saying much. They have
> their ear to the ground and are sawing wood. (Author's
> note: Good trick, and quite possible in Hoosier poli-
> tics.) Editor Wheeler McMillen of the *Republican* is
> the horse with dark blanket on for the Republican nomi-
> nation for mayor. Mac has been importuned by many,
> the laborers and business men alike, to get into the
> race, but up until now he has smiled and smiled and
> said nothing. It may be that he will consent to head
> the ticket under the eagle as burgomeister of the town,
> and might make a corking fine race. He knows the
> game, has a wide acquaintance and grasp of the affairs
> of the municipality. He has the acumen and leadership
> that have made the old wheel horses sit up and take
> notice.

A course of action had to be determined immediately,
before people began to ask questions. The one attributed
by Bowers looked good enough for the time being, to
"smile and say nothing." I had no serious thought of being
a candidate for mayor. No one had importuned. Maybe
three people had said, when the coming campaign was being

discussed, "Why don't *you* make the race?" Since Covington folks were always asking jocular questions, I had assumed that nothing special was meant by this one.

After a week of saying nothing my mind was more clouded
than clarified. Bower's suggestion had aroused no general
uprising of demand that I should stand for the mayoralty
nomination. A few friends expressed hearty endorsement of
the idea. More were conspicuously silent.

A list of the considerations in favor of becoming a candidate were set down.

1] The $500 annual salary for a few hours of new and
interesting work each week would be welcome.

2] To be mayor of Covington at 24, after only three
years' residence, would be an honor highly gratifying to
personal vanity.

3] It should be possible to "perform really valuable service" to the people of Covington.

4] The prestige would be advantageous to the *Republican*.

5] The experience would be worth something.

For the negative equally potent arguments loomed up:

1] Might be defeated for the nomination if there were
opposition.

2] Probably would be defeated for election because of
the usual Democratic majority, and the possible disfavor
of voters toward electing so new and young a man.

3] No mayor is ever thanked, even if he does serve his
community well.

4] The interference of public with private business
might easily offset the $500.

The weightiest reasons plainly were against becoming
a candidate, weightiest of all being the fair certainty of
defeat in the fall election. Then a candidate for the Republican nomination for mayor announced himself, a
popular gentleman born in the town who had never
lived elsewhere. His name was J. W. McMahon, one of
a large Democratic and Catholic family. Because all the rest
of the McMahons followed town pursuits, J. W., who had at
one time operated a farm, was distinguished from his rela-

tives as "Farmer" McMahon, and was so generally known
by that name that few remembered he had not worn it from
birth. Proud of being a total abstainer from both tobacco
and liquor, his one other peculiarity was that he had not
followed the religion of his family. For a living he bought
and shipped livestock and dealt in horses. Enterprising,
industrious, and kindly, he was well respected. McMahon's
announcement appeared to me to leave little reason for
thinking further of running for mayor.

Yet, on the final day for the filing of names to be placed
on the primary ballot, a statement that Wheeler McMillen
was going to be a candidate for the Republican nomination
was made public. Nothing had occurred to change the
course of reasoning that I had followed. I was sure I should
not do anything of the kind. But I wanted to. If defeated,
I would be in no different position than before. If victorious, a new adventure in life was ahead. That seemed
reason enough.

The *Republican's* columns carried the news:

> Two names are filed for the mayoralty nomination,
> Farmer McMahon, who has been in the field for several
> weeks, and Wheeler McMillen, editor of the *Covington
> Republican.*
>
> The filing of two names for the nomination for mayor
> does not indicate that there will be a fight for the place
> on the ticket, the matter being left thus to the Republi-
> can voters of the city to make a choice. Mr. McMahon,
> the first filed, is known to every voter in the city. He
> was born in this community, and has lived his entire
> life here. He has hundreds of friends in town and over
> the county, where his business as a stock buyer has
> taken him, and he is intimately acquainted with condi-
> tions in the city. If nominated and elected the people
> may be sure that he will bend every effort towards giv-
> ing the city an honest and fair administration.

I felt that to praise my opponent was better campaign
strategy than to criticize the gentleman, especially when
the advantage of newspaper control was all on one side. Be-

sides the statements about McMahon were true and would
be taken into consideration by the voters anyway.

Of my own candidacy I said:

> We have known this fellow McMillen for several
> years, and in fact have been closely associated with him
> — too closely to offer any judgment as to his qualifica-
> tions. If nominated and elected he proposes, in brief,
> to observe the oath of office taken by a man on assuming
> the office of mayor, which reads:
>
> "I, ——— ———, do solemnly swear that I will support
> the constitution of the United States and the constitu-
> tion of the state of Indiana, and that I will faithfully,
> honestly and impartially discharge my duties as the
> mayor of the city of Covington, according to law and
> to the best of my ability, so help me God."
>
> He believes that the law can be enforced in Coving-
> ton, as well as anywhere else, and without fear of the
> position of the violators; that the city government can
> be administered with far greater efficiency at much less
> cost than at present; and that Covington can be made
> a better town to live in and to do business in.

McMahon came to the *Republican* office promptly to
proffer his thanks for the compliments. The two candidates
shook hands in an agreement to make no campaign whatever, other than to discuss the situation with any voter who
wanted to talk or ask questions.

Only one further reference to the contest appeared in the
Republican before the primary election. An editorial paragraph remarked that "Being a candidate is lots of fun when
you don't care much whether you win or not."

The truth of the paragraph might well have been challenged. I wanted to win. And once in the race, I rather regretted having started for there didn't really seem to be any
great amount of fun to be had out of the experience.

Both candidates did a fairly honest job of sticking to the
agreement not to make any campaign. Nevertheless, both
seemed to be running almost continually into Republican
voters, and the subject of the primary was almost certain

to come up in the course of a conversation. Each sought to form some impression of how the people were going to vote.

A day or so before the primary, I checked over a list of all the Republican voters in town. I had "happened" to meet most of them, and had heard reports about the inclinations of most of the others. If all cast votes in my favor who had, without being particularly definite about it, in some way indicated that such was their intention, I seemed certain to win with a majority of from forty to fifty. Discounting all those about whose intentions I was not confident a majority of fifteen seemed certain. I could not identify enough who were certain to support McMahon to endanger the likelihood of victory.

The report of the election in next week's paper said:

> The Republican nomination for mayor was won by Farmer McMahon Tuesday by 11 votes majority over Wheeler McMillen. The Republican side of the primary was clean in every respect, no effort being made by either candidate to influence voters by improper means. The contrast to the methods employed in the heated Democratic contest was marked.

"Bill," I asked the foreman the morning after the primary, "who were all the two-faced liars who were going to vote for me and didn't?

"I just saw Farmer McMahon a while ago, and he said he expected to win by sixty votes, but somebody had lied to him, too."

Bill paused to refill with his fine-cut chewing tobacco and looked over the tops of his goldrimmed spectacles with twinkling eyes. "You want to know who the liars are? I'll tell you — the church people. They're the most accomplished liars in this town." With that blast at his favorite target the foreman darted upstairs to his type case.

As an ex-candidate, beaten by eleven votes by a horse trader, I reflected that one fact seemed clear enough. I was not the most popular man in Covington. The defeat was a jolt, though not particularly a humiliation, for in the

calmer moments such an outcome had appeared likely
enough. I had to own that a little humbling probably
would not be a dead loss in the long run. Anyway, soon
something else was bound to happen, and did.

Two short paragraphs in the *Republican* for July 13,
1917, set into motion a train of events that entertained
Covington and all the countryside:

> The annual outburst of speed law enforcement by the
> city administration is due at 6 A.M. Saturday. The
> eruption will probably continue its usual period of
> about two weeks.
>
> A rigid traffic ordinance was enacted by the city
> council last year, partially enforced for a few days,
> and then allowed to lapse into innocuous desuetude.
> Formal notice is now given by Mayor McGeorge that
> "on and after July 14," the measure will again be en-
> forced, altho for how long the proclamation does not
> specify.

A summary of the ordinance's provisions was added to the
warning.

Mayor Tom McGeorge took the warpath promptly. In-
furiated at the intimation that his administration had been
characterized by any fluctuations in the uniformity of law
enforcement, he decided that something should be done at
once to uphold the dignity of his office.

What made the mayor all the angrier was that the facts
were against him. His nearly twelve years as head of the
city government had been marked by sporadic enthusiasms
for enforcing one ordinance or another. He had become
extremely touchy over any criticism on the point. The
snatch of ridicule in the *Republican,* however, had other
purposes than to remind the public that the mayor was not
likely to follow for long his momentary determination to
make all traffic toe the mark. Mayor McGeorge was a Democrat, and the city campaign was on. He had been defeated
for renomination, but no opportunity to discredit the native
capacity of Democrats in public office was ever overlooked
by an alert Indiana Republican newspaper. Beyond that

was an even more specific point. There was talk that the mayor might run for county auditor the next year. He was certain to make a strong county candidate, being well known and popular, with a good business reputation. Foresighted Indiana politics, therefore, demanded that the mayor be presented in as unfavorable a light as possible whenever an opportunity arose.

His business was the sale of farm implements, buggies, and harness. With a large establishment, he had a trade that probably reached over a wider territory than that of any enterprise in Covington. He was one of the best customers of the *Republican's* printing department and advertising columns. Violent political differences between the mayor and the editor had never affected their business relations. McGeorge was big enough to view business and politics as separate fields; more than that, he and I were personally fond of each other.

Mayor Tom was the real government of Covington. A legislative body known officially as the "common council," consisting of five members, was supposed to make the ordinances. This was unanimously Democratic, and the abilities of the majority of the membership were correctly characterized by the official adjective. The "common council," was thoroughly dominated by the able McGeorge. He was Irish, with the racial talent for politics; a slight person physically, with black hair, prominent eyes, an amazingly wide, froglike mouth, and a rumbling voice. His manner was of one born to command. His capacities were recognized beyond the narrow limits of Covington, for the Tri-State Implement and Vehicle Dealers Association had elected him their president.

At Mayor McGeorge's direction, the common council had a year before passed a traffic ordinance that for rigid detail and completeness would have been entirely adequate for a city the size of Indianapolis, a hundred times bigger than Covington. It was far more than adequate for a country town of two thousand people. The angles at which cars should be parked, the spaces that might be used, were elaborately defined. Amongst the minute provisions was one that made it a misdemeanor for a pedestrian to cross a

street intersection diagonally. I suspected that Claude Philpott, the city's attorney, had not bothered to draw up the
ordinance, but had simply sent for a copy of the one in
force in Indianapolis and had presented it to the council as
suitable for Covington. What would happen the first time
Charley Lyons, the police force, obeyed Mayor Tom's orders
to jack up some independent farmer for parking his car the
wrong way was easy to foresee. The farmer would threaten
to trade in Veedersburg or Attica and let Covington get
along without his patronage.

I found no occasion for surprise when a rumor reached
my ears that His Honor the Mayor had been deeply incensed
by the paper's dirty Republican insinuation that his metropolitan traffic measure would not be enforced to the letter
forever. I did get a surprise at the prompt expression of
magisterial resentment.

On the day after the *Republcan* had printed the warning
and cynical prediction, I went home for lunch by the usual
route. At the post office I picked up some mail. There I
opened up my old home town newspaper, the Ada *Herald*,
and while reading it walked to the corner of the square
where Mike Mayer's hardware store stood and took the
usual route to the First National Bank corner opposite. A
diagonal path was worn in the bricks across there, so long
and so habitually had the shortcut been used. When about
to step up on the sidewalk by the bank, I heard my name
called and looked up from the newspaper. There, in the
full panoply of a new uniform and badge, stood Chief of
Police Lyons, ordering the pedestrian to make his crossing
at right angles, instead of diagonally, in obedience to the
city's traffic ordinance.

"I hollered at you and you didn't pay any attention,"
Chief Lyons complained.

"I'm sorry, Charley, I was reading and didn't hear you."

"Well, go back where you started from and cross the way
the law says," he insisted.

"All right, Charley, I'll try to remember to do it right
the next time."

"You'd better go back and do it right this time," the

Chief warned. Being already across, and hungry, I laughed and went on home.

When I returned from lunch, Chief Lyons was waiting at the office with a document in his hand.

"Mac," he said, "I've got a warrant here that Tom had made out for your arrest." His effort to suppress a grin was not very successful.

"Good!" I said. "Do I go to jail now, or later?"

"Well, Tom said to bring you up before him."

"Charley, I've never been arrested before, so I want this done right. Suppose you read me the warrant. How do I know it's a warrant unless I hear you read it?"

"Here, you read it for yourself," Charley proposed. I suspected that Charley's education had not proceeded beyond the fifth grade, and that oral reading of legal papers was not his strongest suit.

"No," I insisted, "Charley, you'll have to read it to me. I'm quite sure the statutes require that the officer of the law must read the charges to his prisoner."

"Well," conceded the Chief, "I can read the darn thing to you if I hafto."

Unlimbering a pair of spectacles from his hip pocket, he hung them over his ears and manfully proved that he could read the warrant. The full text was not without interest:

STATE OF INDIANA,
COUNTY OF FOUNTAIN, SS;

In the City Court, City of Covington.

The City of Covington, Indiana,
vs
Wheeler McMillen.

The plaintiff complains of the defendant and says; that on the 14th day of July, 1917, at and in said city, county and state, the said defendant, then and there being within the corporate limits of said city, did then and there cross the street intersection of Fourth and

Washington streets in said city diagonally and not at right angle with the general traffic on said streets, and did not comply with directions given by Charles P. Lyons, member of City Police Force, contrary to and in violation of Section Three of an ordinance of said city adopted by the council thereof on the 26th day of June, 1916, entitled "An Ordinance to Regulate Travel and Traffic on the Streets and Public Places of the City of Covington, Indiana, and Providing Penalties for the Violation Thereof," to the damage of said city Ten Dollars.

Wherefore the plaintiff demands judgment for Twenty Dollars.

> *Claude P. Philpott*
> Attorney for the Plaintiff.

Charles P. Lyons being duly sworn upon his oath says that the matters and things alleged in the foregoing complaint are true as he verily believes.

> *Charles P. Lyons*

Subscribed and sworn to before me this 14th day of July, 1917.

> *T. H. McGeorge, Jr.*
> Mayor, City of Covington, Ind.

The reading completed, I offered to be handcuffed, but Lyons explained that the irons were not customarily used for minor offenders unless they became violent. Together we marched to the "city hall," where the mayor was found sitting alone in his magisterial chair, waiting for our arrival. Ordinarily he handled routine city business at his desk next door in the implement store, but evidently he wished to make clear that this was no ordinary ceremony. The "city hall," was a storeroom in the building belonging to the "T. H. McGeorge, Sr., Estate," of which the mayor, T. H. McGeorge, Jr., was executor. Legally the estate and the mayor were different individuals, so he was able to rent profitably to the city a business room that otherwise would have been vacant most of the time.

"Are ye guilty, or not guilty," Mayor Tom demanded, with more than a trace of truculence in his booming voice.

"Must I plead to this charge offhand, like this, Tom?" I inquired. "I haven't had time yet to consider it."

"The court will grant the prisoner a hearing, if ye want one," His Honor replied. "Monday at two o'clock, if that ain't too soon."

That was satisfactory. I asked whether I should spend the intervening time in the calaboose.

"Certainly not," snapped the mayor, in no mood for levity.

"Do you want any bond for my appearance?"

"I guess ye'll be here if ye say y'will."

Thus released "upon his own recognizance" as the phrase went, I went over to the law office of Oliver S. Jones. Jones, once mayor himself, was a shrewd, self-educated lawyer notable for his resourcefulness and, although a Democrat, at outs politically with Mayor McGeorge. His contemplative mind and humorous outlook had interested me and I enjoyed the wit that enlivened Jones's talk.

My arrest delighted the lawyer immensely. He leaned back full length and straightened out his wooden leg to enjoy a long and hearty laugh before beginning to plan a scheme to extract the maximum of entertainment out of the situation. A decision was quickly reached that the case was of too great importance to be enjoyed by only one lawyer, so Omar B. Ratcliff was summoned. Ratcliff, an earnest, keen, hard grubbing legal grind, cast in the physical and mental mold of a minor Lincoln, bore a Lincolnian reputation for honesty and simplicity. For years he had invested his earnings in lawbooks until his legal library was said to be the second largest private collection in the state. Later he was to become a circuit judge. "O. B." cackled in dry glee as he heard the situation described.

The defendant opened the discussion. "Gentlemen, the editor of the leading Republican newspaper in Fountain County is under arrest. The real offense is *lèse majesté*. He

has spoken lightly of the Democratic overlord of Covington.
The technical charge is jaywalking. This is entirely too
trivial a matter as it stands. Can't we make something really
big out of this small beginning?"

"I think we might," chuckled Jones through his walrus
mustache.

"Well," added O. B., "great oaks grow from little acorns."

"I hope you're not calling Mac a nut!" Jones's wit was not
of uniform quality.

"His Honor is a very angry mayor. I think we ought to
strike while the mayor is hot," I observed.

"Just what are you driving at, I'd like to ask," Ratcliff
inquired. "Sounds like you might have an idea."

"I have. The mayor is to try this case as a magistrate. He
is not a lawyer. He is bullheaded. I have the honor of sitting here with the two most brilliant lawyers in Fountain
County. My guess is that under the circumstances two clever
lawyers and one modest young editor ought to be able to
work out a plan that will result in great and desirable embarrassment to the mayor of our city. I'd like to embarrass
him enough that he won't be able to run for county auditor."

"So that's it?"

"Well, that's part of it. Now, what do you say Tom will
do if you ask for a change of venue?"

There was only one answer to that — he would refuse. A
dozen years before, when he first became mayor, McGeorge
had refused to grant a change of venue — that is, transfer of
a case to another judge. It so happened that the law of
the state of Indiana was very explicit on the matter. Whenever a proper affidavit, declaring the defendant's belief that
the court was prejudiced, was presented, the court had to
grant the privilege of a change to another court. The facts
likely were that on the first occasion McGeorge knew nothing about such a law. He simply felt that his fairness had
been challenged. The lawyers at that time rode the mayor
on the point, which set him firmly on the course ever afterward.

"I have refused a change of venue in this case. I have
not only refused it now, but as long as I sit as a magistrate

no change of venue will ever be granted in this court," he had proclaimed. Law or no law, Mayor McGeorge had stood on that edict. No change of venue had he ever allowed, and the force of his personal will had been sufficient to prevent anyone ever from making an issue of his illegal procedure. Or perhaps no case had seemed important enough to the persons involved to go to the expense.

So the plot was laid that an affidavit should be offered charging that the mayor was prejudiced against the defendant — about which there would be in this case no possible doubt in the mind of anyone. He would be asked for a change of venue. He would deny the change. If he didn't deny it, there would be victory enough by exposing that he was afraid of the consequences. If he denied it, whatever followed would be clearly illegal. The conspirators hoped that then the mayor would continue the trial, declare the editor guilty of the offense charged — of which there was no doubt — and impose a fine.

This much achieved, I was defiantly to refuse to pay the fine. The customary alternative to paying a fine was to "lay it out," that is to go to jail for a period related to the amount levied. The program was to prod and goad and irritate the mayor into a lively rage so that he would either commit the defendant to jail, or confess that he was afraid to do so.

I entertained no illusion that being sent to jail would arouse the populace against McGeorge or in sympathy for me. As a matter of fact, the town would take the whole thing as a grand joke and delight in the mayor's spunk. Our plot was deeper. Because of the mayor's expected refusal of the legal right to a change of venue, if I were sent to jail I would have a clear case against the city of Covington for false imprisonment, and for cash damages of several thousands of dollars, an amount big enough to make the taxpayers writhe and rise in wrath against McGeorge. After such a blunder, the mayor would cease to be a threat for county auditor. And I might even win some damages, although I knew that hope was slight.

Before two o'clock on Monday the city hall was crowded so full of spectators that Jones, Ratcliff and their client had to edge their way to the front. The mayor's gavel fell with a bang as the Homer Sewell Memorial Clock in the court-house tower struck the hour. The charge was read. Mayor McGeorge sternly addressed me:

"Guilty or not guilty?"

"Your Honor!" Ol Jones, graven of countenance but twinkling of eye, rose on his one good leg and swung his wooden limb into place. "I move that the complaint be quashed."

"Motion denied," snapped the mayor.

"Your Honor!" Jones solemnly read the necessary affidavit and presented the demand for a change of venue to permit trial before an unprejudiced judge.

"Change of venue is denied." The mayor's jaws clicked after the last syllable, as he quickly turned again to the defendant.

"Guilty or not guilty?"

"In that case, Your Honor," Jones calmly continued, "the defendant can take no further part in this procedure, which will clearly be unconstitutional and illegal."

"I want the purpose of this occasion understood by every-body," His Honor said, blandly addressing me, the lawyers, and the crowd, in a suddenly pleasant manner quite as though he were continuing a kindly conversation that had been interrupted.

"There is no desire here to persecute Mr. McMillen. That is not the idea at all. In his newspaper he has spoken flip-pantly of an ordinance of our municipality. According to the charge you have heard read, he has broken a city law and refused to obey a police officer. There is no wish on the part of this court to inflict a heavy penalty upon him, regard-less of the truth of these charges. We are merely holding a sort of court of inquiry, to find the facts, to determine, for his own good and for the public good, whether he maintains and asserts a malicious and disrespectful attitude towards the tokens of law and order."

Mayor Tom could talk like that, without a single col-loquialism, when he wanted to. Whether or not he had smelled the baited trap, plainly enough he sensed trouble. So, with a naïve hocus-pocus that was no less than spectacu-lar, he transformed a trial for misdemeanor into an entirely different form of legal procedure, a court of inquiry — a court of inquiry without the grand jury that Indiana required to conduct such a proceeding, and which belonged in a county court rather than in a mayor's jurisdiction. Nor was he yet through for one afternoon with performing legal legerdemain.

"Now, Charley," the calm magistrate directed, "tell us what happened."

Chief Lyons, under the questioning conducted by City Attorney Philpott, narrated in full detail the story of the occurrence on the bank corner. His testimony was corroborated by Ben Cox, the bank janitor, who while sunning himself in front of the building had seen and heard all that took place between the police officer and the editor.

"Mac, are these boys telling it straight?" asked the mayor, turning to me.

With equal informality I addressed the court. The mayor, having neatly stepped aside from the lariat that had been tossed, I had no reason to care what course the entertainment followed. "You understand, Tom, that we do not recognize this as a legal proceeding. I have no objection, however, to taking part in what appears to have become a friendly chat. Charley and Ben have given substantially accurate accounts of what happened."

"You made some rather sarcastic references in your paper last week. Do you approve of this ordinance?"

"I do not approve of that part of the ordinance that restricts the uses of the streets by pedestrians. Make the motorists observe reasonable precautions while in motion and people on foot will be able to look out for themselves in all the traffic we have here. However, I do believe that as long as you keep the provision on the books and as long as the officials try to enforce it, a citizen should be willing to obey it."

"You have admitted that you didn't obey," declared His Honor with suddenly renewed grimness. Once more waving his magisterial wand he vanished the statutes of Indiana and closed his "court of inquiry" with a verdict — another phenomenal performance since a court of inquiry is supposed merely to determine and report facts. "Then you're

guilty. The court finds you guilty of the charge as preferred. As I said, there is no desire to inflict a severe punishment. The court sentences you to apologize to Officer
Lyons."

There was a gasp of amazement amongst the spectators,
including several lawyers who had come in to see the show,
over this remarkable sequence of judicial actions. The defendant and his attorneys put their heads together for a
quick consultation. Jones and Ratcliff agreed with their
client that it would spoil a very pleasant afternoon to decline an offer so magnanimous as the privilege of making
apology to Charley Lyons, especially as no previous expression had indicated that the officer, or anyone else, had suspected that the chief was the individual offended. The warrant had specified that the city had been damaged, but had
said nothing at all about the feelings of the officer. I therefore rose, waited until complete silence blanketed the room,
then delivered the most oracular apology I could extem-
porize:

"Officer Lyons, no disrespect to the majesty of the statutes
of this magnificent municipality, as they are incarnate in
you, nor any affront to the dignity of your uniformed person,
is excusable within the boundaries of this corporation, nor
at the intersections of its streets. Had my auricular senses
reported your objurgations, I should most assuredly have
deviated from my illegal course. I most sincerely deprecate
any humiliation, any . . ."

At this point the risibilities of Attorney Jones could stand
the strain no longer. The sight of the blank and puzzled
face of Officer Lyons, who stood stiffly at attention while
being mystified by my stream of apologetic polysyllables, was
too much for Ol. His guffaw rang through the room, and
was joined by a full chorus of roaring laughter from the
crowd.

Officer Lyons' face relaxed and was wreathed in smiles
as he shouted, "Whatever it was you said, Mac, it's all right!"

Mayor McGeorge's gavel crashed down on the table. The
veins were swelling in his neck and purple ire blazed in his
countenance for one moment: and then he barked, "Case
is dismissed!"

The sequelae of the trial were less dramatic. Officer Lyons, deciding after all that he had been offended, but by the mayor rather than by the editor, resigned his position and turned in his badge.

Thomas H. McGeorge, Jr., in his capacity as a merchant of farm implements and vehicles, came to the *Republican* office the next week with an order for two thousand full page circulars plus a full page advertisement in the paper, and lingered for a half hour to chat over various matters of local business interest; thereby conveying plainly that he was not a man to let a political dispute or a momentary rage stand in the way of healthy business relations and pleasant personal friendship. The printing and advertising orders were extremely welcome. The business struggle had been growing more and more uncomfortable.

14

Tight Squeezes

"THIS JOB," I wrote to a friend one day, "is a constant succession of financial crises, fiscal emergencies, pecuniary exigencies, and other bad fixes of a monetary nature."

The business habits of Covington ranged from easy-going to lackadaisical. "Here it is, come and get it if you want it," most of the shopkeepers seemed to say under their breaths to a world in general and to no one in particular. High pressure salesmanship did not exist nor did high pressure collection methods. Credit to almost anyone who said "Charge this!" was the rule, and no businessman, unless he were in desperate need of cash, ever hurried those who were "slow pay." It was not customary, and he feared to lose even a slow-paying patron. A reasonable percentage of credit losses was accepted as one of the inconveniences of being in business. Accounts were commonly permitted to run for the full year, the last week of the annum being the customary time for settlements. Then the plumber would present his account to the grocer, who would bring out his charges against the plumber. The larger debtor was expected to give a check for his balance. If he could not, the amount was entered against him as of January 1, and an effort would be made to work or trade back to an even position. This process would be followed all around the business community. Farmers, laborers, and others were counted upon to pay in enough cash for day by day requirements.

As a salesman of advertising I was not aggressive nor highly persuasive. Much as I enjoyed meeting my fellow businessmen I was reluctant to press them hard to buy the space on whose sale my success depended. The job printing department lacked equipment and skill to produce superior work, for which Covington had no demand, so prices had to be competitive on the low scale which prevailed. I found it difficult to estimate costs on other than standard jobs. The job printing accomplished no more than to help bring in a little cash to pay wages and overhead.

The subscription list grew slowly. The actual cash-paying circulation, I had found, was not one thousand but fewer than eight hundred. Merchants who advertised and some who did not received free copies. A lengthy list of township and county officials and lawyers who placed legal notices expected their subscriptions to be complimentary. Various others whose names appeared on the mailing list as delinquents were prompt to protest, when bills for arrears were sent, that Clifton had given them the paper for some past favor and that they had never been cash subscribers.

A quiet, well-dressed stranger came by one day. He offered to check all delinquents in the county and to collect from those actually indebted. He went out Monday mornings for the week. For three Saturday afternoons he returned and meticulously reported his calls, his failures and his collections. He turned in forty to sixty dollars each time. On the fourth Saturday he did not return, nor did he ever show up again. In time a few of the receipts he had signed were exhibited to me, enough to indicate that he had absconded with some collections. How much I never knew, but it could have been no great amount.

I had no automobile. Even if I had owned one not much time could have been spared for selling subscriptions. Such agents as had been persuaded to try had not worked steadily. Yet I was convinced that a much larger circulation could be obtained. The paper was not yet as good as I thought I could make it, but it was doing a fair job of covering the county's news, and I was sure it had a bit more sparkle than other local weeklies in the area.

While I was looking for ways to build up the list, along early in the second year a businesslike young stranger came in with a proposal. Did I want an extra thousand subscribers? It was simple. Run a contest. Put up an automobile for first prize, add a few other prizes, and soon a lot of people would be out hustling for subscriptions. The young man's name was Reynolds. He produced evidence as to results his contests had produced elsewhere, evidence which I verified by correspondence. He was employed by a company which made a business of such contests, and if I accepted his proposal was to manage the contest himself. His company was to receive some percentage of the cash receipts above the cost of the prizes.

I liked Reynolds. He looked and talked like a square-shooter. Despite my first issue's pronouncement against circulation gimmicks, I felt that the *Republican* needed one.

"But," I protested, "I haven't enough cash to buy the prize automobile."

"We can get terms on the car," he assured me, "and a cut in the price in return for the advertising it will get."

So we signed an agreement, and Reynolds went to work. Before long he had a reasonably good list of entrants, and subscriptions began to roll in. We bought the automobile, a 1915 Maxwell touring car, and used it to stimulate the eagerness of the contestants, as well as for occasional Sunday pleasure trips.

By the end of the eight weeks' contest period the leading entrants were working frantically. One or two late starters began to loom up formidably. Each week, of course, standings were published. Leaders considered holding back some of their orders until the end, and some did so. As the deadline hour approached on the last night one young farmer stood at the office counter filling out subscription order blanks, writing checks, consulting his bank balance, wondering whether to gamble a few more five-year gift subscriptions. I am sure all his relatives and friends received the paper long after their interest in Covington news, if they had any, had been fully satisfied. I grew uneasy as I watched him, and kept open a vigilant eye to detect any possible collusion with the contest manager. I wanted no unpleasant repercussions afterwards. There was no collusion, I was fully satisfied, but the young fellow won the Maxwell. I had not anticipated the likelihood that the top prize might go to someone who would give away as

well as sell subscriptions. Fortunately, the other winners
did not protest and appeared to be happy with their prizes.

The contest doubled the circulation. The cash returns
paid for the car and other prizes; Reynolds appeared to be
pleased with his share. I had cash to make another payment
on the paper, and to pay off obligations, but not much more.
However, I had collected in advance a substantial propor-
tion of normal subscription revenue for two or more years
in the future; besides, I was obligated to buy twice as much
paper and print twice as many papers. If the contest was
a "success" it was also a failure unless I could sell additional
advertising at higher rates. And that I did not do. The net,
I eventually discovered, was that I had had another experience, with some gain in that at least the paper was reaching
more people.

Setting the type for an issue of the *Republican*, small as
the six-column, eight-page sheet seemed, was a major task.
The compositor had to reach into his case for each letter,
place the letter in the "stick," then reach for another. A
single column of type contained about five thousand letters,
punctuation marks, and spaces, so that an issue with twenty
or more columns of home-set news matter meant reaching
into the type-case upwards of a hundred thousand different
times. Then after the paper was off the press, the type had
to be replaced letter by letter before another week's composition could begin. From two to five typesetters were employed to do this work.

The idea of owning a linotype had sounded like too expensive a luxury to contemplate. I was surprised when a
salesman came along one day and offered to sell a machine
and accept, in monthly payments, less than my payroll had
been for typesetting alone. He made a sale, and the magical
machine that cast its own type in entire lines proved to be
a genuine economy. I undertook to master its workings so
as not to be helplessly dependent upon a machinist, and
before long was able to manipulate the keys at a fair speed,
as well as to solve such mechanical mysteries as presented
themselves.

A few trying experiences intervened. I had learned how
to heat the metal to the right temperature and to keep the

casting mechanism working until, while rushed late one night, the machine's initial good behavior was interrupted. Instead of casting the usual neat line it squirted hot metal in various undesirable directions. For a half hour I patiently cleaned up the mess and tried again. Another splatter resulted. When that had been cleaned up I went home to sleep, hoping that when the metal had cooled and been reheated the work could proceed. The morning brought no better results. A desperate search through the manual disclosed no clue. A frantic telephone call for the salesman-mechanic who had installed the linotype found him in Cincinnati. He instructed me to move one small lever and try again, while he held the phone. That was the answer, and we had no more trouble.

Bill, the foreman, soon learned to run the machine. However, it was so easy to use the linotype keyboard in place of the typewriter that I found myself turning notes and ideas directly into type. Thereafter Bill and I kept the shop running without additional help.

But even that was not economy enough.

Usually local accounts were kept paid. It seemed important to maintain a reputation for meeting obligations as they came due. With the urgent need for immediate working capital, I had instituted the custom of presenting monthly bills, and of collecting as closely as was possible. When business was reasonably good, outside obligations were met as they came up. The small cash balance I foolishly undertook, at first, to divide between the Citizens Bank and the First National Bank. Although the amount was too small to provide a profitable account for either bank, I felt that as a new man I ought not to show partiality.

I knew that a good businessman always took his discounts. A paper bill came along that was quite a bit larger than the supply of funds to meet it. Reasoning that the bill was for several months' supply of paper, and that the discount should be saved, I borrowed a hundred dollars from the First National Bank. When the ninety-day period of the note expired, I told the cashier that I would like to pay fifty dollars and renew the balance for another ninety days.

"You don't need to pay any of it now if you need the money," the cashier said.

Immediate uses for the fifty dollars were plentiful, and I was then confident of the future, so I not only renewed the note for a hundred dollars, but accepted the cashier's pleasant proposal to make the total a hundred and twenty-five. When the next three months had flown the note was again renewed, and perhaps still once again. Then a day came when the cashier referred me to the president of the bank about a further renewal.

"We always take care of our own customers," the president said brusquely. "Now, I notice some of your checks on the Citizens Bank have been presented here. We want all your business. Bring your entire account here, and I will renew this note. Otherwise, I'll ask you to pay it."

I walked out with a promise to return in the afternoon. Perhaps the demand was good banking business, but it felt like coercion. I liked the people at the Citizens Bank better. But what could I do? I didn't have the hundred and twenty-five dollars, and had no exact idea as to when I would have it. I already owed the Citizens Bank a larger amount, which they had obligingly lent and renewed from time to time. I went in to see Worth Reed, the president of the other bank, and reported the facts.

"Just now I can pay neither him, nor you. I am telling you this not as a banker, but as a friend whose judgment I respect. How shall I handle the matter?"

From our first meeting I had taken a liking to Worth Reed, who was quite unlike the traditional country banker. Reed was, in fact, not a banker originally. After thirty years or more as a school teacher he had inherited control of the Citizens Bank from his uncle, its founder. Nevertheless he understood thoroughly the requirements of sound banking and operated the institution successfully.

"How much did you say you owed the other bank?" Mr. Reed inquired.

"A hundred and twenty-five."

"And how much do you owe us, you say?"

"Two hundred and fifteen."

Reed pulled the ends of his mustache. After gazing for a period out over the courthouse square, he took a pad of blank notes from a pigeonhole of his rolltop desk and filled in the date.

"Do you owe anything else to anybody?"

"Nothing pressing, Mr. Reed, except forty or fifty dollars in small bills for supplies."

"Hunh! Well, you ought to have a little to turn around with."

With Spencerian flourishes Reed made out a note for two hundred dollars and pushed the pad over in front of me.

"There!" he said. "Sign on the dotted line."

"But Mr. Reed! The way things look just now my name on this note isn't worth a damn. Not that I don't appreciate ——"

"Sign on that line," the banker interrupted curtly.

I took the pen and wrote my name as directed. Worth Reed pulled the note over and with a bold flourish placed his signature on the lower line.

"I guess that'll make it good with the bank," he remarked drily. "Now, go pay that son-of-a-gun his hundred and twenty-five dollars!" Then, softly, he added:

"We need young fellows like you in this town."

The name of Worth Reed was forever blessed in the mind of the young man who heard those words at a moment when Covington seemed full of worries and scant of sympathy; a friendship was sealed that was to endure.

"He didn't even ask me to close out my First National account," I reflected on the sidewalk. I hurried over to pay off the note and to transfer what remained of my balance to the Citizens Bank. To my amazement, the First National's president came to the *Republican* office the next week to order a series of advertisements, and long remained a friendly customer.

Not every uncomfortable situation was solved quite so agreeably, although by stretching dollars to the limit, paying the few that could be found whenever demands became insistent, I managed to keep creditors convinced that I was honestly intent upon paying every just bill.

Once an unjust claim was presented. The bill, for $53.67,

was received in the mail from a Covington man with whom I had done some business which had terminated in a misunderstanding. I had considered the matter fairly and decently closed. The claimant by a tortuous course of reasoning, arrived at the conclusion that the $53.67 was still due him. His bill was ignored, as were two or three subsequent duns. Finally the claimant's affable red-faced lawyer, who was later disbarred, brought the bill in one day and demanded a payment. He threatened suit. I pronounced the claim fraudulent and refused to discuss the matter further.

Nevertheless, I was badly worried. A suit against me would for many reasons be embarrassing, even though I were victorious as I felt I would be. I had never been sued, and was not emancipated from the opinion that participation in litigation was not wholly righteous, no matter how innocent one might be. I even thought seriously of paying the claim as the cheapest and simplest way to close the controversy. Reflection dissuaded me from doing that; I would, I thought, then always curse myself for being bluffed into a cowardly act.

"I'll be in to see you once more Monday morning," the lawyer announced one Saturday. "Blank says to give you that much more chance — if you don't pay then, I am directed to file suit."

A carpenter who was making a small repair in the *Republican* office, and who at the moment had been out of sight behind a cabinet, overheard the lawyer's threat. After the door had closed he stood up and said, "Is that pious old Methodist hypocrite Blank up to his old tricks?"

"I guess he is, if this is an old trick." The carpenter was a trustworthy friend to whom the situation could be sketched.

"The old skunk! He would try to put something like that over." Removing his nail apron, the carpenter hung it over the back of a chair and started toward his home. In a few minutes he returned and handed me an old letter.

"I done some work for him in his back office a few years ago," the carpenter explained. "I found this here letter in a funny place, back behind some things where it wouldn't have fallen, but had to be *put*. I expect he was in there readin' it and somebody come in, maybe his wife, so he had to get it out of sight quick, and then he must 'a' forgot it.

"Anyway, I had to read it, and I says to myself, why, that old coot! Passin' the plate in church every Sunday, too! And I just thought to myself, by gol, this'll come in handy some day, so I took it home and put it away. Maybe it'll help you shut him up."

I read the letter. The fervid contents were illuminating, especially in view of its recipient's local reputation as a pillar of respectability. The gentleman was supposed to be a close dealer, and not above taking a little undue advantage in money matters. That he was also a Romeo was a revelation.

The ethical advisability of using such a letter to terminate the unjust claim against me was debated over the weekend. Ordinarily, I reflected, to use such a weapon would be little other than blackmail. Was I even justified in possessing the missive? Neither I nor the carpenter who had given it to me had any right to it.

By Monday morning I reached the decision that here was one instance where two wrongs would make a right. When the lawyer stepped into the office I had just tapped out the last lines of the letter on my typewriter, with several carbon copies.

"My client wants to know what you're going to do about that bill," the attorney said.

I handed the bottom carbon to the lawyer.

"Ask your client what he wants to do about this letter! Here is the original, if he wants to see it."

The legal gentleman glanced hastily over the letter, laughed, and walked away without a word. The text of the letter, written from Indianapolis, was:

Sat. 3.30 P.M.

My Dear Sweetheart:
Rec'd yours of yesterday this A.M. Glad to get, dear, though it brought me disappointment. I had no reason to feel sure you would be here this eve, yet I did. Oh, I want to see you so badly, dear, I am almost crazy.

Now you think me foolish, perhaps. Oh, well, I am only a "kid" in some things. Have worked so hard, I know but one thing, that is, I am a very tired little woman. You, darling, are much worse off than I, in that work is not with me an absolute necessity. It is with you. That makes it so much harder. However, I could not be content without some thing to do. Am not built to sit around with hands folded. (some one at door). Why do not women who have nothing to do stay away from those who have. Both of us will I am sure feel a whole lot better after we have had a visit together. What sweet ones we have had. I, too, live them over many times. A sweet, beautiful picture, memory presents, makes me more anxious, more impatient, for a repetition. Know, darling, you must be tired and need a *good rest.* You shall have it, too, when you come. I am just waiting. Pet grows more and more restless, wants her stick of candy. You must come and bring it, soon.

Trip to Seymour Monday called off, and I am glad, but I will spend Sunday night with mother as planned. Now you are not coming this evening I will go to Columbus at 5 P.M. returning tomorrow (Sunday) evening. Will look for letter Monday A.M. Hope you have no harder, no more unpleasant task for Sunday than writing me.

Sorry Mrs. is sick; that adds to your burden, of course. Wish conditions were such I could help you in your work. Believe I could be really a help. What a great pleasure it is to do for those we love and who we know appreciates our efforts. What is there I wouldn't do for you? I study your wishes, your pleasure, and try to govern my actions accordingly.

You do not say how you feel, still getting better I hope. Can "She and He" be too "good?" I think not. You cannot wish more ardently to be here than I do to have you. The last time I felt I had entered into the portals of heaven — the pleasure so exquisite — what could be sweeter when love prompts all? Nothing!

Returned from Terre Haute 9 P.M. last evening

pretty well tired out; to bed 11,30, up this A.M. 5,30, have done a lot of work, had several callers, and now in fine condition for a rest if only *you* were here.

In your letter Sunday tell me all about your dear self, your sorrows as well as your joys. You seem to be a little blue. Can I help you in any way, dear? Come soon as possible, but I know you will do that. Must close for this time, finish some work on hand, and that must get out before I leave.

Do not ever feel that you are entirely forsaken, that no one cares, etc. A little woman who lives in a big City cares. But darling, must say Goodbye. God bless you, sweetheart, is the prayer of —— with love and kisses ——

Neither the lawyer nor his client ever again mentioned the $53.67. Nor, curiously enough, was any effort made to recover the original of the letter.

On one other occasion the force of the law was invoked to compel the payment of an account, this time one whose validity I could not dispute. By the terms of the purchase, I was to pay $500 on the first of each July and January, until the complete price was discharged, with interest at seven per cent on the deferred amounts. Never had I imagined that Januarys and Julys could crowd the calendar so closely. No sooner was one $500 note taken up than I had to begin working desperately for fear I would be unable to meet the next one. I had been saved on occasion by the receipt of additional generous help from the hard won proceeds of the home farm in Ohio, from where Father kept an interested eye on my progress. Eventually there came a January when the $500 was not ready. Having a reasonable expectation of being able to raise the money in a few weeks, and feeling that the parental kindness ought not to be imposed upon further, I kept the facts to myself and desperately tried to hurry the accumulation of the necessary sum. When this $500 would be paid, and one more installment the following July, the mortgage would be discharged in full.

Except for an occasional reminder from the bank, which

had the note for collection, no pressure had been felt. I had no doubt that I would be given time to find the money. Payments of sums due were exasperatingly deferred. A slump in the business volume piled up greater difficulties. A large legal publication that had been promised failed to materialize. Then one day the blow fell.

"Something over here I think you ought to see," the county clerk, Homer McKinney, said on the telephone. "Come over right now."

"Over there on my desk," McKinney said with a nod, when I arrived to find the clerk busily engaged with other callers. On the desk I saw a yellow-jacketed legal paper on which was typed:

THOMAS A. CLIFTON ET AL.

vs.

WHEELER McMILLEN

— — — — — — — — — — — —

Foreclosure of Chattel Mortgage

I sat down and, through half blinded eyes, read the thing through. In the dry verbosity of legal phrases it meant that I had to get that $500, and get it quick, or the mortgage on my newspaper and plant would be foreclosed, and I would lose the business and all the money that already had been paid. The injustice of that rankled, and I inwardly cursed Clifton, though reason insisted that the man was entitled to his money and I knew that probably Clifton needed it. I sat looking at the blank wall. Where to turn I had no idea, but one thing was sure — that mortgage must not be foreclosed; if I could avoid it, even the fact that I had been sued must not be spread upon the records to be advertised to the public. Shortly I heard the clerk's callers depart, and turned to find the sympathetic McKinney looking at me. An idea formed.

"Homer, has this thing been entered on the docket, yet?"

"Not yet. I haven't had time. I called you the minute they left."

"Homer, you have to go over to the post office after the mail, don't you?"

"Why, I guess it's about time."

Probably the clerk suspected my design, but his countenance revealed nothing except anxiety to go over and get his mail. I waited until I saw Homer enter the courthouse yard on his way back from the post office. Then, putting the yellow legal document in my inside coat pocket, I walked out and headed toward my own office. My bowels quivered and hung heavy from their diaphragm.

Taking the document out of the courthouse did not disturb me. I knew that McKinney would not worry about its disappearance, for if worst came to worst, the clerk knew that it would be returned in time for entry on the big leather book, one of the kind that cost sixty dollars. The abstraction relieved the clerk of the obligation to make the entry at once, as he was normally supposed to do. If he couldn't find it, he couldn't enter it, yet he knew it would be "found" before any embarrassment could be caused by the delay in entry. The problem of getting the $500 and of saving the paper was acute. Something had to be done and done quickly. Yet there seemed to be nothing that could be done.

Back in the office, I listlessly straightened up the counter and desk to give my hands occupation while racking my brain to think up some scheme of earning, collecting, or borrowing the necessary sum. Nothing that I could think of seemed to be practicable. As the day passed the outlook appeared more and more hopeless. Every way out that could be imagined was checked and rejected. That night an ordinarily sound sleeper tossed in his bed, unhappy and awake, until nearly dawn.

The next forenoon my father-in-law dropped into the office on one of his social visits, infrequent because we saw each other daily on the street.

"The girl says you didn't sleep very well last night," he remarked cheerfully.

"Not very. I usually sleep pretty soundly, too."

"I just wondered if you might be worried about something."

I admitted that I had been trying to solve a little problem. Questioned, I stated the facts.

"Well, for God's sake, why didn't you come and tell me? Fellow paid off a note last week, and I've got some money that's not working. You might as well have it as some one else — I can watch you, and some of these fellows that borrow money are hard to keep an eye on."

I tried helplessly to express my thanks and relief, but my words were brushed aside. "Don't bother about that," Mr. Doane said brusquely. "What in hell is a father-in-law good for if he can't help a fellow out?"

So that problem was solved, temporarily. The Clifton mortgage was paid off in full, and new notes made out to Mr. Doane for the amount advanced. I retained the legal paper from the clerk's office as a souvenir. The debt remained, but at least it was in the generous and tolerant hands of a gentleman who delighted in secret kindnesses. Gratitude was added to the high respect I already had for my new creditor who was eventually paid in full.

15

Covington's World War I

EUROPE WAS a tremendous distance from Covington in the spring of 1914 when the orioles began to weave their hanging nests on the endmost twigs of the elm branches. Events that were transpiring in England and France and Germany might as well have taken place a century or so before, for all the county seat cared. The sense of geographical remoteness was just as vague. George Washington and Lloyd George were about equidistant. Only Morris Herzog was a cosmopolitan; he had made voyages to visit relatives in Germany, and may have paused once in Paris. A teacher in the high school, Verna Glascock, had toured England and the continent. Most of the people had as much expectation of sometime taking part in the War of 1812 as they had of ever crossing the Atlantic Ocean. Europe was so remote that whatever happened over there was too far away to be important or even interesting. It just didn't matter.

When the orioles spread their wings to go south that autumn, Europe had moved measurably closer to Covington — and was still comfortably far away. The impact of armies in Belgium was heard, though dimly. The Indianapolis and Danville newspapers were filled with war news — news of places and names that Covington could not pronounce and had never suspected of existing. People were heard sometimes to say that they wished the war would end, so that the newspapers would again print something interesting, by which they meant events that occurred in places they knew about.

Covingtonians were not sailors, nor ship owners, nor were they consciously engaged in any form of foreign trade. The war in Europe seemed to be no concern of theirs, except that prices were showing signs of rising. Only Herzog or Julius Loeb, and maybe a family or two of recent English origin, had relatives abroad.

"Do you think the United States will get into the war?" was a casual question sometimes heard. The answer was always negative. Why should our country cross the Atlantic to mix up with so insane a conflict, for which no reason could be perceived except the Kaiser's ambition to rule the world?

"What are they fighting for?" No one was able to offer any explanation other than resistance to the German militarists. The bloodshed and the suffering were deprecated. One who lived in Covington was sorry that people over there were killing each other. But, if they wanted to fight, let them fight.

Strictly devoted to events and ideas purely of local interest, the *Republican* carried no war news. That was left to the city dailies. Only now and then did an editorial reference to the war appear to suggest that Fountain County was becoming increasingly conscious of Europe's closer approach.

A movement is on foot for the establishment of a military battalion at Indiana University. Europe is today furnishing argument enough against any further steps towards militarism in this country. Indiana has been famous for its statesmen, its literary and industrial giants. It has done its part in the nation's wars. The establishment of a military course in our state university is on a plane with a movement to restore Jesse James and negro slavery.

The community may not have agreed with me on that point. Fathers and grandfathers had engaged in the Mexican and Civil Wars; warfare was accepted as glorious and noble. The school books said it was. Training to bear arms

would probably have been endorsed by most of the people.
In May, 1915, I probably did express the prevailing sentiment:

> The American public would commit a grave crime to
> urge upon President Wilson war between this nation
> and Germany . . . But what would be gained by sacri-
> ficing millions of our young men and billions of our
> dollars in an effort to avenge the Lusitania's dead? . . .
> Fighting does not convince anyone, though it may shut
> them up.

Three months later a news item revealed that the carnage
of the battlefields was bringing new money into the community. Since the Europeans were fools enough to squander
their substance in fighting, there seemed to be no reason why
we should not take their cash. This article may have been
the first intimation to former owners of the eventual destina-
tion of the horses for which buyers were bidding higher and
higher prices:

> More than $150,000, according to men who know,
> has passed thru Covington into the hands of farmers
> and horse owners in surrounding territory in exchange
> for horses to go to the European war. Next to Dan-
> ville, this city is the largest horse center for several
> counties around. Farmer McMahon, P. J. McMahon
> and Charles Shepherd here have been buying horses for
> export for more than a year, and hundreds of horses
> purchased by smaller buyers in five counties come into
> Covington to the larger firm. The local men have pur-
> chased more than a thousand horses since the beginning
> of the war. The animals are shipped out rapidly, and
> the European demand is growing rather than decreas-
> ing. Their average life on the battlefield, according to
> reports, is from three to ten days.

As the war in Europe continued, the possibility that the
United States might become involved became more apparent
to Covington. The "outrages" upon American shipping, es-

pecially when committed by the Germans, were increasingly
resented. The Allied propaganda about the "Huns" bayo-
neting babies and raping women began to take hold. The
blood of ambitious youth began to stir at the waving of
distant flags and the tattoo of far away drums. One fine
young man, George Coffing, made his way to Canada, enlisted in the British air forces, and was killed in a crash at
an air school in Scotland. The Atlantic grew narrower.

Prices of farm products increased. Jobs became more
abundant in the cities, and the drain of youth to the industrial centers was accelerated by the manufacture of war
materials for the Allies. A Cleveland brick yard advertised
in the *Republican* for laborers at $3 to $3.65 a day, rail fare
returned after ninety days work — big wages for boys from
a ten-dollar-a-week town.

The election of 1916 came. Woodrow Wilson "kept us
out of war" and won votes in Fountain County as a result of
the slogan. No source of information that trickled into
Covington revealed that Wilson knew we were doomed to
be swept into the European maelstrom. Wilson was inaugurated. Then, suddenly, with little more warning than
a submarine could give, the terrific news came that the
United States had declared war against Germany.

The act was instantly applauded. Those few who did not
approve kept silent and quietly or otherwise determined to
do their full shares toward the victory. Our country, right
or wrong, was a sentiment unanimous. Besides, the Kaiser
and his inhuman Germans had to be stopped. One who had
no other comprehension of the issues at stake could readily
believe that if the Huns were not defeated in Europe, they
would sweep across the ocean that once seemed so wide and
attempt to conquer the western hemisphere. Covington was
convinced that the picture of the German as a destroying
fiend was correct. Well, our American soldiers were the
boys to put a finish to Germany; it wouldn't take long when
we got in.

One warm Thursday night in April, 1917, the county's
leading men came quietly to a meeting in the courtroom.
After it adjourned I walked thoughtfully back to the office.
The paper was nearly all made up for the press next morn-

ing. I lighted the gas to heat the metal in the linotype pot, and moved half the type from the front to inside pages. With the biggest type in stock I set a headline that crossed the whole top of page one:

FOUNTAIN COUNTY MEN, IN SPIRIT OF 1776,
PREPARE TO HELP MEET NATION'S NEED
FOR FOOD WHILE WAR LASTS

The metal was hot. I placed a magazine of twelve-point type, a large size, in the machine and sat down before the keyboard. Before I left the office at midnight a new front page was ready for the press.

There was less than ten dollars' worth of commercial advertising in the issue. I made up my mind as I walked home to list the paper for immediate sale, hoping to be able to enter the first officers' training camp at Fort Benjamin Harrison.

In double columns twelve-point, the front page told the story of Fountain County's first warlike move:

No bands were playing. No men in brilliant uniform were marching to the thrilling tones of fife and drum. No magnetic orators were stirring souls with impassioned voices and eloquent phrases. No vast multitudes were cheering.

There was merely a meeting of some 175 Fountain County farmers and businessmen, with perhaps not more than a dozen curiosity seekers besides. There was some matter of fact discussion of a few practical matters. That was all.

Yet in its nearly a century of history, this county has witnessed few more deeply significant meetings that this sober gathering of farmers and businessmen in the courthouse Thursday night, come upon short notice from the eleven townships of the county, upon the call of the Governor of the State, to plan their part in the momentous world conflict into which our nation has deliberately entered.

The United States, our country, to battle for the principles of humanity and justice, and, too, for its own honor, has crossed from the happy and prosperous plains of peace over a Rubicon into the sulphurous craterland of war. There is now no turning back.

. . . .

There was no mad waving of the spangled banner, no solemn hush of impending doom. In the characteristic Hoosier business manner, committees were appointed and methods were discussed.

The object of the meeting was quickly outlined after County Agent Rosencrans had called the body to order, when Walter M. Moore, manager of the Covington Grain Company, read the letter from Governor Goodrich.

. . . .

Said the Governor: "The man who grows our food is no less a patriot than the man who shoulders a gun."

The talks were brief, spirited, practical, prophetic of what Fountain County will do.

Among the speakers were Mayor T. H. McGeorge, C. E. McClure, V. E. Livengood, Harry Glascock, William Madigan, and Worth Reed. Mr. Reed said, "A man can be a patriot in the corn field as well as on the battlefield; in a ditch on a farm as well as the first line of trenches."

A committee, the members of which were C. E. McClure, M. F. Livengood, Dan W. Carpenter and George McMurtie, was appointed to define a course of action and to name a community leader. Their report appears on this page.

Manford Livengood, county superintendent of the schools, Tuesday received authority from State Superintendent Ellis to announce that high school boys who left school now to take employment on farms will receive all credits towards graduations the same as if they remained in school. The view is held that in this year of the nation's need every hand possible will be needed in the armies, in the munitions plants, and on the farms.

J. W. Harrison, president of the Attica National Car Coupler Company, who repeatedly refused munitions contracts from European nations, will manufacture munition products for the United States, and the Attica high school boys who take employment in his factory will receive the school credits for their work there.

In the endeavor to increase the production of Fountain County, the first problem that confronts the farmer is the question of obtaining adequate labor to handle the farm work. This difficulty in a measure will be solved by the activities of the office of County Agent Rosencrans, who will have a list of all the boys and men he can obtain out of the schools and elsewhere who will be available for farm work. No effort will be spared to carry through to a successful finish Fountain County's determination.

The 5-acre corn contests will be used with more energy than ever in stimulating corn yields. This work is already very well under way.

The greater food production movement is sweeping the county with enthusiasm. A lively meeting was held at Attica last night. Every vacant lot there will be farmed this summer. The Commercial Club is taking hold with a vim. Newtown tonight will devote its Community Club's meeting to this topic. At Veedersburg Monday night the tabernacle will be turned over for a monster mass meeting of the community.

In Covington the City Beautiful movement, which was already under way, will be swung into cooperation by its leading workers.

"England expects every man to do his duty," Lord Nelson told his men at Trafalgar in 1805 as they went into the famous battle that annihilated the French and Spanish fleets. So, today, Uncle Sam expects every citizen to do his duty.

FOUNTAIN COUNTY WILL GIVE GOOD MEASURE!

The entrance of the United States into the conflict wrought no quick transformation in Covington. The issue of the *Republican* that carried the grandiose account of the county's first war meeting also contained the explanation of Zeke Evans, the barber, as to why he charged the full price of twenty-five cents for cutting the hair of Vawt Livengood, the baldest member of the bar. "Tain't for cuttin' his hair," Zeke had said, "it's for huntin' for his hair." The people were well aware that they would be called upon to play a part. Some of their boys would enlist in the army. Taxes of course would be raised. There was no question about the willingness to do whatever was required. But such things were arranged in Washington, and in Indianapolis, just as this meeting had been called by Governor Goodrich. In the meantime, the life in town was to follow the usual routine of work and rest, with moments of fun interspersed.

Europe was no longer four thousand miles and a hundred years away from Covington when the orioles began weaving the 1917 nests. The hale young single men began wondering how they would look in uniform, how they would feel crouching in a trench to shoot at Germans. Mothers and fathers of eligible cannon fodder suffered flashes of discomfort at the battlefield headlines.

Down in Washington the President and Congress were talking about a law that would reach into Covington as no federal law had ever done before. "Selective conscription" they called it. The draft! Washington was no longer just a place where the President lived and the postage stamps were printed. The draft law idea was repugnant, at first; it seemed to mean that no one could avoid going into the army. Then realization dawned that a draft law with teeth might be just as well; the sons of the rich and powerful would have to go to war just the same as the sons of the farmers and merchants of Covington. The people wanted first to be assured that the draft was going to be fair.

"We favor selective conscription if that is what it is. But we do not propose blindly to endorse any law," the *Republican* said.

The enthusiasm for food production brought the "farm-

erette" craze down upon the country as one of the by-prod-
ucts of war. The contempt of a countryman for the spurious
dress-ups of the metropolitan press had to be expressed:

> Almost any society chick who can get in front of a
> camera with a hoe in her hand can get her picture in
> the city papers these days. She doesn't even have to be
> pretty. We would like to get some of these city folks
> out here in Fountain County, where we could show
> them some real women farmers — girls who are driving
> teams to plows and planters, not to get their pictures in
> the papers but to get the corn in. We would like to
> take these imitation folks out east of town where the
> other day Mrs. Ray Keefer was driving a big team and
> planting rows so straight that a cyclone wouldn't warp
> them. We would like to take these metropolitan made-
> moiselles up into Shawnee township where the Galloway
> girls rode the plow this spring.

An early June issue reprinted — by request — a letter to
the editor from Covington's most prominent German citizen,
Morris Herzog. The letter, breathing patriotic fervor for
the land of his adoption, had originally been printed in February when the shrewd Morris foresaw that the severance of
diplomatic relations with Germany was prelude to war;
Germany was his fatherland he said, but, "coming to this
land of promise when a mere youth, I am, perhaps, pecul-
iarly fitted to appreciate patriotism in its truest sense. I hope
that war with Germany may yet be avoided, but in the event
that it is inevitable, my allegiance, my sympathy, and my
assistance are pledged to the country that I have long known
as my home. . . . Nine times have I crossed the ocean, but
each experience has served to strengthen the ties of my allegiance to my adopted country, and I have always returned
proud and happy to be a citizen of the United States, with
increased love for my country and for my flag."

Herzog's assertion was, perhaps, unnecessary. The neighborhood had no doubt of his loyalty. And the liberality
with which he supported every "drive" more than proved
his promise.

An interesting poster was printed in the same issue:

SWAT THE ROOSTER
June 18 to 23
ROOSTER WEEK!

3,000,000 dozen marketable eggs are spoiled every year in Indiana by Mr. Rooster.

Hens lay as well or better without the ROOSTER and it is a waste of feed to keep a useless ROOSTER

Pen Up the Rooster or Sell Him!
Remember, 2¢ Lb. Premium Paid for Roosters During Rooster Week

Show Your Patriotism! Produce Infertile Eggs!

SKIDOO THE ROOSTER

G. W. ROSENCRANS
County Agricultural Agent

The sequel appeared shortly afterwards:

The horrors of war were fetched home to Fountain County this week when thousands of widows were made as by a single sweep. In every barn yard there is deep mourning — and perhaps in some cases deep rejoicing, depending upon the esteem in which the deceased was held by his numerous wives. This is rooster week; though doubtless chanticleer thinks it is no time for a rooster to be around. A Veedersburg poultry house reported at Wednesday noon that up to that hour from Monday morning they had slaughtered more than a thousand roosters.

By this time 206 names had been enrolled in the local Red Cross. The *Republican* printed the names each week as new members signed up. The pressure of social compulsion! Your name had to be on the list or you were — a new and ugly term that quickly caught on — a slacker. Two or three stubborn and contrary citizens, not unpatriotic but only resentful of being ballyhooed into line, got themselves talked about unpleasantly. Across the whole top of the front page, in eighteen-point type, was an appeal:

"THE RED CROSS on the Battlefields of Europe is the Emblem of Life to the Dying; of Health to the Sick; of Hope to the Hopeless. Next year Fountain County Boys, our own Flesh, will be Bleeding on those Battle Lines. Will you refuse the dollar that may bring your neighbors' and your Boys back sound and whole? The Red Cross Calls for $100,000,000 this week. Fountain County's Quota is $7,500. Send your check AT ONCE to Worth Reed, Treasurer."

The county raised not $7,500, but $10,000.

An unexpected happy by-product from the Red Cross effort was reported from a township across the Wabash in Vermillion County:

Under the flag of the Red Cross, the warring factions of Highland township joined hands Wednesday evening, after months of bitter enmity. Around $500 was realized for the Red Cross at the Orchard Inn, near Gessie, in an auction of goods donated by citizens of the township. It was estimated that 3,000 people attended.

Eugene and Perrysville have been centers of the Highland factions. The hostilities were opened when the new school building at Perrysville, one of the finest of its kind in the state, was proposed. Eugene objected to paying taxes for Perrysville's greater benefit, and Perrysville had no idea of letting Eugene have the building. The battle was waged persistently, nor did firing cease when the cornerstone of the handsome structure was laid.

But when the Red Cross banner was waved, the whole township fell in line and went to work. Perrysville led off. Now the township branch is the second largest in the county. . . .

Highland township folks are happy over having found something to agree upon, and predictions are made that amity and friendship once more will reign within their borders.

Other war news was good news:

J. E. (Bud) Stucker, who resides near Aylesworth, sold his rye crop last week to Ed Foster, the Aylesworth grain merchant, and it brought him an average of $54 an acre. A. T. Claypool in the same neighborhood did nearly as well, his rye crop having brought him an average of $50 an acre.

Registration day came for every male of military age. The county found 1,497 enrolled, 971 eligible for exemption.

Weeks before, the hotter blooded boys had begun to enlist in whatever fighting unit they could find. Two high school seniors ran away and found their way into a camp at Hattiesburg, Mississippi. Frederick Boord, son of the senator, carried on the military tradition of his Civil War veteran grandfather. Clyde Clawson joined the navy. Dr. Aldridge was soon in England, a captain. Many others did not wait for the draft.

"How to Knit Socks Sweaters and Wristlets for Soldiers" was the subject of a full column of directions that ran on and on: "Turn, slip 1, purl 5, purl 2 together, purl 1. Turn, slip 1, knit 6, slip 1, and pass it over slipped stitch, knit 1."

A boxed statement thereafter appeared every week:

The *Republican* wants the address of every soldier from this section who will be interested in the home news. They'll all be interested. It is our desire to send a paper to all the boys every week, free of charge, that every one of them may have a real letter from home weekly. All that is necessary is to furnish us the address. We'll do the rest.

My favorite "ear" — a boxed message at the right or left of the name of the paper — had long been "Why subscribe when you can borrow?" I claimed at least two families read every copy. Now the "ears" were given over to war slogans.

Mid-September found the front page nearly solid with local war news, if two divorce suits could be so classified. And there was big news:

Business will be suspended for an hour and a half here today while the entire county pays honor and bids farewell to the sixty men who will go on the 12.17 train to Camp Taylor at Louisville. The schools will be dismissed and the pupils will parade to the station with the soldiers, G.A.R., Red Cross and other organizations.

The sixty men gathered at the courthouse Thursday afternoon. At the roll call every man was found to be ready to go, so it is expected that the five alternates will not get away. . . . Apparently the great majority of the men were in good spirits, and all ready to prepare to exterminate the Hohenzollern dynasty.

The sixty names were printed in boldface capitals. Headlines:

PLAN TO PUSH NEXT LIBERTY BOND ISSUE

STATE RED CROSS FINDS FOUNTAIN COUNTY HARD AT WORK

WAR WORKERS ALL TO GATHER HERE TUESDAY WITH STATE COUNCIL OF DEFENSE

WHY UNCLE SAM ASKS FARMS FOR 10,000 ACRES OF WHEAT . . .

Many people wonder why the government urges a larger production of wheat in preference to corn and other foodstuffs. Wheat is the food staple of Europe. Europeans know nothing of corn. They have no mills in which to grind it. Corn meal will not keep for a long period, and even if it did, European soldiers would have to learn to use corn products.

Advice from Rosencrans told how to make the yields bigger.

A five-columns-wide photograph of the draft group and a three-column picture of the train departure graced the next week's front page. One of the boys who gaily climbed aboard was the first from the county to be buried in France.

He was "just a fellow around town," a laborer, whose comrades, when they came back, organized the Wilbur Fulton Post of the American Legion.

A letter from Clyde Clawson of the navy, from "somewhere in France," was sprinkled with repetitions of a new parenthetical phrase "(deleted by censor)."

The language of a full page advertisement, appealing to Liberty Bond subscribers, was less than moderate:

SEND OUR BOYS TO BERLIN AND BRING THEM HOME SOON

BUY A LIBERTY LOAN BOND — THE SAFEST INVESTMENT ON EARTH

Every Liberty Bond bought in Fountain County will HELP WIN THE WAR. It will help to conquer the outragers of Belgian women, to defeat the Hohenzollern system that left Belgian children to die, nailed to barn doors. The money you invest in Liberty Bonds will help to win a righteous war of the people of the USA, to make a world safe for our individual rights. Any man who says or believes that the 4 per cent Liberty Bonds issued by the U. S. Government will ever sell for less than par fails to believe in the integrity of his government and is talking for the Kaiser.

Belief or not, the bonds did in a few years "sell for less than par." The county quota, ten per cent of bank resources, was $335,000; $400,000 worth of bonds was subscribed.

A new "horror" of war to inhabitants of a valley of plenty astonished and disturbed the people:

SUGAR SCARCITY IS EYE OPENER HERE

A foretaste of what they may experience before many months with other commodities was experienced this week by Covington people, when, by reason of a scarcity of sugar, local groceries declined to sell the saccharine substance except in small quantities. Most of the stores sold only a dollar's worth to a customer Saturday, and

this week the amount was generally reduced to 50 cents'
worth. Some of the groceries had none at all this week,
and many jobbers had none to supply them.

The sugar stringency is widespread, the same course
being followed in a great many other cities. Sales have
been limited to enable the stores to accommodate as
many customers as possible, and to prevent hoarding
by those able to buy in large quantities.

In some instances people sawed the air over the
matter, though as a rule they accepted the fact willingly
and evinced a gladness to do their part. It is believed
by federal authorities that the sugar scarcity will be
over in a few weeks, when the 1917 crop of beets and
cane has been run into the refineries.

I asked a question on the street one morning, and printed
the replies:

"WHAT WOULD YOU DO TO THE KAISER
If Asked to Sentence Him?"

CHARLES CHENEY: I would run him down to the Big
Rock with my hounds and let them chase the son of a
gun off into the river.

HON. W. B. HARDEN: I would sentence him to go to
church regularly.

S. B. WALKER: My suggestion would not look well in
print.

TOM EVANS: I don't know. I have to think that over a
while.

OLLIE HARDEN: I'd put him on exhibition in the United
States at a dime a look, and give my patrons leave to
throw anything at him they wanted to.

Random bits of local war news:

FRANK AND EARL LITTLE
ENLIST IN 2ND ARTILLERY

Dear Folks: Received your letter this morning and
was glad to get it. I suppose you will be surprised and

glad to hear that the names of your two sons are under the list of Volunteers to help win the world war for democracy. We enlisted last Friday night in the Second Indiana Artillery for the Duration of the war.

That Fountain County farmers will not receive less than $15.50 for their hog crop is the slightly qualified declaration of Herbert Hoover, federal food administrator.

"The prices," Hoover's statement reads, "so far as we can affect them, will not go below a minimum of about $15.50 per cwt for the average of packers' droves on the Chicago market until further notice.

Asa Osborn and Son's advertisement: YOU CAN HELP HOOVER AND YOUR COUNTRY   Use these items to save sugar: Syrup, sorghum, molasses, honey, dates, prunes, raisins, figs, jams, jellies, fruit butters and maple sugar. To Save Wheat Flour: Animal fats; In Place of meats needed at the Front.

Late in January of 1918 an order that astonished Covington brought consciousness of the war home with new force:

BUSINESS SUSPENDS FOR "HEATLESS" DAY

With an aspect more funereal in every way than on the dullest Sunday, the business section of Covington last Monday observed the first of the ten heatless days ordered by the federal fuel administrator to conserve fuel and to enable the director general of railways to get the eastern freight situation relieved from its congested condition.

Banks, post offices, restaurants, and county offices were about the only open places. Groceries and butcher shops opened part of the day. But two or three lights burned on the square on Monday night.

The war prosperity that industrial centers experienced did not come to Covington. Higher prices for agricultural prod-ducts had begun to raise farm income a little, and accelerated slightly the currency circulation in town, but very slightly. The repeated campaigns for Liberty Bonds and for war charities kept the community drained of cash. No prosperity at all reached the *Covington Republican;* advertising fell off until the task of making ends meet became more irksome than ever to the young owner who was more editor than businessman.

A year earlier, in the fervent days that followed the U.S. declaration of war, I had listed the paper for sale, intending to enter the officers' training camp at Fort Benjamin Harrison. No buyers appeared. The draft authorities placed me in a fourth classification. As time permitted more deliberate thoughts about the war, enthusiasm for military service waned. Although other young men were making such sacrifices, I was loath to lose the newspaper property, and no one else was available to carry it on.

Summer and fall dragged on, while I speculated about the future. There seemed to be none for me in Covington. I had found no formula to make the town grow. Though dreams had come of expanding the printshop, or perhaps eventually of creating some new type of publication for wider than local circulation, I saw no gifts within myself for doing either.

Then one cold and stormy January day Charley Lowe stomped into the office — "Commodore" Lowe of ferryboat fame. Shaking the sleet from his overcoat he proclaimed, "I want to buy this here newspaper."

Charley was an unwearying jokester. I looked to see what gag was forthcoming. "Well, make a good offer," I parried.

He made an offer, and plainly he was serious. That he had no qualifications for publishing a newspaper I knew, nor did I propose to concern myself about his motives. Chances were that he intended to run for county office, or that he might be acting as agent for the former owner. His check was sure to be good at the bank.

We haggled a while until he raised the offer by $500. It still was less than I thought the property should bring, but I wanted out. Next day we closed the deal.

The news that Charley had bought the paper created much more of a sensation around town than the fact that I had sold it. Retired farmer, ex-thresherman, ex-ferryman, jokester, no one would have been surprised had he done anything else. But he was hardly expected to be an editor.

"Always wanted to be an editor," he said solemnly.

Morris Herzog asked the two of us to visit his store. "Charley, I haf a present for you. If you vill put this on, and you and Mac valk around the square, I'll gif it to you to keep."

He produced an ancient, stove-pipe silk hat, beautifully lined with red silk. Its vintage must have been 1888. Charley delightedly donned the hat and, arm-in-arm, he and I paraded around the courthouse square.

Gayer of heart than for months I composed, on the linotype that my fingers were soon to touch no more, a valedictory screed:

To the end of my days on this terrestrial sphere, my four years in Covington will remain with me as a delightful memory; and I prefer that they will continue with me so — as a memory.

In four years here I have had a large measure of interesting and profitable experience. I have accumulated some information that I didn't have when I blew into town on a snowstorm in February, 1914, and have also learned that there is some information lying loose around in the world that I have not even yet corralled. I have acquired since moving to Covington the best wife I ever had or ever expect to have, established a home, and we have a boy who's "just like his father was before him." I have been denounced publicly from the tabernacle pulpit and the saloon bar, and also arrested for infracting the sacred ordinances of the city, superintended a Sunday School and demonstrated that a man can gain a wider reputation by going without a hat or doing some other fool thing than he can by sheer ability. I have learned from personal contact that Covington has, strutting under the mask of respectability, some of the most damnable scoundrels who ever sat in a

church pew, and some people whose friendship is so
genuine that it needs no trade mark. I have learned
that no community where the business leaders smile
upon each other face to face and at other times kick
each other on the base of the spinal column can enjoy
the fullest measure of prosperity.

. . . .

I want to register my profound gratitude to those
who in any way have contributed to building the paper;
to the steady subscribers who are every editor's joy; to
the corps of capable community correspondents who
have weekly written their budgets of the events in their
neighborhood am I especially grateful, for their columns
are important; to the attorneys who have directed to us
their legal notices; to the patrons of our job department; and to every merchant of the city, both those few
who have advertised with comparative regularity, and
the ones who in an ungoverned fit of wild extravagance
have courted bankruptcy by advertising as much as two
dollars' worth every holiday season, some years. . . .

The city of Covington has my very sincerest good
wishes. . . . I have been asked to venture a prediction
as to the future of Covington. Would you have my
answer, note that my index finger is pointed to the
past. . . .

This experience has been good for me. I am content
if, in any measure, I have contributed anything of value
to the community.

The boy enthusiast who had bought the *Republican*
four years before had not outgrown flamboyancy.

"Contributed anything of value to the community?" I
wondered, and doubted. With a degree of pride I read the
"obituaries" by brethren of the press in neighboring towns.
One fellow-editor had sensed my question. Perhaps he had
asked it for himself and was giving an answer such as he
wanted to hear.

"It can truly be said," wrote the Fountain-Warren *Democrat* of Attica, "that Mr. McMillen's four years in Covington

have been fruitful of good. He fought vice and stood for those things which elevate. He was active in all organizations for better social conditions. Covington has gained by his having lived there."

"Gained what?" I was inclined to doubt those kind words. A little entertainment, perhaps. No visible evidence could I perceive that the town was better or different physically, socially, morally, or intellectually.

The four vivid years had advanced my own education. I had learned more about people and about living, maybe a greater total of practical and useful knowledge, than would have been acquired in a university. I had found out that the necessary art of making a living was not to be taken for granted, and that it might demand something more than merely being willing to work at something one liked to do. I had not quite learned that he who attends strictly and well to his own business frequently serves best in this world (and perhaps was never to learn that) but I had made some headway toward comprehending the idea. I knew more than before about the importance of plain arithmetic. I had not found out what I might be good for, nor what were all my limitations. I was richer in experience, still rich in youthful hopes.

It was almost exactly on the fourth anniversary of my arrival in Covington that we left. The greatest profits of the four years were with me — the lovely and gay and sensible young wife at my side and our baby son in my arms. We climbed aboard the little train, "the crawfish special," that followed the tracks up the old towpath to the main line . . . and on to the future.

A soft sun warmed the first of March air. The whistling snowstorm that had greeted my arrival came to mind.

"Epitaph for a young editor," I said to Dorothy. " 'He came in like a lion cub and went out like a lamb.' "

Afterword

That was 1918; and here is 1968! One can look back over a half century and muse that Covington was, to use a term then seldom heard, an underdeveloped town. Even more evident, it had an underdeveloped editor.

What has since happened to the editor forms no part of this story, except that in at least forty of these fifty years he has found occasions to return for glances at Covington.

By some standards, the town remains underdeveloped. The rows of maple trees still shade the sidewalks in summer; grown more venerable, on many streets their branches meet high over the pavements. Day or night, one can walk where he chooses with no apprehension that he will be attacked or robbed. The air is still unpolluted. The continuous noises, the stenches, the crowded loneliness that the highly developed cities provide are absent. Traffic is heavier, but no real problem. Nearly everyone knows nearly everyone else. As they did in 1918 and long before then, people talk about each other and tend to know each other's affairs. When sickness or death befalls, they rush to extend sympathy and to offer help.

Growth, if measured only by numbers of people, has been slight. The census in 1890 reported nearly 2,000 souls; sixty years later, only 2,235. When 1960 came around the count had risen to 2,759.

No one nowadays enters or leaves by rail. The tracks are there, and a car of coal may be left on the switch, but the three Big Four passenger trains that once shuttled each day between Indianapolis and Peoria have reached their final terminal. Even the depot has been dismantled. The Wabash Railroad long ago tore up and sold the rails from the "Towpath" branch that followed the ancient canal northward to meet the main line. For those who may find it inconvenient to drive their own cars, buses stop twice daily.

Have the people changed, too? The reminiscent stroller along familiar streets will have to stay a few days to find out. He will, nevertheless, notice outward signs. The beards are gone, for one thing. Fifty years ago at least a dozen prominent citizens, mostly of Civil War vintage, wore full beards, chin whiskers, or goatees. Free-swinging mustaches were fairly common. Safety and electric razors and changed styles have prevailed. Not even a hippie beard had appeared as of 1968.

The barber shop, where a haircut, shave, shampoo, shine and a bath were once available, and where even on the busy Saturday nights one was welcome to loaf, now sells little other than the haircut. Men shave themselves, and shampoo under their showers. Bathtubs were not rare in 1918, nor the other indoor plumbing every house now has, but the shower was something one only heard about.

Saturday night has all but vanished, too. At one time no storekeeper was surprised if he did more business on Saturday night than he had done through all the previous days of the week. Farmers came in with eggs and butter to trade for groceries. Town people stocked up for the week ahead, or went downtown just to see who was there. A former townsman, if he had been away for a year or so, could need a full two hours to make his way around the four sides of the square greeting and visiting with acquaintances. Now Saturday night is nearly as quiet as early Sunday morning.

In the more leisurely days when a man went "downtown," that is, around the square, he could always find places to sit down for a talk and someone to talk with. Not only in the barber shop, but in the tailor shop, the pool room, the lawyer's offices, the grocery or drug stores, or in almost any other places of business he could find a spare chair and a welcome. He can still talk, but the places to sit down are fewer and offer a bit less welcome for mere conversation.

The tempo is faster. The time for aimless chat, however pleasant, seems now to be restricted to that innovated period, the coffee break.

The stores, of course, are different. Seven or eight grocery stores and a butcher shop or two used to purvey the foodstuffs; the owner and his family tended the store, for long hours, with maybe a delivery boy or spare clerk to help. The visitor now can find only two such "family" stores, one serving the neighbors near the grade school and the other out on Liberty street. Inquiry reveals, though, that the big chain supermarket (IGA) — where the lumber yard used to be — employs some two dozen people and supports about the same number of families as did the numerous little old stores, and its people work fewer hours. The variety and quality of foods it offers throughout the year must have advanced the local level of nutrition.

The town folks call attention to the new buildings. The WPA in 1936 tore down the rather stately but outmoded pre-Civil War courthouse, uprooted the more than fifty beautiful old trees, and erected a conventional but more efficient housing for the county offices. The Masons have for themselves a new home out Liberty street. The post office, no longer in a rented store room, now functions in handsome brick on the corner where Pete Schma's livery barn stood. A substantial school gymnasium was built a few years ago. A new high school structure, they report, is soon to rise. It will cost $1,800,000, a sum that would have evoked both awe and incredulousness in 1918. The school district now includes three neighboring townships; and the people believe in education.

What can one say when he finds more churches than ever before? Are Covingtonians more religious, or more sinful and more in need of religion? The Methodist church structure has been enlarged and improved, and a prosperous congregation attends. One change: the Presbyterians have lately merged with the Methodists. The Baptists, with perhaps the largest membership, the active Fifth Street Church of Christ and the old "Little Brick," now called the Seventh Street Church of Christ, all have added to their buildings. The Catholics, too, have improved their church building but have now only a weekend priest who drives down from Lafayette.

These were the old groups. New since 1918 are the Church of the Nazarene, a small congregation with their own frame building; The Assembly of God, some twenty years old, and the Bethany Full Gospel group with a new church. Six of the ten churches have resident ministers.

One hears that new organizations, the Lions Club, the Jaycees, Boy Scouts and Girl Scouts carry on constructive projects. Businessmen of Fountain County and its neighbor across the Wabash, Warren County, have joined in an active Bi-County Chamber of Commerce. Two Covington sororities, Psi Iota and Tri Kappa, aid charitable causes and support scholarships for high school graduates. Of these, only Tri Kappa can boast a half century of Covington history. A museum in the courthouse and a restored grist mill south of town attest to interest in the new Fountain County Historical Society.

During the depression years the *Covington Republican* was sold to its Democratic competitor, the Covington *Friend*. Both papers continue to appear weekly, more or less identical except for their mastheads, but with a new wealth of local pictures. Both are now owned by a chain publishing organization which has absorbed a dozen small papers in the area; each has its local editor. Over on the northeast corner of the square, where groceries were sold for seventy-five years, the Danville *Commercial-News* maintains a daily staff and competes stiffly with the local weeklies.

The saloons that flourished in 1918 gave way to prohibition. Three taverns now cater to the thirsty. Alcoholic beverages can be purchased in one of the groceries and in one of the two drug stores.

Do people have as much fun now? Once numerous small social clubs were made up of congenial couples who met weekly at each other's houses, ate an evening meal together and then played cards or otherwise entertained themselves. Home talent plays and entertainments, unless given by the schools, are no longer heard. But if no television aerial rises over a roof, there is a 500-foot tower at the edge of town and cable TV enters the home at a monthly fee. More people

travel to see America; many of the elderly migrate southward for winter months. The old county fair ground has
been made into a community park with a big swimming
pool, lights for baseball and football games; the old race
track now serves for horse shows and rodeos. With play-
grounds for the youngsters, the picnic area attracts family
reunions and in summer a big tent shelters a roller-skating
rink.

What, by the way, became of the youngsters one knew
fifty years ago? They scattered, most of them. One made
his fortune as a manufacturer in Missouri, another became
an executive in a Michigan chemical company, and a third
rose to be commandant of the United States Marine Corps.
Several chose educational fields, as teachers, administrators,
lecturers, and writers of school materials. One who stayed
home, except for a spell in the Seabees, served as mayor for
twenty years besides achieving success as a contractor. One
of the girls married her childhood beau while he was still
the red-headed partner in the main barber shop. He later
prospered as an automobile dealer. She went further, serving for ten years as a member of the national House of
Representatives and longer as Indiana's Republican National Committeewoman. An industrious clerk in Herzog's
store back when, now has a son who is Congressman from
the Seventh Indiana District, and lives in the home town.

Politics, apparently, engrosses Covington as deeply as
ever. At the last election the vote for mayor was a tie. Not
for many months did any Hoosier legal brain discover a way
to decide whether the Democrat or the Republican was entitled to be His Honor. Meantime the town managed without knowing for sure whether it needed a mayor at all.

Changes? Yes! Progress? Yes! The biggest change came
along after 1955 when Olin-Mathieson chose to locate a new
Cellophane plant on a 660-acre site two miles west of town.
Construction men came to Covington, liked the village, and
decided to stay. Management men came in, some from
North Carolina, some from Iowa, and built or acquired
homes. New jobs opened for almost any qualified worker.
The plant contributed much to the 500 jump in the 1960
population count, and to the four new subdivisions where

modern houses have risen in old pastures and fields. Other factors played a part. The gravel pit, apparently owning an inexhaustible supply of pebbles, has grown much larger. And now, when anyone who has a job can afford an automobile, dozens drive daily to Danville and on paydays bring new money home from the manufacturing plants and offices there. Two small garment factories, apparently well established, supply local jobs. The town has moved well beyond the stage where it was only a haven for retired farmers.

The new houses, the old houses with central heating and plumbing and new decorations, the bright cars and the more fashionable garbs all proclaim a prosperity far greater than the average Covington person could expect five decades ago. More youngsters finish high school, many more go to college. The rumor even circulates that, after the next census, the law may require that the volunteer fire department, with its recently new building, two-way radio equipment and modern motors, may have to be supplanted by a paid fire-fighting force.

Underdeveloped? Yes, no doubt by urban measurements. As hundreds of other pleasant small towns across America's midwest and elsewhere have done, Covington has progressed, but not too far. A local citizen recently wrote: "Covington is a comfortable place to live. Untouched by the fierce competition of an industrial metropolis, ignorant of the bitterness of strikes and segregation, unhampered by the inconveniences of bigness, the people of Covington have developed the art of living as a friendly and gracious art, casual and relaxed. The sport shirt is more common than the dinner jacket."

Americans might be happier if more could find just such an underdeveloped environment in which to spend their lives.

Index